Red Sniper on the Eastern Front

Red Sniper on the Eastern Front

The Memoirs of Joseph Pilyushin

Joseph Pilyushin

Edited by
Sergey Anisimov

Translated by
Stuart Britton

Pen & Sword
MILITARY

Publication made possible by 'I Remember' (www.iremember.ru) and its director Artem Drabkin

First published in Great Britain in 2010 by
Pen & Sword Military
an imprint of
Pen & Sword Books Ltd
47 Church Street
Barnsley
South Yorkshire
S70 2AS

A CIP catalogue record for this book is available from the British Library.

Typeset in Ehrhardt by Phoenix Typesetting, Auldgirth, Dumfriesshire

Printed and bound in England by the MPG Books Group

Pen & Sword Books Ltd incorporates the imprints of Pen & Sword Aviation, Pen & Sword Maritime, Pen & Sword Military, Wharncliffe Local History, Pen & Sword Select, Pen & Sword Military Classics and Leo Cooper, Remember When, Seaforth Publishing and Frontline Publishing.

For a complete list of Pen & Sword titles please contact
PEN & SWORD BOOKS LIMITED
47 Church Street, Barnsley, South Yorkshire, S70 2AS, England
E-mail: enquiries@pen-and-sword.co.uk
Website: www.pen-and-sword.co.uk

Contents

List of Illustrations

Yosif Pilyushin.

Pilyushin's commendation for the Order of the Red Star.

Registration card of Pilyushin at the Frunze plant where he worked from 1945 till 1950.

Sniper training.

A sniper-instructor who has been decorated with the Medal for Bravery.

Snipers of the 32nd Army after receiving their decorations.

Snipers of the 104th Rifle Division on 15 March 1943.

Snipers on the Karelian front.

A sniper in the firing position.

Snipers in the firing position under different conditions.

A sniper of the 104th Rifle Division of the 19th Army posing with his rifle.

A sniper decorated with the Order of the Red Star.

Translator's Introduction

This is an abridged version of Red Army sniper Yosif [Joseph] Yosifovich Pilyushin's memoir, first published in 1958 under the title *U sten Leningrada [At the walls of Leningrad]*. It has recently been republished for the fourth time under the title *Snayper Velikoi Otechestvennoi [Sniper of the Great Patriotic]*, which is indicative of its enduring popularity in Russia.

As is typical for Russian World War II veterans, Pilyushin reveals little about himself or his background before the war. From his memoir, we know only that he was born in Belorussia, and that he had a wife and two young sons and was working at a Leningrad factory when the war broke out.

Pilyushin was born in 1903 in the village of Urbanovo in Belorussia. Thus, he was already 38 years of age when the Germans invaded in 1941. He was called up for the Red Army in 1926, and after his discharge into the reserves, he went to Leningrad, where he worked at the Arsenal factory as a welder. Like many young Soviet men and women, Pilyushin learned to shoot through his membership in the *Osoaviakhim (Soiuz obshchestv sodeistviia oborone i aviatsionno-khimicheskomu stroitel'stvo SSSR* – the Union of Societies of Assistance to the Defence and Aviation-Chemical Construction of the USSR), an All-Union society that offered preliminary military training in things like flying, marksmanship and parachute-jumping. Apparently, Pilyushin never received any specialized sniper training.

Pilyushin marched off to war in July 1941 as part of a hastily-raised workers' battalion, mobilized to defend the city of Leningrad. According to him, the battalion became part of the 105th Separate Rifle Regiment, though he fails to identify the specific division of people's militia to which the regiment belonged. However, Pilyushin spent most of his war in the 14th Red Banner Rifle Regiment of the 21st NKVD Division, which later became the 109th Rifle Division. His remarkable skill as a sniper was recognized when he was awarded the Order of the Red Banner. He was credited with 136 kills.

Unusually for a Red Army soldier, Pilyushin's entire war experience took place on the approaches to Leningrad or in the trenches surrounding the city. In fact, he received a disabling wound that took him out of the war in early 1944 in very nearly the same place where his war had begun in 1941, lending a unique symmetry to his part in the war.

After the war, Pilyushin returned to work at the Arsenal factory, until his war wounds resulted in his complete blindness by the mid-1950s. Unable to work, that is when Pilyushin sat down and dictated his memoirs.

There are several reasons for the book's lasting popularity in Russia. First is its surprising (for a book first published in 1958) relative lack of communist-era rhetoric and Party propaganda. Pilyushin is fiercely loyal to his motherland, but when he writes of the successful defence of Leningrad, he credits the soldiers defending it and the citizens of the city itself, not the Communist Party or the Supreme High Command. Second, the book pays frequent homage to the city of Leningrad and its besieged residents, and gives us a clear picture of their terrible ordeal. In addition, the book is almost lyrical in its descriptions of nature, which the author uses to draw a sharp contrast with the devastations and horrors of war. Finally, Pilyushin's memoir is as much about his comrades and combat-friends as it is about himself, and we see the costly toll of the war as he recounts the maiming and death of his combat-friends and family members.

The original book was not free of some inaccuracies and embellishments, which I have corrected or removed for this English-language edition. For example, Pilyushin writes constantly of encountering 'enemy submachine-gunners' in the summer of 1941. In fact, machine pistols were still rare in the German Army in 1941, and carried only by paratroopers, platoon leaders and squad leaders. German infantry at the time was still equipped primarily with the Karabiner 98k rifle. Where appropriate, I have edited the manuscript to address this and similar problems, and removed a couple of side stories due to length considerations.

Finally, I wish to thank Rupert Harding at Pen and Sword for commissioning this memoir, and Pamela Covey, whose careful copy-editing, proofreading and eye for detail have yielded a clearly improved manuscript.

Chapter One

My First Shot at the Enemy

Leningrad . . .

The streets and squares were filled with sunshine; golden spires gleamed brightly against the blue sky, and the gardens and parks were alive with fresh greenery and colour. I had seen all these things many times, but now the beauty of my native city seemed especially attractive.

At noon on 23 July 1941, together with other new recruits I was marching through the streets of Leningrad towards the front, in the direction of Narva. We gazed at the streets, buildings and parks and silently said goodbye to our homes and families. The Narva Gates receded into the distance, but still we kept glancing back at the city.

Immediately upon arriving at our destination, we became part of the 105th Separate Rifle Regiment, which was assembling in an attractive little village. That same night, our company was assigned to man combat outposts. We headed off towards the banks of the Narva River. The commanders and Red Army men strode silently, keeping their weapons at the ready.

Private Romanov and I picked our way through some low undergrowth along the banks of the river. Petr was moving in front of me so stealthily that not a single branch rustled and not a single dry twig snapped beneath his feet. Whenever my head or shoulder brushed up against some bushes or an incautious footstep broke a twig, Romanov would stop, turn around and whisper through his teeth, 'Quiet!', wrinkling his broad forehead in consternation.

Reaching the place that our commander had designated, we lay down beneath a low-growing willow. Below us, the water was flowing in a broad current.

The mysterious silence of the woods was unsettling, and our ears pricked up at any soft rustle. Everything around me seemed unusual; even the starry sky seemed to be suspended just above the tips of the pine trees. The birds had long ago fallen silent; only somewhere in the rye, something was repeating a monotonous call: 'Peets-polots, peets-polots, peets-polots . . .'

1

A thin shroud of morning fog slowly rose above the river and meadows. On the edge of the woods, concealed among the overgrowth, a field dove began its mournful call: 'Ooo-ooo.' A magpie began to warble in a birch grove. A squirrel, its head tipped to one side, looked down on us with its bright little eyes and loudly chattered while hopping from branch to branch.

At dawn, our company commander Senior Lieutenant Kruglov showed up. He dropped down onto the grass next to Romanov without taking his eyes off an isolated cottage on the other riverbank. The home seemed to be empty and abandoned: the windows and door had been boarded up.

Suddenly I saw a gate in the fence that surrounded the yard slowly open. A tall woman emerged, stopped, and looked around. She was dressed in a long black skirt and a blouse with unusually wide stripes. A yoke lay across her shoulders, with a basket of laundry hanging from each end. The woman walked directly across a field to the river. Reaching the bank above the river, she placed one basket on the grass, and with the other slowly made her way down to the water's edge.

Gazing at the woman, I thought of my native Belorussia. There were many times when my own mother had hoisted a yoke with baskets onto her shoulders, and headed for the Sor'ianka River to wash the laundry. 'Where is she now?' I asked myself. 'Has she remained in German-occupied Belorussia, or did she manage to leave with the other refugees?' With pain in my heart I thought of my family, which I had recently left behind in Leningrad: 'What are my wife and children doing now? How are they?'

I recalled the early morning in June, when a messenger from the district recruitment centre [*raivoenkomat*] had knocked on my apartment door and handed me a summons to appear immediately at an assembly point. I quickly gathered my things and stopped in front of the bedroom's closed door. I badly wanted to see my wife and children one more time, and have a quick talk with them before my departure. I took hold of the doorknob . . . but stifling my internal emotions, I released it and strode resolutely away from the room.

Kruglov's soft voice interrupted my reflections: 'Comrades, for some reason this woman isn't hurrying to do the laundry. Take a look at her.'

Kruglov crawled on his belly to the edge of the woods. The woman was standing on the bank, and shading her eyes from the sun with her hand, she was looking towards our side of the river. Romanov and I took a close look at her face: Romanov through his binoculars, and I through the telescopic sight on my rifle. The face was long and somewhat gaunt, with a sharp nose and chin; the closely-spaced eyes reminded me of a fox's.

Apparently satisfied, she squatted down, pulled a thin cord with a weight on one end from the basket, and deftly tossed it into the water. Then with one hand she grabbed an article of clothing from the basket and slowly began to wash it. Meanwhile, she carefully wound the end of the cord around her other hand; as soon the weight appeared, she immediately tossed the soaked piece of clothing into the basket, stuck the cord down her blouse and left the riverbank. Glancing one more time in our direction, she easily lifted the yoke with the baskets and hastily returned to the cottage, walking with a man's stride.

Kruglov crawled back to us. 'Well, what do you think?' he asked us.

'It's all very suspicious, Comrade Commander,' Romanov replied.

'I think so too . . . But we mustn't show ourselves. We need to keep watching . . .'

'But she might leave.'

'Don't worry; some of our guys are over there in that little village.'

Walking up to the fence, the woman grabbed the gate latch, took a furtive look around and, apparently noticing nothing out of the ordinary, stepped into the yard. Once through the gate, she tossed the laundry baskets against the fence and quickly strode over to the doors of a shed.

Romanov gave a soft whistle, and commented, 'You must have come a long way, you devilish *frau,* to wash laundry in a Russian river.' Then he quickly added: 'Look, look, Comrade Commander; that laundress is raising an antenna!'

Petr Romanov was a radio operator by military training, but in civilian life he had been a German language instructor. His powerful physique was like that of a village blacksmith. Cheerful and clever, he easily got along with people and made friends quickly. However, he had one flaw: he was too excitable. Even now, he tensed up all over, as if ready to hurl himself across the river.

'Easy, Romanov,' Kruglov said as he laid his hand on Romanov's shoulder. 'The German scout will only report what he saw: there are no Russians, the crossing over the river is clear, and the water is of a certain depth. That's just what we need.'

We all liked our company commander Viktor Vladimirovich [Kruglov] from the first meeting with him. His swarthy, somewhat oblong face radiated an inner tranquillity. His large blue eyes, thick eyebrows, firm lips and absurdly white teeth gave him a youthful look and immediately made a lasting impression.

Military Orders decorated the commander's chest. From word of mouth among the troops, we knew that he had participated in the Finland campaign [the so-called Winter War with Finland] and had already participated in more than one clash with the German occupiers. While listening to the commander, I scanned the opposite bank like an owl, fearing that I might miss the enemy, which had to be somewhere nearby.

Suddenly the sound of motors carried from the opposite bank, and soon we saw enemy motorcyclists speeding across a field. There were ten of them. 'Greetings,' I thought to myself. 'Here's our first meeting, and how many more such meetings lie in our future?' My hands unconsciously gripped my rifle more tightly. I looked over at Kruglov. His face was impassive, but his eyes were burning with a malicious fire.

'You see how the enemy is operating,' he said. 'First they sent out a scout with a radio, and after him, a reconnaissance squad on motorcycles.'

The Senior Lieutenant looked sternly at us: 'I'm warning you: not a single shot without my command.' With that, he crawled off towards the location of a signalman in the forest.

The German motorcyclists drove up to the riverbank, shut off their motors, and without dismounting, began to look attentively at our side of the river. Then one after the other they hopped off their motorcycles, and holding their submachine-guns at the ready, moved towards the river.

Romanov elbowed me in the side and whispered: 'No way! Have the swine decided to cross over to our bank?'

'How should I know? We have to wait for orders . . .'

The Nazis cautiously walked down to the water's edge, removed canteens from their belts, and filled them with water.

Romanov muttered through his teeth: 'Eh, if only we could fill their bellies with something other than water!'

'Everything in its own time . . .'

We examined the German motorcyclists with curiosity. Their faces and uniforms were dusty from the road. They had potato-masher grenades on their tightly-strapped belts, and steel helmets on their heads that settled down almost to the level of their eyes. My conscience compels me to say that for some reason, I wasn't feeling any hatred towards the German soldiers at that time. The hatred came a little later, when I witnessed the death of my comrades and the brutal cruelty of the fascist executioners.

High above us in the sky, a dogfight was playing out. An enemy plane, enveloped in a black cloud of smoke, swiftly plummeted towards the ground. A black spot separated from the burning aircraft, tumbled through the air, and then seemingly came to a brief halt as a parachute canopy blossomed above it. Under the canopy, the pilot was swinging from side to side as he drifted downward.

With agitation Romanov and I watched what was happening in the sky. From time to time we nudged each other in the side and said something, passionately hoping for the victory of our pilots, who were duelling with the Messerschmitts. The German motorcyclists were also distracted by what was happening above, seemingly surprised by the sight of a handful of Russian 'falcons' courageously taking on a larger number of German aircraft. Quickly exchanging a few words about something, the motorcyclists returned to their mounts and quickly drove away.

Romanov again turned in my direction: 'Don't be surprised by what I'm about to tell you. There will be a battle soon . . . who knows when we'll have a chance to speak calmly and leisurely again.'

I looked into his eyes. They were affectionate and trusting. Romanov pulled a photo out of the pocket of his combat blouse and extended it towards me. I saw in the photo a man about 35 years old, whose face looked very similar to Romanov's: the same affectionate eyes, smooth high forehead, and sharp chin. Returning the photo to him, I asked: 'Is this your father?'

'Yes . . . But I've never seen him. He left for the war back in 1914; I was born about a month after his departure. Later my mother told me that he was killed on the banks of this very river in 1917. You can understand my feelings: I can't take a step back in any direction from here.'

Romanov was perceptibly agitated, and he pronounced those final words rather loudly. Company commander Kruglov was lying nearby and heard everything. 'And who told you that we would be retreating from these banks?' the Senior Lieutenant asked. Romanov didn't reply. 'We will fight here for our fathers and brothers, who were victorious for us on these fields during the civil war, and we will fight here for Soviet power,' Kruglov added.

A certain while passed, and then again the sound of motors carried to us from the opposite bank. I spotted a new group of motorcyclists hurrying towards the river. This time, an armoured car was leading them.

The German armoured car stopped by the cottage. Two officers leisurely stepped out of the vehicle. As they did so, a tall fellow also dressed in an officer's uniform approached them. Observing the Germans through my telescopic sight, I immediately recognized in the tall officer's face the 'woman' who had measured the river's depth that morning. Motioning with his hand towards our bank, the scout was saying something confidently to the other officers, who frequently consulted outspread maps. 'Soon, their forward units will come up,' I thought.

How much time passed in the waiting, I don't remember. Then suddenly not far from me a shot rang out, and immediately machine-gun fire and rifle fire shattered the calm over the Narva River.

I quickly selected my target – the tall officer. I hastily took aim and fired my first shot. The German rocked sharply and slowly dropped to his knees, then to his hands. Propping himself on the ground, he tried to push himself up, but simply couldn't lift his now heavy head. With that final effort, he fell awkwardly onto his chest, his arms splayed in opposite directions.

Seeing the first German that I had killed, I didn't feel any sense of satisfaction, just some sort of dull pity for this man. After all, I was no longer firing at targets, as I had done in the *Osoaviakhim*, but at a living being. All of this flashed through my mind like lightning, but I immediately and automatically began to search for a new target, in order to repeat what I had already started.

When the battle sputtered to a close, Kruglov gathered us all together and with an irritated tone that we didn't understand, shouted: 'Who fired the first shot?'

We were celebrating our success, but our commander was furiously swearing at us: 'Do you understand what you've done?! We might have dropped many more of them here, if you had carried out my order.'

Private Gerasimov, who was standing next to me, deeply sighed, took a step forward, and without looking at the commander, acknowledged in a deep baritone voice: 'My nerves couldn't take it any longer, Comrade Commander.'

Chapter Two

A Successful Ambush

When our company returned to the battalion's location that evening, a deep trench had already been dug and carefully camouflaged. The other soldiers were eating dinner, talking over the day's events in muffled voices, washing their mess tins, filling their canteens with fresh water, or checking their weapons.

Our sleep that night in the front lines was very restless: each of us woke several times during the night, and listened with concern to the distant rumble of artillery fire, coming from the direction of Kingisepp. Not a single sound was audible from our unit's positions. Everything was done silently and without conversation. Our sentries paced cautiously, their eyes constantly looking towards the opposite bank of the river, where we were expecting the enemy's appearance.

Many of the soldiers slept on the bare ground, tightly squeezing their rifle to their chest. Their sleep was light; they were ready at any minute to get up and go into battle. Those who could not sleep sat in groups and led whispered discussions. They were remembering their factories, their collective farms, their families. Each of us was hiding our concerns deep inside our hearts, although we tried not to think about the dangers that loomed over us.

The faint sound of engines hummed in the sky. Airplanes were heading to the east; obviously, towards Leningrad.

'They've slithered up, the snakes,' Romanov said. 'Who knows, perhaps they'll even drop a bomb on my home.'

I felt a stab of pain in my heart. Feeling my own sense of helplessness, I couldn't stay still. I quickly smoked one cigarette after the other, pacing back and forth along the trench. The beauty of the 'white night' shimmered.[1] The rumbling noise of aircraft passing overhead filled the air.

---

1. Due to the high northern latitude of the city, during much of the month of June and until mid-July, the sun never sets far enough below the horizon in the St. Petersburg (formerly Leningrad) area for the sky to get dark. The streetlights are not even turned on. Russians thus call this the period of 'white nights'.

Several days passed. We spent our time working with shovels and axes to deepen and reinforce our trench. There were light skirmishes with enemy reconnaissance groups on the opposite bank of the Narva River. It seemed the adversary was giving us the opportunity to grow accustomed to life on the front lines, before hurling his full strength at us.

I closely examined the comrades around me. Everyone was behaving differently before the battle. Some were endlessly checking their weapons over and over again. Some were carefully adjusting their equipment. Some smoked cigarette after cigarette without interruption. A few slept soundly.

On the opposite bank of the Narva it was quiet, like on the first day of our arrival here. Now and then glancing at my watch, I waited for when Viktorov, the company commander's messenger, would return with fresh mail. Off in the distance, beyond the forest in the direction of the city of Narva, there were sounds like a rumble of thunder. The sharp report of gun volleys followed. Then everything merged into a constant roar of battle.

In the trench, two soldiers unfamiliar to me were standing around a heavy machine gun. One was older, and moved without haste; the other was a young guy, rapid in his motions. The young soldier was plainly nervous.

The old soldier gave a laugh: 'What, Grisha, are you a bit scared?'

'Of course, Uncle Vasya, I've never heard these sounds before.'

'You'll soon hear enough of it; you'll get your fill of it . . .'

With that, Uncle Vasya stretched out on his back, pulled an overcoat over his head, and immediately began to snore.

Viktorov didn't bring me any desired word from Leningrad. Downcast, I returned to the company command post.

Romanov was sleeping beneath the spreading branches of a spruce tree. Light brown curls of his hair were scattered across his tall forehead, partially concealing his dark-complexioned face. His new khaki combat blouse seemed to make him look younger. The company political officer Vasil'ev was lying beside him. He wasn't sleeping: by the light of a torch, he was reading a letter he had just received from his wife. I stretched out next to him.

I had often met Vasil'ev before the war – we had worked together at the same factory and I was well acquainted with him. He had got married literally just a few days before the war. Now, observing the joy with which he was reading and re-reading the letter, it wasn't difficult to understand how much pain Vasil'ev was carrying inside caused by the separation from his wife. By his nature, Vasil'ev got along well with people. He quickly gained the trust of the soldiers and commanders, though he himself wasn't much of a military man.

From the depths of the forest, a command suddenly rang out: 'Stop!'

Vasil'ev quickly turned towards me: 'Who's shouting?'

We braced ourselves for an exchange of fire, but nothing happened. Silence settled over the forest. Moonlight fell upon the forest clearing, and we spotted dark figures creeping across it before disappearing into a forest thicket. It was impossible to determine who it was. I nudged Romanov in the side, and he instantly woke up and grabbed his rifle, but the company commander seized him by the arm: 'Calm down!'

Soon the snipers Sidorov and Ulyanov approached us, conducting a stranger in civilian dress. Sidorov reported to Senior Lieutenant Kruglov: 'We detained a couple of men in the forest clearing, at the bend in the river. One of them put up resistance and we had to kill him, but we took this one alive. They were operating this radio' – with that Sidorov handed over a small metal case, which held a radio. 'The operator was trying to contact someone: "*Der Tiger.*"'

After briefly questioning the scout, Kruglov immediately set off for the battalion command post to report on what had happened. He took Ulyanov and me along with him.

Major Chistyakov, a tall, thin man with piercing, deeply-set eyes, opened a map as he listened to Kruglov, and began to examine it for the forest clearing, where the enemy scouts had been detained. Pointing at a map quadrangle he had circled with a red pencil, he thought aloud: 'This isn't just a forest clearing. This is a temporary airfield, abandoned by our pilots.'

'What if we contact the Germans over the radio?' Kruglov proposed.

'No, we shouldn't do something like that now. First of all we must let the regiment commander know.'

Senior Lieutenant Kruglov, Ulyanov and I were ordered to set out immediately for the regimental command post and to report on the activities of the enemy scouts. We ran the 3 kilometres to the command post in ten or fifteen minutes. Lieutenant Colonel Agafonov attentively heard us out, stopping us only to ask us some questions and to clarify certain details. Finishing his cigarette, he walked over to a table and ran his hand over his greying hair, lost in thought.

At last he spoke to his chief of staff: 'The Germans already know our position. It is fully possible that under the cover of darkness they'll make an assault crossing to seize this airstrip.' The Lieutenant Colonel's fingers drummed nervously on the table. 'Not a single telephone call to the battalion commanders! The Germans might be listening in. We need to set up an ambush around the airfield as quickly as possible.' The eyes of the Lieutenant Colonel were burning with intensity. 'If the Germans pay us a visit, we need to arrange a warm welcome for them. Do you clearly remember the enemy's call signs?'

'Yes, Comrade Commander!'

'Tell Chistyakov that I won't object to any attempts to contact the Germans over the radio. Just make sure the battalion commander keeps me constantly informed of events. Thoroughly interrogate that German and send him back to us.'

When we returned to the battalion, Romanov strode over to the prisoner. The German was short and scrawny, with a frightened, ashen face.

'Who were you talking with, and what are your call signs?' Romanov abruptly asked in German. The prisoner, seeing the Russian's threatening expression, quickly answered, 'I was communicating with my commander. I don't know what he intends to do.'

Romanov caught each word of the German, and distinguished the slightest nuances in his speech. Kruglov walked up. 'Oh, I can see you're on good terms,' the company commander said, turning to Romanov. 'Well, that's not a bad thing. A German is a man and he wants to live, but now a fascist is a beast, and let him expect no mercy from us.' Romanov translated the Senior Lieutenant's words for the German.

'Herr Officer,' the German scout hastily spoke up, in a heavy burr. 'They're not fascists, they're German soldiers ...' Kruglov interrupted the German: 'Enough of your lying! You did your duty, and revealed the location of Soviet forces in this area to your commander.'

Romanov set up the radio; I donned the earphones and listened in. Above us was a clear, starry sky, but the airwaves were full of sounds. Dozens of voices were speaking – Russian, German, and Finnish. They were crying out call signs; from every direction, voices were demanding, calling, requesting.

Kruglov squatted next to the radio: 'Well then, should we give it a try?'

'I'm ready, Comrade Commander.'

Romanov took the headset from me and raised the mike to his mouth: '*Achtung, achtung! Hören Sie, hören Sie, "Der Tiger," "Der Tiger," "Der Tiger." Ich bin "Elefant", ich bin "Elefant."*'

The Germans were silent. Romanov repeated the call. Several more seconds of agonizing waiting passed. But then amidst the chatter on the airwaves, he heard the call signs and the words: 'Why have you been out of contact for so long? Report immediately, is everything quiet in your sector?' Taking Kruglov's dictation, Romanov transmitted: 'Everything's quiet in this sector. There are no Russians.'

Elements of our regiment had already taken position around the airfield in the form of an L-shaped ambush. Two companies of the 1st Battalion were occupying the northern side of the field; the 3rd Battalion was covering the western side. The southern approach to the airfield had been kept free of troops, but it had been mined.

... Next to me on the forest's edge, two soldiers had concealed themselves behind a heavy machine gun. I noticed that one of them could hardly lie still for a minute.

'You, Grisha, don't be so nervous,' one of the soldiers said reprovingly to the other. 'In our business, fortitude is necessary. Also, it's embarrassing in front of your comrades – they'll see it and laugh at you later.' Grisha responded in a faltering voice, 'Don't scold me, Uncle Vasya, I'm trying . . ..' I suddenly recalled that I had seen these two soldiers in the trench that evening during the artillery barrage. Now, just as he had then, Uncle Vasya was instructing his young team-mate.

The moon illuminated the entire field. Tall willows were standing on the riverbank; in front of us were some tall weeds into which soldiers had settled. To the right of us, some anti-aircraft guns opened up on the sound of engines passing overhead. Golden explosions appeared high in the sky.

About this time, Zakharov crawled up to us, accompanied by the soldier Bulkin. Swearing furiously but silently, the platoon commander pointed out a place for him next to us.

'What, were you planning to run, you damned wretch? You don't want to fight?' Zakharov clenched his fists.

The platoon leader told us in a hurried whisper that he had bumped into Bulkin as the private was crawling away into the depths of the forest.

'What are you saying, Comrade Commander?' Bulkin tried to excuse himself. 'I wasn't running away; I was looking for some water, I wanted something to drink.'

'Then why the devil do you have a full canteen of water hanging from your belt?'

Bulkin audibly snuffled, his cheeks quivered, and his eyes were darting from side to side.

Zakharov threatened him with his pistol: 'If I catch you one more time, justice will be swift.'

Suddenly, in the moonlight I could see shadowy figures emerge from the direction of the river and begin to advance across the airstrip. The

German infantry soldiers were moving cautiously. Behind the advance, I could see other Germans hastily setting up machine guns, the barrels of which were pointing in our direction.

Then suddenly a green rocket soared through the sky in a large arc, before falling into the middle of the airfield. Immediately, all our heavy and light machine guns opened fire. German soldiers toppled heavily to the ground; others started to crawl away, while a few got up and ran for the steep riverbank, in order to find cover from the heavy fire.

The young soldier, who had been so nervous before the start of the battle, rose onto his knees, and feeding another belt of ammunition to the machine gun, shouted at full voice: 'What, vermin, has it become hot for you?' Uncle Vasya, wiping the sweat from his brow, calmly replied, 'Grisha, this heat is a different matter . . .'

The fighting continued for about two hours. The Germans furiously clung to the riverbank and resisted our attempts to drive them back across the river. The smell of gunpowder smoke filled the air. Only with the coming of dawn was the last pocket of resistance wiped out.

Under the light of the morning sun, we buried eight of our comrades who had fallen in the night combat. My eyes began tearing as I looked down on the faces of our dead friends, with whom just a few hours before we had been talking and laughing. Among the killed was our platoon leader, Ivan Sukhov. Petr Romanov replaced him.

Chapter Three
Fighting on the Narva River

That evening, as soon as the twilight started to gather, Romanov ordered the sniper Volodya Sidorov and me to scout towards the river. 'If you discover anything important, return immediately,' Romanov told us.

Reaching the edge of the forest, we lay down among some scrub brush, and started straining to hear and see anything that we could in the soft glow of the 'white night'. An hour passed, and then another. Everything was quiet. The moon glided upon a thin ripple of clouds, now and then hiding behind loosely spreading clumps of swamp alders, or casting a bluish light upon the misty meadows. Sheet lightning from some distant thunderstorm flickered against the backdrop of the pale sky. Carefully watching the opposite bank of the river, from time to time we exchanged a few words.

'Did you get a letter?' Sidorov asked.

'No, did you?'

'I also didn't.'

Vladimir hunched his shoulders from the chill, damp air, and then spoke again: 'There's a lot of dew. Look, there's some fluff in the air, but you can't make out whether it's from a poplar or the ground.'

My team-mate was a native of Leningrad; before the war, he had worked as a lathe operator at the Red Candidate factory. His family lived on Polyustrovsky Prospekt, from where he was anxiously waiting for some news. Sidorov spoke up again: 'You know, I'm worried for my wife. I didn't manage to say goodbye to her. The day before the war started, she left on a business trip to Minsk. My 10-year-old daughter accompanied me to my departure for the front.'

Sidorov took a look around, paused to listen, and then shifted a little closer to me. 'You can imagine,' he fervently began to whisper, 'three weeks have passed since I said goodbye to my dear daughter, and even now her little arms seem wrapped around my neck. I close my eyes, and I can see her tear-stained face.' We lay for several minutes quietly, each of us wrapped in his own thoughts.

Time passed, the sky grew darker, and the first stars began to appear. Vladimir broke the silence: 'Left in limbo . . . that's the soldier's lot.'

Sidorov was a good sniper; there was something almost feline in his habits. He could sit motionless for hours, without taking his eyes from the object that had caught his attention. He had exceptional hearing, but his vision wasn't as sharp as mine. Something stirred in the bushes. Sidorov whispered: 'Listen, something's rustling.'

Suddenly I spotted a rabbit. Hopping out onto the edge of the forest, the little creature sat down, took a quick look around, and with its front paws washed its whiskered little muzzle. Then it leisurely hopped towards a patch of clover. On the fringe of the forest, an owl began to hoot loudly. Then again it was quiet . . . Suddenly Sidorov grabbed me by the arm: 'What's that? Someone's crawling . . .'

We became alert. Several minutes passed, and soon a man appeared in front of us. The unknown man was crawling, breathing heavily, and stopping every now and then. When he crawled over a little mound, I caught sight of his dishevelled hair and a grimaced expression on his face. From what he was wearing, it was impossible to determine whether he was a soldier or a civilian.

The stranger crawled along on his left hand; his right hand was holding a pistol. Then he dropped his head and began to groan in pain. We crawled over to him. The man lay motionlessly, still holding the pistol. I took the gun from him. He made no attempt to resist. Sidorov rolled the man over. He was breathing fitfully through an open mouth. His face was damp, and his eyes wandered aimlessly. His clothes were torn and covered with grime, and his right shoulder was wrapped with a bandage, on which dark spots showed.

Sidorov unfastened a map case from the wounded man's belt and handed it to me. Then he began to examine the man closely.

'It's a German,' Sidorov said. 'There's an eagle on his belt buckle. Perhaps he's one of those that we hit yesterday. I can't figure it out – where has he been hiding?'

We tried to rouse him back to consciousness. Sidorov grabbed his canteen. As soon as the stream of cold water fell into the wounded man's mouth, he convulsively snatched the canteen with both hands and began to gulp down the water greedily. A shiver ran down his body. Then he wiped his damp face with his hand and began to mumble something. It was clear that he was delirious.

Then the delirium seemed to pass, and our prisoner suddenly hoisted himself on his hands into a half-seated position, and began to search the grass for his pistol. Failing to find it, he dropped back to the ground, and began moaning softly, biting his lips.

We began to discuss what to do. Go back to the company command post, or keep watching? It was possible someone else might show up . . .

We decided to head back to our company commander Kruglov right away with the wounded man. The German was very weak. Sidorov gave him a lump of bread and a flask with water. I'd never seen a man consume bread and water with such avarice before.

When we led the wounded man into Kruglov's dugout, we found all the platoon leaders gathered there. As the senior in rank, I reported: 'Comrade Commander! We took this prisoner in the meadow; he was crawling from the woods towards the riverbank. We didn't conduct a thorough search. We took a pistol and a map case from him.'

Kruglov ordered Romanov to interrogate the prisoner, while taking the German's pistol from Sidorov: 'A Luger semi-automatic. I know them well; the Finnish officers had them.'

The prisoner was a certain Major Strauburg.

'I'm grateful to your soldiers for the care they gave me,' Strauburg announced. An arrogant little smile flickered across the German's face. He wiped his angular forehead, and then turning to the Soviet officer, he said with confidence, distinctly pronouncing each word: 'Do with me as you wish . . . but we will take Leningrad.'

'Thank you for your candour, but also understand: our city will never be German. You'll crack your teeth on this walnut.'

The German lifted three fingers to his forehead in salute. Then he turned around with difficulty, and paced out of the dugout into the trench, where two guards were waiting to escort him to battalion head-quarters.

Kruglov opened up a large map that was in the map case and began to examine it carefully. Then he turned to the platoon commanders and said: 'There it is, the direct road from Kingisepp to Narva. If the enemy seizes it, our forces won't be able to hold either place. Having cut this road, the Germans will outflank us and force us to retreat. Here, comrades, is the great responsibility that we bear.'

Kruglov carefully folded the map back up, placed it back in the case, and then handed the case to a runner to take it to the battalion command post. The company commander then announced that according to intelligence reports, the enemy outnumbered us by several times over. We had one advantage: the river in front of our companies' trenches, and the difficult forested and swampy terrain on our flanks. Enemy tanks couldn't pass here, but we faced a tough fight with infantry, supported by artillery and aviation.

Kruglov paused to listen to something; then he slowly walked to the door, cracked it open, and asked: 'Do you hear that sound? The Germans are bringing up troops to force a crossing. We will not let them onto our bank! We will defend the Narva-Kingisepp road to the death!'

He turned towards the plank beds, upon which the platoon commanders were sitting: 'Don't think that death is frightening only to us. No, the Germans also fear death. Endurance, cunning, mutual support – that's our strength. One more thing – we must constantly face the enemy. Teach this, and only this, to every soldier and officer. If we turn our backs, we're done for. Then you're no longer a force, but a target . . .'

When we left the dugout, it was five o'clock in the morning. The air carried the loud sound of motors, which quickly grew. Immediately airplanes appeared from behind the forest treetops. They were flying so low that their light shadows raced across the ground.

The soldiers pressed themselves tightly against the walls of the trench, but having spotted the five-pointed stars on the planes' green surfaces, they enthusiastically began waving their hands. The planes were our bombers, returning from a mission behind German lines.

At six o'clock in the morning, an enemy reconnaissance plane – a Henschel Hs 126 – appeared. It fled at the very first shots from our anti-aircraft gunners.

Again everything fell silent. This eerie calm before the battle gripped us all in a state of nervous tension. The soldiers were unable to keep still. They kept shifting grenades from one niche to another, wiping cartridges again and again, or repeatedly checking their weapon. Each minute in the nervous wait before a battle seemed like an hour. Only the eyes of the fighters remained calm. They were ready at any minute to face what was worrying their minds and hearts.

Eight o'clock. Now the sun's rays were reaching the bottom of the narrow trench. There were the vague sounds of the forest.

Next to me, Uncle Vasya was busying himself at his machine gun. As always, he moved deliberately, was spare in his motions, and he was preparing for battle with great prudence.

'Look, Grisha, how everything's turning out all right for us because of you,' he said to his young friend. But Grisha didn't respond. He wiped his smooth face with his sleeve, and puffed himself up a bit. Taking on a serious demeanour, as if he hadn't heard this praise, he was trying in every way to act like his 'senior'.

Uncle Vasya by his nature was a somewhat reserved, very tranquil man, who liked to listen more than talk. He always took his work seriously, and carried out the commander's orders precisely and unquestioningly.

Grisha worked to clear a little more space for their position, and then inserted his spade back into its case, walked over to Uncle Vasya and said inquiringly: 'Vasiliy Dmitriyevich, yesterday you promised to tell me how you beat the Whites in the civil war.'

'To tell you the truth, Grisha, I really don't feel like talking about that now. Our victories – and there were a lot of them – are sometimes attributed only to the cavalry, while we, the foot soldiers, seemingly didn't even fight.'

The machine-gunner smacked his weather-beaten lips, as if trying to taste something, and thoughtfully looked up at the sunny sky: 'It was hard for us to fight back then: we didn't have enough bread or equipment, and we counted every cartridge. I dragged this little friend (and he gestured at his machine gun) along military roads for three years of war, cleansing our native land of the Whites. Once it happened that we were chasing the White Poles back towards L'vov. Then one evening, cavalry unexpectedly charged at us from some woods, and I had only three belts of ammunition. The guys were swearing at me for all they were worth: why wasn't I firing? But the platoon leader was lying next to me and saying, "Wait a bit longer, Vasya, until the Whites gallop up that little rise, and then cut them down, the devils."'

'And did you wait?' Grisha asked.

'Of course, the commander's word is law. I'm gazing at this wave of cavalry, at their flashing sabres, and I felt ants running up my spine. After all I was younger back then than you are now, Grisha, but I was patient. As soon as the cavalry emerged from the low ground onto the rise, that's when I cut them down!'

Yershov, knitting his brows a bit, glanced over at the attentive Grisha. He slowly finished his cigarette, and then continued: 'That's just one story I've told you about, son, but at the front it happens that the enemy will attack you suddenly, and then Grisha, picture for yourself how you'll bang away at him with a little more fervour.'

The company commander walked up to us and said: 'Get ready for battle, comrade snipers! Look for the officers and machine-gunners, and don't forget about our flanks! The more of these uninvited guests you shoot down, the easier it will be for us. And you, Uncle Vasya, keep the ford under fire and look after the edge of the forest.'

I watched as a strange, unfamiliar smile crossed my team-mate

Sidorov's face; he was pale, and his lips were slightly quivering. 'He's a bit afraid, likely,' I thought to myself. But then I realized that I probably looked the same way. Kruglov disappeared around a turn in the trenches, but his words lingered: 'Get ready for battle, comrade snipers!'

About ten o'clock in the morning, our artillery fired a salvo from far behind our positions. The air trembled. The thunder of the guns carried throughout the forest, rolling from one end to the other, and then died away in the deep morning silence. Suddenly the earth began to moan. It seemed to rise up a little and shake from side to side. The cannonade filled the forest with a ferocious roar. In the grain field and the meadow, puffs of smoke and fire rose into the sky.

We were bewildered.

'What have our artillerymen thought up?' Sidorov became agitated. 'There wasn't any order to attack, but they're firing anyway.'

'And what are you thinking . . . the artillery only shoots before an attack? No . . . it's going to wear down the fascists, you'll see, and it's going to reduce their momentum,' Ulyanov answered in a hoarse voice. He wiped an eye with his palm and then pressed it to the eyepiece of his telescopic sight. His hands were shaking slightly.

Soon the Nazis returned fire. The forest resounded with shell explosions. Fires were burning everywhere. Ancient trees were cut down like blades of grass. At first the enemy shells exploded behind our forward positions, but then the explosions began walking back towards us. The seething avalanche of fire grew and began to chew up more and more of our defensive lines.

Romanov came up and looked at us: 'Well, comrades, has this trifle caused you to lose heart?'

Sidorov snapped back: 'And just what do you have, an iron spirit?'

'No, not iron . . . But here it is, the real war!' Romanov said.

He covered his face with his forage cap. Dust and smoke filled the eyes, nose and mouth, making it hard to breathe, and caused a dry cough. The artillery duel lasted for about an hour, but it seemed to me that an eternity had passed. When everything finally settled down, the howl of shells and the thunder of explosions continued to ring in my ears.

How much time then passed – minutes or hours – I don't recall. Suddenly Sidorov tugged at my sleeve: 'Hug the earth. Look, Germans!'

Enemy tanks were moving across the field towards the riverbank, zigzagging like hares making for a burrow. But first one, and then another armoured vehicle shuddered to a halt and began to emit smoke. They had struck a minefield. Other tanks, increasing their fire, drew nearer to the river. German troops were running after them. Firing disorderedly, they were bawling, 'Lia, lia, lia . . .!'

Our artillery started firing over open sights. As soon as the infantry approached to within firing range of our rifles, we opened fire. Romanov shouted: 'Guys, see that lanky officer? Shoot him!'

Sidorov fired and the German fell. I took aim at the thickset soldier who had been advancing beside the officer. The bullet dropped him at the feet of his commander.

At that same minute, our heavy and light machine guns opened fire. The German infantry was cut off from their tanks and pinned down.

On the opposite riverbank, across from our company's position, three enemy tanks and two self-propelled guns had been immobilized or wrecked by mine blasts. Our minelayers' labour hadn't gone in vain. They were a great help to us in repulsing the tank attack.

The first enemy attempt to force a crossing had no success. After a short pause, a new infantry attack followed, but this time with major air support. Bomb after bomb fell on our position. The earth again started to tremble and shake. Ancient pine and fir trees, torn up by their roots, were hurled high into the air. It seemed that you were no longer on terra firma, but on a shaky footbridge across stormy sea waves.

A thick layer of smoke and dust hung over the battlefield. At five paces, it was impossible to see what your comrades were doing. Shell fragments ploughed the earth, and it seemed nothing living could withstand this blind force of metal. Only the insurmountable desire to see the enemy's death forced us to tear ourselves from the embrace of the earth, hastily pick out a target and fire. Then again we would hug the earth, taking shelter from the bullets and shell fragments.

To experience all of this in the very first battle was very difficult. Everything we experienced, though, contributed to our combat education, which you can't receive in any university.

A sense of self-preservation and desire for victory suggested how and where to take cover from fragments and bullets; they teach you how to use properly every fold in the ground, and help you find a place where you might best be able to kill the enemy with the least danger to yourself. I don't believe anyone who says that soldiers don't fear death in battle. No matter how he tries to show himself to be a brave man, when a bullet creases his temple, he can't help but flinch, and hurl himself to the ground.

Combat is a very tough deal. It demands every bit of strength from the soldier. In the warrior's trade, nothing is done on the off-chance or done halfway and there's no allowance for the soldier's fatigue or lack of preparation. You're placing your stake not only on your ability to fight, but also your inner qualities. If you fail to notice something, or delay just a bit, hundreds of your comrades will pay for your error with their own blood and lives. At the least moment of calm, a soldier will literally collapse and immediately fall asleep, while still gripping his weapon.

The Germans launched a second attack on the banks of the Narva on this day. But this one, too, was beaten back everywhere.

A second day of fighting on the Narva arrived. With the first rays of the sun, everyone was already on their feet. Sidorov and I were standing in a narrow slit trench, next to a fortified bunker that sheltered Romanov's platoon. Senior Lieutenant Kruglov was present and speaking in a comradely voice about the previous day's fighting, about our courage and fortitude, and about our blunders and mistakes. I was standing next to the entrance, trying not to miss a single one of the commander's words.

Soon the company *politruk* [political leader] Vasil'ev walked up to us. He took me by the elbow: 'Today I received a letter from my comrades back at the factory; they're writing that the Germans still haven't bombed the city. The factory is operating in a new way. They're asking how we're fighting.'

He handed me the envelope, and then turned to the soldiers standing around us: 'Well, guys, have you become acquainted with the Germans? Have they showed their faces yet today?'

'Not yet, Comrade *Politruk*,' Sidorov replied, 'we must have thrashed them yesterday. Apparently, they still haven't woken up!' Sidorov gave a smile.

The *politruk* added: 'Yesterday the Germans were probing our lines, but today, likely, they'll hit us with everything they've got. So – hold on.'

We started smoking.

'When the tanks and infantry appeared on the bank' – I heard the voice of the company commander speaking – 'You opened fire on them. That's fine. But you forgot about the enemy machine-gunners. Since they don't advance, you think they're not dangerous . . . No, that's not correct. After all, we weren't attacking, but the foe ran away from our machine guns.'

'One more thing,' Kruglov added. 'We don't know how to take cover. During the air attack, platoon leader Vesyeloye didn't get his men under cover in time. And what happened? He himself was killed and placed his men under fire. Senseless hot-dogging is equivalent to the most serious crime. To die at the front is a simple matter, but everyone wants to live.'

Kruglov walked over to squad leader Zakharov. Smiling, he affably laid a hand on the sergeant's shoulder: 'Well now, will we take heed of our mistakes?'

Zakharov, sensing the gazes of his comrades, replied: 'One never stops learning, Comrade Commander. But we'll survive. We really gave it to the Germans yesterday!'

We hadn't had time to grab a bite for breakfast, when the Germans started laying down an artillery preparation: once again, shellfire started to rage over our trenches. As soon as the storm of fire started to slacken, the company commander's order rang out: 'To your places!'

The bunker quickly emptied. In a low crouch, Sidorov and I made our way to our sniper emplacement. In our protective shelter, we shook off the sand and took a seat at the embrasure.

'You hunt down the machine-gunners,' said Sidorov, 'and I'll take care of the officers.' With that he placed his eye against the eyepiece of his scope. A shot rang out. Vladimir glanced over at me: 'That's it for one of the bastards.' Then he resumed shooting.

I didn't have to search long for machine-gunners: Germans were crawling across the field towards the river, and there were so many of them, it seemed that the earth itself was moving.

Five Nazis brought up a heavy machine gun to the edge of a birch grove. I had time to shoot two of them, but the remaining Germans abandoned the machine gun and took cover in some bushes.

Clouds of smoke started spreading across the battlefield. It became increasingly difficult to spot enemy targets. A pile of cartridge casings had accumulated around Sidorov. Soon my own rifle grew so hot, it was impossible to touch the breech. Then I picked up a captured light machine gun and crawled out into the trench. Not far from me, Drozdov was firing his bipod-supported Degtyarev light machine gun. It seemed that with his strong hands, he wasn't holding a machine gun, but a light walking stick. On his long, rough-hewn, begrimed face, only his alert eyes and yellowish teeth were visible. Drozdov was firing coolly, in short bursts. Noticing me, he shouted: 'Come on! Give it to them, sniper! Kill them, the vermin! We won't let them reach our bank!'

As I was reloading the machine gun, something struck my head so violently that I reeled. Clutching the side of the trench, I was barely able to remain on my feet. Gold spots flashed in my eyes, and the sounds of battle around me became heavily muffled. It was astonishingly quiet. I wiped my eyes and took a look around. Drozdov was lying on the bottom of the trench, his arms outspread . . . on his face there was not even a hint of a tormented grimace signifying a pending death, and his thick black curls lay strewn across his forehead. His eyes were slightly squinted, as if still taking aim for the next shot. Drozdov was dead, his finger still clinching the trigger of his machine gun.

Private Lesha Bulkin suddenly darted past me with a bundle of grenades. He adroitly leaped onto the parapet, then quickly crawled to a large shell hole and took cover in it. Just then, I spotted an armoured behemoth with a black cross on its side emerging from the water onto our bank . . .

At last Lesha raised his head, and from the resolute expression on his face, I realized that he had decided to take on the tank with his grenade bundle. Bulkin rose into a crouch, and when the tank neared his position, he tossed the grenade bundle against the side of it.

I didn't hear the explosion but a hot blast wave struck my face. When I looked back at the tank, I saw blue tongues of flame lapping along its side and turret.

Romanov ran up to me; he was shouting something and waving his arms. But I didn't pay any attention to him. At that minute, all my thoughts were focused on the fervent hope that the Germans wouldn't spot Aleksey Bulkin, who was crawling back towards us. A lot of time has passed since that day, but I can still see the young soldier with the shining eyes crawling back to our trench.

I spent the rest of the day lying in the bunker. Romanov visited me there several times. He tended to me like a brother, seeming to suffer more from the concussion than I was. My hearing gradually began to return, and as soon as it became dark, I returned to the trench, although my ears continued to ring and crackle. The comrades were finishing their work to restore and strengthen the firing positions that had been damaged by shells. On the slope of a forest ravine, we dug a fraternal grave for those of our comrades who had been killed in the battle.

We were suffering deeply over the death of our friends. Company commander Kruglov crouched on one knee by the edge of the grave. The wind was tousling his blond hair, his face was stern and mournful, and his eyes were reddened. It seemed that parting from these heroic warriors, he had immediately aged by many years.

A gusty breeze rustled in the forest. Soldiers and commanders with bare heads were standing by the fresh grave. *Politruk* Vasil'ev, in a hoarse, agitated voice read out the names of the fallen comrades, and then a Red Army farewell volley rang out. Machine-gunner Stepan Semyonovich Drozdov was also lying in this grave.

. . . In the trench, the cook Seryezha Katayev greeted us. The tasty aroma of hot cabbage soup wafted from the flasks he had brought with him. No matter how sad we were, our stomachs still let us know that we were hungry. After all, we hadn't had anything to eat since breakfast!

'Come on up, fellows, you've had enough fighting for the day – it's time to eat!'

'Seryezha, take a look, where's the sun?' Sergeant Akimov was pointing at the crescent moon.

'It's not my fault that you got tangled up in fighting with the Germans from early morning, and then spent all day with them.'

'Give us some vodka, Seryezha!' someone shouted.

'Ha! Don't ask for that . . . my business is only cabbage and porridge. If somebody wants a little more, come on up!'

Romanov extended a tobacco pouch towards me: 'Have a smoke, the *politruk* will soon be arriving; he's going to be telling us about the latest events at the front.'

The troops gathered around the commander's bunker. Gradually, a leisurely conversation developed.

'Lesha, how is it that you got caught crawling away through the bushes during that night fight with the paratroopers, but today you took on a tank all by yourself?' Sidorov asked Bulkin.

The whiskerless soldier shot a not particularly friendly glance at Sidorov before replying: 'Iron must be forged in order to get steel, don't you know?'

Vasil'ev stepped out of the command bunker. The soldiers fell silent. The *politruk* pulled out a notepad, and then took a look around. A starry sky spread out above us, and a gentle breeze was carrying the astringent scent of the pine forest. The setting made your head spin and your heart wrench for peaceful, familiar places.

Vasil'ev started the discussion: 'From prisoner interrogations, we know that the fascists are not stopping whatever the losses. Do you see?' Vasil'ev gestured towards the opposite bank of the river. 'They're quiet now, but those still remaining will continue to push forward towards our Leningrad. The Germans have captured Luga, and are trying now with their right wing to cut the last rail line, connecting Leningrad with the rest of the country.'

The Red Army soldiers were squatting, leaning against the trench wall. The faces of all were sombre. Uncle Vasya was absent-mindedly rolling a cigarette with shaking hands, and tobacco spilled out onto his knees. He again stuck two fingers into a tobacco pouch and pulled out a little wad of tobacco, but his trembling hands were unable to roll another cigarette. His sunburned face was lost in thought. Grisha was sitting next to him, automatically levelling the cartridges in a belt of ammunition, from time to time throwing a hostile gaze in the direction of the enemy.

'Yes, comrades,' the *politruk* continued, 'it's hard for us to withstand the enemy pressure. We've already been fighting here for six days. Our task remains the same – to wear down the fascists' forces, to kill their soldiers, to blow up and burn their tanks and troop transports, to drive the Germans from our land. The Hitlerites still have a lot of tanks and self-propelled guns, but we don't fear them. We learned how to kill them over twenty years ago.'

I watched as Lesha Bulkin lowered his head, picked up a pebble, and began tossing it from hand to hand.

'We will not let the Germans into Leningrad! That will never happen!' the *politruk* concluded.

The new day on the banks of the Narva River began completely unexpectedly for us: as soon as dawn began to glimmer in the sky, our air force pounced on the German positions. That is when I saw how Soviet pilots wage war, how the Germans rushed about, not knowing where they might find shelter on Russian soil, where they might save themselves from death. How happy were our soldiers and officers! Without any misgivings, we emerged from our cover, and a few men even hopped up onto the breastwork, shouting as they shook their rifles: 'Give it to them, the vipers, give it to them! Work them over!'

The smoke from our bombing attack gradually dissipated in the rays of the sun. The Russian land again laid spread before us, torn by fragments and shells. From mouth to mouth, the commander's order was passed along the trench: 'Everybody take cover!' The trench line instantly emptied. Romanov, Sidorov and I stopped at a machine-gun bunker and quietly smoked a cigarette. Through the half-opened door of the bunker, I heard Grisha's voice: 'Uncle Vasya, will the Germans come calling today or not?'

'It's hard to say, Grisha . . . but if they come at us, it won't be as quickly as it was yesterday. Our falcons [a reference to Soviet pilots] entertained them today.'

When we entered Sergeant Akimov's bunker, his squad had already gathered there for breakfast. The squad leader cut off a piece of bread, slowly salted it, and at the moment he wanted to take a bite, a shell exploded just outside the door. The door burst wide open and we were covered with dirt and smoke. Mess kits fell to the ground, and the Red Army men rushed to their machine guns and rifles.

'Well these Fritzes are indeed quite the jokers; they won't let a man have a bite in peace, and they thought to dust my morsel,' Akimov said as he shoved the piece of bread into a pocket.

Senior Lieutenant Kruglov paced along the trench from soldier to soldier, giving them encouragement: 'Well, fellows, our bit of fun has arrived! There's no reason to be bored now. Don't spare the ammunition. We have plenty of it.'

Another shell exploded nearby. The blast wave tore the machine gun from Uncle Vasya and hurled it onto the breastwork. Grisha, without stopping to think, leaped up onto the parapet, grabbed the machine gun and dragged it back into the trench. Next he quickly unfastened the canteen from his belt, cautiously lifted Uncle Vasya's head, and raised the canteen to his lips. Propping Vasya against the wall of the trench, Grisha set the machine gun into position again. A long burst whipped across the surface of the river.

Enemy soldiers were emerging from the water onto our bank. It was the first time I'd ever seen Germans so closely. Their distinctive 'coal-scuttle' helmets sat low above their brows, their faces distorted with fear or combat lust, their widely-opened mouths . . . They were evidently shouting something, but the cacophony of battle sounds drowned out their voices. The Germans were firing on the move, and their bullets struck the breastwork, raising little fountains of dirt.

The Nazis were trying with all their might to gain a foothold on our bank, but they couldn't overcome our resistance. One after another, they began scuttling back to the river. However, only a few of them managed to make it across to the opposite side.

By evening, the din of battle on the Narva River slowly began to subside. The acrid smoke of battle gradually dissipated. Silence settled over the trenches. Not a single blade of grass stirred, not a single leaf rustled . . .

Just a few days ago, we had admired the birch groves, the blooming meadows, and the sea of uncut grain. Now everything had been blasted or ploughed up by bombs and shells. Wherever you looked, there were destroyed tanks and self-propelled guns . . . and corpses. Where the isolated farmstead had been standing, there was now only a blackened wasteland.

Dropping to his knees, Grisha shouted into Yershov's ear: 'Uncle Vasya, we've drowned the fascists in the river!' But the machine-gunner didn't hear Grisha. Gripping the wall of the trench, he stood up with difficulty, and then leaning on the shoulder of his comrade, he looked at the opposite bank. Without a word, he embraced Grisha and kissed him firmly on both cheeks.

Early on the morning of the seventh day on the Narva, everything around again began to shake and became shrouded with smoke. Advancing behind their artillery barrage, German infantry tried again to force a crossing. I watched as one officer crept along behind the ragged line of advancing infantry. He was holding a 'potato-masher' grenade in one hand and a Mauser pistol in the other, with which he was motioning his soldiers forward.

Company commander Kruglov ran up to Sidorov: 'Do you see the fascist officer?'

'I see him, Comrade Commander.'

'Then why are you simply admiring him?'

A shot rang out and the officer collapsed face-first to the ground. Sidorov glanced at me: 'How many of them do we have to our score? We kill them, we kill them, but they just keep coming, like devils from a swamp.'

'Look sharp, or else we'll miss again.'

Vladimir began to fire shot after shot. The sun's rays couldn't penetrate the dense clouds of smoke that had gathered over the battlefield. Riflemen and officers squinted, searching with irritated eyes through the smoke for targets. Failing to see one, they fired blindly.

Romanov was standing next to me. He pointed out three enemy tanks to me: when and where they had crossed the river, I hadn't seen. The tanks were firing at our machine-gun nests from point-blank range. Our artillery was unable to help us: the dense forest and the tanks' close proximity to our trenches prevented their fire.

At the platoon leader's order, five of us set out at a crawl with grenade bundles to intercept the tanks. Sidorov and I moved in front, with Sergeants Zakharov and Akhimov and Private Sergeyev in trail behind us.

In these minutes, I wasn't thinking about anything other than my one desire: to halt the Germans here, on this river. Sidorov was the first to toss a grenade bundle under the tracks of the lead tank. The blast wave pressed me to the earth. Moments later, a second grey behemoth emerged from the cloud of smoke, which we targeted with Molotov cocktails and grenades. The third tank disappeared.

If the fighting subsided in one place, it immediately flared up in another. Riflemen ate on the move, without putting down their weapons. Yet no one complained that they no longer had strength to continue fighting. Battalion commander Major Chistyakov was together with us in the trenches. He gestured towards the Germans, crawling in our direction: 'They've stopped running at full height! They're attacking on their bellies.' The Major looked at us: 'We've forced the Germans to the ground! We won't let them get back on their feet; they won't get very far on all fours.'

Major Chistyakov gazed at the Germans with an evil grin on his freckled face. His jaws were tightly clenched. The Major was resolute in combat. He wasn't afraid to face death. We loved our battalion commander and always tried to protect him from an enemy bullet.

Despite our fierce resistance, by the end of the day German armour-carrying assault infantry had managed to force a crossing of the Narva. A critical situation had arisen on our bank. The German tanks and storm troopers were directing a ruinous fire. At this decisive moment, our air force came to our assistance. Several armoured vehicles were destroyed in front of our eyes in the span of a few minutes. The remaining vehicles hastily retreated.

In the pre-dawn hours of 8 August, German bombers dropped thousands of incendiary bombs on the forest. Within several minutes, fires began to rage. German artillery then opened a harassing fire on the area to hinder our efforts to fight the fires. The battalion's soldiers and officers quickly worked to establish a fire break and dug a new trench on the northern side of a ravine. Sappers, our inseparable friends, set off anti-tank mines – the blast waves helped extinguish the flames.

The next day, the Nazis didn't resume their attacks. Kruglov compiled a list of our losses. The list was long, filled with familiar names and the names of friends. Kruglov slowly rose from his seat; his face was ashen and crestfallen, and the hair on his temples had turned silver.

'Take this to battalion headquarters,' he said, handing the list to his runner. As the messenger was heading out of the dugout, he added, 'Don't forget to bring back the mail!'

Politruk Vasil'ev and I headed to the battalion headquarters on different business. We didn't return until after midnight. Many of our comrades were sleeping. Sitting on a box of cartridges, Kruglov was reading a letter by the light of a candle. A child's unsteady handwriting covered the sheet of paper resting on his knees. Kruglov silently handed the letter to Vasil'ev. The *politruk* took it and read it aloud:

My dear Papa! Where are you now? What is going on? I don't know; at night I wake up, think of you, and cry. Mama also cries. She tries to hide her tears from me, but I see them. Papa, I'm keeping your first letter from the front. Papa, quickly finish this war and come back to us. I want so much to be back together with you! I kiss you firmly, firmly.

Your son Tolia.

This letter touched my heart. I didn't bother to hide my feelings.

Kruglov, with no embarrassment, kissed his wife's and son's letters, folded them neatly, and stuck them into his tunic pocket. For some time, he remained sitting, deeply lost in thought, morosely gazing in the direction of Leningrad.

Vasil'ev broke the silence: 'What did your wife write? How is she managing without you?'

'She's very worried about us.'

'Yeah, it's tough. My wife is worrying too. And you don't know how to soothe them.'

Only then did Vasil'ev hand Kruglov an order from the battalion commander. The company commander read the order several times. Then he looked disbelievingly at the *politruk*: 'Is this true?'

'Yes . . .'

'Does that mean we're retreating?'

'The Germans have taken Kingisepp; they might encircle us.'

Kruglov impulsively stood up, left the bunker, and walked over to a machine gun. A long burst of machine-gun fire rang out among the scattering of rifle shots. It seemingly communicated the rage of a man, who without sparing lives had defended every metre of native soil here.

But an order is an order. We abandoned our lines on the Narva River, which had become soaked with the blood of our comrades.

Chapter Four

A Soldier's Conversation

That night our regiment fell back to the Luga River with a forced march, and by dawn we were crossing to the eastern bank of the river in the area of Aleksandrovskaya Gorka, covering the Kingisepp-Krikkovo road. After the eight days of fighting and the exhausting night march, many of the soldiers dropped to the still dew–covered ground and immediately fell asleep, as soon as they had reached the trenches.

Sidorov and I were sitting on the edge of a ditch, not far from the highway. Romanov stood next to us, leaning against the trunk of an old birch tree. Petr's unshaven face, thickly covered with stubble, was sullen. That night, together with some radio operators who were tuning their sets, he had heard some German radio transmissions. The German radio was announcing: 'A three-day march remains to Moscow, and to Leningrad less than that. Today our forces took the city of Kingisepp and entered the outskirts of Leningrad.' Romanov, squinting, was looking in the direction of the city of Narva, where fighting had continued all night long.

Yershov and Grisha Strel'tsov were setting up their heavy machine gun in an open position near the road. From time to time, they also intently gazed at the opposite bank of the Luga River, where we were expecting the enemy's appearance.

'You, Grisha, say that old friends are forgotten,' Yershov spoke up.

'What, isn't that so?' Strel'tsov replied, sticking alder branches into the ground in order to conceal the machine gun.

'No, and again no, Grisha!' Yershov stated emphatically, while checking the full ammunition belts in the cases. 'Old friendships don't die.'

Vasiliy Dmitriyevich [Yershov] was speaking about friendship enthusiastically and fervently, as if it was the loftiest human feeling. At that moment his eyes were shining brightly, and his face was literally transformed as he spoke. Akimov spoke up: 'Uncle Vasya, have you ever cried?'

'I've cried, Senia; oh, how I've cried. It happened back in 1920, when the Whites killed my front-line friend.'

Yershov fell silent. The other soldiers began to busy themselves with their tobacco pouches.

Prime movers clattered past us on the road, towing long-barrelled guns. One truck after another, loaded with cases and barrels, rolled down the road, emitting clouds of blue exhaust. Cars slipped past us almost silently. Artillerymen were sitting in the trucks, on the gun carriages, even on the gun barrels. Their faces were gloomy, their uniforms smudged with grease and covered in road dust. They were our artillerymen, falling back from Kingisepp to new positions. They were looking with concern back in the direction of the city, where large balls of fire were soaring into the sky and muffled explosions could be heard.

'They're burning the city, the vermin,' Sidorov angrily whispered through his clenched teeth.

Romanov glanced at the growing conflagration in Kingisepp. 'My native town,' he said grimly.

The sun began to set. A chilly breeze was blowing in from the Narva harbour. No matter where you looked around you, there was not a single standing building: everything had been burned or had collapsed, as if a hurricane had blown through here.

But how dear was this scorched native land to me and my comrades! Our hearts were touched by each small, withered shrub, each blackened stone, and every scorched chimney. And I thought about the great courage with which these exhausted men, who fell fast asleep at any hour or perhaps in the limited minutes just before a battle, were defending their land.

The soft, rosy glow of the sun fell upon the cobblestone road, which stretched across the gently rolling terrain like a grey ribbon. Here and there it disappeared into small thickets, only to re-emerge on gentle slopes. Now the road was orphaned and empty of people.

Major Chistyakov with the regiment chief of staff was checking our lines. Carefully stepping around the slumbering men, the officers attentively examined each bunker and firing position.

The next morning, soldiers who had been defending Kingisepp began to approach our lines. A large group of Red Army men suddenly emerged from some woods and entered our lines. An officer was among them; two red pips were visible on his dusty shoulder tabs. With a precise step, the Lieutenant marched up to battalion commander Major Chistyakov and reported in a clear voice: 'Company commander Khmelev. We defended Kingisepp to the last possibility . . .'

Khmelev fell silent and lowered his head. His combat friends were standing at attention next to the Lieutenant. The stern faces of the privates and junior officers were begrimed with smoke and their eyes were reddened.

Khmelev was around 30 years of age and well-built. There was not a trace of timidity on his manly face. His grey eyes were open, penetrating and resolute. The Order of the Red Banner was decorating the Lieutenant's chest. He was holding a German machine pistol and had one of our Mosin 1891/30 rifles slung over his shoulder.

'I request permission, Comrade Major, to fight the Germans here together with you. . . . I don't know where our headquarters is.'

'I'll get in touch with the regiment commander, to see if he'll authorize it – please.'

The battalion commander and chief of staff disappeared around a turn in the trench. We surrounded Khmelev and his men. Someone passed around a tobacco pouch.

Rolling a cigarette, one short soldier exclaimed: 'Now this is a defensive line!' as he surveyed his new surroundings with interest.

'Leningrad gals built these lines for us,' Romanov said.

'Leningrad gals!' the short soldier repeated, his eyes twinkling. 'What sort of little gift should we send them in return?' he asked thoughtfully, puffing on his hand-rolled shag.

'What sort of gift for them? Let's toss the enemy from our land, then we'll bow low before them and tell them, "Thank you, dears, time will remember your work!" That's our best gift,' Romanov replied.

We all fell silent for a spell. One of Khmelev's soldiers broke the silence: 'Hey! It'd be a fine thing now to get acquainted with your cook. To tell you the truth, we haven't had a bite to eat since yesterday.'

Sidorov shook his fist at him: 'No, brother, first you'll tell us why you abandoned Kingisepp to the Germans!'

'Abandoned? What, have you gone crazy?' The soldier turned to the sergeant standing next to him: 'Comrade Commander, explain to him, please, or else he'll keep talking rubbish.'

Sergeant Rogov, a husky man of middle age with a broad face and high cheekbones, scowled at Sidorov: 'You know, in the area of Kingisepp and Sapsok we beat back ten or eleven tank attacks a day, and if it hadn't been for the enemy air force, we wouldn't have retreated! The fascist vultures didn't let us breathe. Now if we'd had better air cover, then things would have turned out differently . . .'

'According to you, it seems, our pilots aren't doing anything,' Sidorov retorted.

'They're flying, but we still have few planes. I pity them; they're dying right in front of your eyes . . .' Rogov waved his hand in annoyance. 'Eh, a few more planes and we'd show the Germans a thing or two . . . Neither tanks or assault guns are as frightening as air power. You can stick a grenade bundle under the tracks of a tank or assault gun, but just try to toss a grenade into a plane!'

Rogov was silent for a moment or two, then continued: 'In the area of Ivanovskii, I encountered the commander of our forces himself, General Dukhanov, and asked him, "Comrade General, where is our air force?"'

'Well, how did he answer you?' Ulyanov quickly asked.

'What could he say? He squinted and looked up into the sky . . .'

The Sergeant inhaled deeply, before continuing: 'You say we retreated, and abandoned the city to the Germans. As if we just let Hitler have it, our Soviet city, like we don't need it. Isn't that your opinion?'

Sidorov amicably laid a hand on the Sergeant's shoulder: 'But all the same, brothers, you gave up the city, didn't you?'

Rogov's face flushed, and his hazel eyes flashed angrily. He gazed directly into Sidorov's eyes and in a firm voice retorted: 'And just how are you fighting? Likely, you were the first to flee from the Narva!'

'We had orders.'

'Aha! While we were driven out by force . . . Just stop and think, who's right and who's guilty.'

Kruglov quietly listened to the argument. He knew that the troops were anguished over our failures, and didn't want to intervene.

But Khmelev turned on us, and heatedly said: 'You think we don't know how to fight or are afraid to die. This is nonsense! Look, for example, on the left of our regiment, the 2nd People's Militia Division was fighting. Many of these men were untrained and poorly armed. They only had enough cartridges for two days.'

He stopped as if trying to recall something. Then he continued: 'A militia member Petrov was lying next to me in a shell crater. Before the war he had worked as an engineer at the ship-building factory in Leningrad. When the German infantry attacked, Petrov met the fascists with grenades. As soon as the attack was beaten back, he quickly crawled out to a dead German and took his submachine-gun and magazines. If only you had seen how his face was shining! "Now this is a different matter," he said. "Just teach me, Comrade Commander, how to use this thing." When the Germans started coming at us again, Petrov fired the submachine-gun, emptying one clip after another. Suddenly he stopped firing. I asked, "What's happened?" He replied, "Just a scratch on my

right hand . . . It's nothing, I'll shoot at them with my left hand."
Wounded, he continued to fight . . .'

Lieutenant Khmelev continued in admiration: 'Leningrad volunteers!
What men! Knowing nothing about military tactics, they're blocking the
foe's path to Lenin's city with bayonets and grenades.' Then Khmelev
shook his head: 'They say we're retreating because of our weakness. What
weakness! If only we had more tanks and planes . . .'

Sidorov waved his hand in vexation: 'All right, guys, that's enough . . .
you're embittered. Let's give you something a bit better to eat.'

We ate in the open trench. An enemy Hs-126 reconnaissance plane
was circling overhead, trying to spot our positions. Enemy artillery was
sporadically shelling the highway.

After the meal, one of Khmelev's men – Fedia, a stocky fellow about
25 years old – grabbed an accordion and took a seat on the edge of a trench
shelter. He glanced around mischievously, and then started running his
fingers over the two rows of keys.

A young soldier came running out into the middle of the glade, gave
his blond curls a shake, raised a bowed arm above his head, waved it in
the air and started to dance.

The soldiers started to cry out: 'Volodya, let's have it!'

Fedia started to work the bellows, tapping his feet to the rhythm, and
sang: 'It's Saturday today; you're my lady, you're my ma'am!' [The first
line to an old, popular folk dance song.]

The sounds of the accordion drew an audience. Even our neighbours
on the defence, soldiers of a people's militia battalion, came to listen, and
among them were two young women with medical kits. One of them, with
dark eyes and a kind, open face, plainly loved to dance, and she was
tapping the toe of her unseemly large combat boots to the beat of the
music. She was so light and lithesome, that it seemed the slightest nudge
would send her flying into the air like a feather.

The militia men began to shout: 'Get our Shura out here! Shura!'

The dark-eyed nurse Shura with the medical bag over her shoulders
stepped forward, put her right hand to her waist, raised her left hand
above her head, and waving a kerchief, began to work her shoulders.
Stamping out a lively rhythm, she started to sing: 'And tomorrow's
Sunday; you're my lady, you're my ma'am!'

Our hours of merriment were short. Suddenly the fun came to an end
as quickly as it had started. Again the sound of engines began to hum in
the air, and the order rang out: 'To your places!'

Kruglov walked up to Khmelev: 'Comrade Lieutenant, you've been ordered to head to the rear with your fighters to the reassembly point.' We warmly said our goodbyes to our comrades. Khmelev said upon parting, 'Don't be blue; we'll meet again.'

Life soon surprisingly confirmed the Lieutenant's words. We indeed met again, but under very different circumstances.

Chapter Five

On Reconnaissance

The German forces, having seized the city of Kingisepp, hurled fresh infantry and armour in pursuit of our retreating units, with the aim of breaking through to the Gulf of Luga and encircling the group of Soviet forces defending the city of Narva. All day long on 11 August, Soviet aviation bombed enemy concentrations near the Salka River. Large groups of aircraft from both sides were locked in constant aerial battles.

More and more fresh infantry and artillery units made forced marches to reinforce us. A people's militia division was holding the defensive line on our right flank.

Towards evening, an exchange of rifle and machine-gun fire started up. At this time, a group of Ju-87 dive-bombers appeared in the sky. They operated just as they had previously over the Narva River. The leader rocked his wings, the Stukas shook out into a chain, and the dive-bombers went into a dive on our positions at the edge of the forest. The piercing howl of sirens rang out. We were hearing them for the first time. For the uninitiated, this terrifying sound was even more frightening than the whistle of a falling bomb.

Just at that moment, when the men were afraid even to move a muscle, a long burst of machine-gun fire cut through the air. I raised my head for a moment and immediately saw one of the diving Stukas go into a spin. The pilot tried to pull out of it, but couldn't do it. With a howl and a loud explosion, it smashed into the ground on the edge of the highway.

The machine-gun burst seemed to wake the men up, and shook them out of their daze. Rifle shots began to ring out. The word was passed down the trench line: Uncle Vasya had shot down the Junker. It was the first time we had fired at the enemy aircraft with our rifles and machine guns.

Uncle Vasya was kneeling behind his Maxim machine gun. His chestnut-coloured hair was dishevelled, and his eyes were shining. Mixing his words with choice swearing, he shouted, 'Load it with

35

armour-piercing! With armour-piercing!' In front of us and behind us, everything seemed to be on fire: the haystacks, the woods, knocked-out tanks and downed aircraft.

The Germans launched their attack. Romanov and Ulyanov were firing from Degtyarev light machine guns. I was sitting in the trench, re-loading empty drums for the machine guns and passing them to my comrades. Nearby, next to a shattered dugout, the soldier Kazaryan was lying face down. I thought he was dead. Kruglov ran up and wanted to take the light machine gun from the fallen soldier. But as soon as the commander touched the barrel of the machine gun, Kazaryan hopped to his feet: 'I'm guilty, Comrade Commander, fear overcame me. The Fritzes have dropped a lot of bombs.' Kruglov pointed at us: 'What do you think, their hearts are armoured?' Kazaryan set his machine gun on the edge of the collapsed dugout and opened fire.

A loud moan suddenly came from beyond a turn in the trench not far from me. I handed over a loaded drum and ran to give assistance. Sergeant Ukhov was sitting with his back against the wall of the trench, trying with both hands to close the wound torn into his lower abdomen by a shell fragment. In a quiet voice, he asked for something to drink. I gently laid him on his back in order to bandage the wound, but as I was unfastening his belt, he died. I watched as the colour drained from his face, and as an unexpressed word solidified on his lips – 'drink' . . .

The fighting continued all day. Despite repeated attacks, the enemy was unable to break through our defences and roll up the Soviet units, defending the Luga.

As soon as it began to grow dark, Senior Lieutenant Kruglov ordered me to accompany him to battalion headquarters. I followed him. The evening was surprisingly tranquil. It was hard to believe that the enemy was just several hundred metres away. The Germans were apparently planning something. However, this evening they had changed their normal tactics: they didn't illuminate no-man's-land with flares, and didn't send bursts of machine-gun fire across it from time to time. 'How can one understand the enemy's intentions?' I thought to myself, walking behind the commander.

We entered Major Chistyakov's bunker. It was cramped, with a very low ceiling. The chief of staff, the commissar and an unfamiliar major were all present. As I learned later, the major was the commander of the division's reconnaissance.

The discussion was short. Chistyakov ordered Kruglov to scout the enemy in the battalion's sector.

'A difficult assignment,' I thought. We all knew Kruglov was an experienced company commander, but he wasn't a scout. Reconnaissance
was a new business for us riflemen as well. On the way back, the
company commander didn't utter a single word. He was also plainly
concerned about the task he had received.

While we were gone, the front had come to life. Flares soared into the
sky, and there was the persistent chatter of machine guns.

Kruglov assembled a scout team carefully, but quickly. The members
had to be ready for anything, and prepared for any surprise. *Politruk*
Vasil'ev organized a watch over the Germans' outposts and firing
positions. By midnight, everything was ready for the reconnaissance
team's departure. I was among the group of twelve men selected for the
mission, as was Romanov, for his excellent German language skills. 'It's
good we're going out together,' he told me as he offered me a friendly
handshake.

When everyone had gathered, the company commander briefly laid
out the mission: 'I ask you to remember not to do anything without my
orders. The scout's strengths are in concealment and decisiveness. He
appears where he is not expected. But if he is discovered, he must
disappear as quickly as he had appeared.'

Kruglov turned to me: 'What, a bit frightened, Pilyushin?'

'It's my first time to go on reconnaissance, Comrade Commander . . .'

The *politruk* pointed out to us the locations of the enemy's heavy
machine guns, took our personal documents, and carefully checked our
gear. We were all wearing German camouflage smocks. 'Good luck!' he
said as we left. The first to clamber out of the trench were Kruglov,
Romanov, Ulyanov and I; after a few moments, the rest of the group
departed to follow us.

The German machine-gunners were firing unceasingly. As soon as
one machine gun would fall silent, another would open up. Thus, taking
turns, they kept our lines under constant fire.

We crawled forward without stopping. Now and then flares soared
into the sky, in the light of which I soon noticed freshly-constructed
earthworks. They were the enemy's forward outposts, just some 40 to 50
metres away. Directly in front of us, a machine gun unexpectedly began
working.

We froze, firmly hugging the earth; the tracer bullets grazed the
blades of grass. But suddenly the German ceased firing. We crept
forward another 30 metres.

Taking cover beneath the German breastworks, we began to listen in on the Nazis' conversations. At this moment a German, who had just reloaded his machine gun which was standing in plain view, opened fire again. Shuddering on its long legs, like an enormous mosquito, the machine gun rapidly chewed through and spat out a belt of ammunition. With his ammunition now evidently exhausted, the machine-gunner quickly tossed aside the empty ammunition case and set a new one in position next to the gun. Coughing, he then disappeared back into the trench.

Kruglov gave a hand signal; we quickly climbed over the breastworks and dropped down into a shallow trench. 'We'll wait here for the machine-gunner's return,' the company commander whispered. 'Then you'll have a chance to chat with him, Comrade Romanov. We need the password.' We scattered to the right and left, concealing ourselves behind turns in the trench.

In the depths of the enemy's defences, nothing was visible. There was just the dark outline of the forest against the backdrop of the sky. Somewhere quite close by a muffled engine was running. Apparently, German tanks or armoured halftracks were nearby. We waited impatiently for the return of the machine-gunner.

At last we heard footsteps. Romanov and I were standing around a corner in the trench, just a few metres from the machine gun, and waited for the German to approach. But as if to spite us, he was in no hurry. We watched as the German stopped and took a look around. He grabbed a cigarette from out of his pocket and lit it up. The flare of the lighter illuminated the fascist's whiskered face. Then he deeply stuck his hands into the pockets of his trousers and started walking in our direction. We lay low. About 20 metres from us, he suddenly stopped and looked up at a rising flare. In its light, he evidently caught sight of something in our trenches, and resolutely headed for the machine gun. Reaching the turn, he bumped into the muzzle of a gun, dropped the cigarette from his mouth, and instantly raised his hands.

Romanov asked him, 'Password?' The German didn't answer immediately. Kruglov disarmed him and told Romanov, 'Get the password, but warn him – if he's lying, we'll kill him.' Romanov shoved the German away from the machine gun and threatened him with his fist: 'I'm warning you, if you give us the wrong password, you'll be killed.'

The German soldier was so frightened that he couldn't say a single word. But when he felt a dagger pressed against his chest, he suddenly blurted out in a quavering voice: 'I swear on my life. Our password is "*kugel*".'

'Where's your regiment headquarters?'

'I don't know.'

'Your battalion?'

'I don't know.'

'Where's your company commander?'

'Here, beyond the third turn in the trench.'

'What's that noise we're hearing?'

'Tanks . . .'

After the brief interrogation, the German was sent back to our trenches under the escort of two of the team. After they left, Kruglov told us, 'If the German was speaking the truth, we'll get something done. But if he was lying, it's going to be difficult. Let's check the password anyway.'

We moved out towards the edge of the forest, with Romanov and Ulyanov moving in front. After about 50 metres, we encountered a different German with a light machine gun in the trench.

Romanov shouted, 'Halt!'

'*Dummer Kerl*,' the German barked in reply.

'Password?' asked Romanov.

'*Kugel*!'

Romanov lowered the barrel of his submachine-gun. The German walked up to us and asked, 'Where are you going?'

'We're scouts, planning to pay a visit to the Russians. They've established a foothold on the other side of that brook.'

The German raised his hand to his helmet in acknowledgement: 'I wish you luck.' Then he leisurely strolled past Romanov. But when he drew even with Ulyanov, he suddenly collapsed to the trench floor – Ulyanov had thrust a knife into his side.

Beyond the third turn in the trench, we discovered a dugout, from which conversation and laughter were coming. Here, apparently, was indeed the company commander. The German machine-gunner had told us the truth.

We went about another 150 metres – and ran into a second heavy machine-gun position. We found another machine-gunner slumbering beside the gun, his back against the trench wall. I saw Romanov quickly cover the German's mouth and swing his other arm. The German didn't manage to cry out. With his second knife blow, Romanov finished him off.

Just short of the forest, the trench took a sharp angle to one side. We stayed in the trench and began to observe. We saw a sentry standing next to a tank in some low underbrush. It was impossible to move into the forest without being noticed. There was only one way forward: we had to take out the sentry.

Kruglov handed this assignment to Romanov. He was supposed to lead our small group towards the sentry, while Ulyanov and I followed him at a short distance, as if we were his messengers. The German didn't even hail us; he just kept softly whistling a tune. Walking up to him, Romanov asked him for a smoke. The sentry hastily pulled a box of matches from his pocket and compliantly offered it to Romanov.

'Can you tell me, Herr Officer, what time it is?' he asked.

Romanov glanced at the illuminated numbers on his watch dial: '1:45.'

Having smoked, Romanov handed the matches back to the sentry. At the moment the sentry was sticking the box of matches back into his trousers with his right hand, Romanov struck his temple violently with the butt of his pistol. The sentry crumpled to the ground, and Romanov fell on top of him. Romanov covered the German's face with his chest and made sure the German's right hand stayed in the pocket. Ulyanov and I helped Romanov carry the German into the woods, where the rest of the team was waiting for us. We took a good listen . . . All was quiet. About 300 metres into the woods, we discovered another tank. We could see the dim outlines of its turret and long gun barrel against the night sky. The tank crew wasn't sleeping. The driver's hatch was open, and a little lamp was glowing inside the tank: the tankers were playing cards.

We cautiously crept along the edge of the forest and counted eight tanks. Kruglov ordered Sergeant Major Kudryavtsev and two sappers to lie down near the tanks and keep watch on them, while he marked the tanks' positions on a map and led us towards a supply road, running through the woods in the direction of Kingisepp.

When we approached the road, we heard the sounds of a harmonica. We went a little further and discovered an automobile. Its doors were open, and someone sitting on the running board was playing a simple tune on the harmonica. Another man was standing beside the car. A submachine-gun was dangling from his neck. He was poking at something in the sandy road with the toe of his boot and whistling along with the harmonica.

For several minutes, staying concealed in the trees, we watched the Germans. It seemed clear: they were waiting for the return of their commander, who was somewhere nearby. He was the one we were seeking.

Suddenly to the left of us there was a scraping sound, and a panel of bright light cut through the night gloom. Two Germans dragged someone barely capable of standing through the open door of the bunker. Two more Nazis stepped out of the bunker after them. Having quickly discussed something, two Germans went back into the bunker and firmly closed the door behind them. In the darkness, we lost sight of the others. After a few seconds, through the sounds of their steps, we could determine that they were moving towards the car. Soon we caught sight of their silhouettes by the side of the road.

The man, who the fascists were dragging, suddenly stood up and tried to shake off the grasp of the Germans holding him, but he couldn't remain standing. Falling to the ground, he tried with his hands and feet to fight off the two escorts who were ganging up on him.

We heard a burst of Russian: 'Kill me, vermin, I won't tell you anything! My comrades will avenge my death!'

One of the Germans struck him on the head with something. The driver and soldier by the car rushed up to help the escorts, and the four of them hurled the Russian into the automobile.

In front of our eyes, they were torturing a Soviet man! We were ready to rush the executioners and tear them to pieces. But Kruglov gave no signal. The driver started the car and the vehicle slipped away into the darkness.

'What? We didn't rescue one of our own,' I said with clear indignation to Romanov in a whisper.

'On the Narva we gave one of their captured officers bread,' Sidorov said between his clenched teeth, 'while they, the snakes, torture and abuse our people.'

At that moment a group of soldiers appeared on the road. They were stopped by a sentry. A change of the guard occurred. As soon as the group moved away, a new sentry was holding his submachine-gun at the ready. Taking a careful look around, he then started pacing along the road.

We waited to see what our commander would decide to do. Senior Lieutenant Kruglov gave a hand signal to Ulyanov and Sidorov. Carefully picking their way from tree to tree, they made their way to the side of the road and dropped into a prone position. Soon the sentry passed them on the other side of the road. Waiting several seconds, Ulyanov and Sidorov crept after him before dropping prone again. When the German returned again, they rushed him. I heard only a muffled wheeze.

Kruglov ordered me and Ulyanov to follow him, while the others were to remain in position and monitor the road. Without any particular stealth, the company commander approached the bunker and kicked in the door. Two German officers were sitting behind a table: one was leaning over a map, while the other was saying something over the telephone.

Kruglov shouted, '*Hände hoch!*' The officers, leaping to their feet, raised their hands and looked at us with widely-opened, terrified eyes. We disarmed them, and then gathered up the map and some papers.

We returned to the woods in a file. Kruglov and Romanov took the advance, while Ulyanov and I followed behind with the German officers. The rest of the scout team followed us. The night had become darker. We imagined an enemy soldier behind every tree.

One of the officers was constantly mumbling and shaking his head occasionally. Ulyanov whispered to me, 'A good catch! But how will we haul him in?'

The sappers joined us at the designated place. 'A lot of Germans passed us heading for the trench,' reported Sergeant Major Kudryavtsev. 'The tanks are still parked where they were.'

We took cover in some brush close to the forward trench. Once again, the ground around was being illuminated by flares rising into the sky over no-man's-land. By the sounds and low conversations, one could guess that new German squads were moving up into the forward trench.

I was standing next to Kruglov, and when the next flare soared into the sky, I looked at his face. It seemed even more stern than usual, and his eyes were staring into the darkness. Wrinkles creased his prominent brow. The commander was searching for a way out of a difficult situation. Suddenly his face brightened, a smile played across his lips, and he gestured for Romanov to join him: 'Take the uniform and cap off an officer and get dressed in them.'

No one knew what the commander was thinking. Romanov got dressed in the uniform of a German Hauptmann. It was almost impossible to recognize him – he looked completely different. Kruglov looked Romanov over carefully, and then said: 'OK. Go alone into the trench and call for the officer in charge. Tell him that you're searching for Russians that have infiltrated into the rear. If the officer detects something wrong, shoot him with your pistol – that will be a signal for us to come immediately to your assistance. If everything goes well, summon us.'

I walked over to Romanov: 'Petya, ask the commander to take me with you. You understand anything might happen.'

Kruglov allowed me to accompany Romanov and handed me his captured submachine-gun. Together, we set off towards the German trench. Once we reached it, Romanov leaped into it without a second thought. I followed him into it. We wound up face to face with a German soldier. Romanov ordered him to summon the officer in charge immediately. I felt as if I was standing on a white-hot sheet of metal, not the ground. Not even two minutes passed, when we saw an officer making his way through the trench towards us. The soldier wasn't with him.

The German pre-empted Romanov. 'Take over this sector of the trench,' he said. Romanov saluted the officer, but said: 'I don't need a sector. I'm conducting a special search. Russian scouts are operating somewhere behind our lines. I've been ordered to capture them when they try to return to their own lines. Get your men out of here; we must operate secretly and take the Russians alive.'

'Just a minute, I must clarify this matter with the battalion commander!' With that, the German disappeared into the darkness.

Romanov whispered to me: 'Quickly, go get our guys. While the Germans are talking things over, the fellows can carry away the prisoners; the Senior Lieutenant will decide the rest.'

Without wasting a second in the trench, the scouts headed by Kruglov dragged the bound prisoners off through some tall grass towards our lines. At the commander's orders, the sapper Kudryavtsev remained behind with us. After some time, the Nazi officer came running up to us: 'They're already searching for the Russian scouts. They're asking you to come to the telephone.' The German then looked over Romanov's shoulder suspiciously at me.

At that moment Romanov struck the German's head with the butt of his pistol. The officer sank to his knees. To our left, quite nearby, a machine gun began to chatter. 'They've detected us, the vermin,' I thought. 'Will we ever reach our homes again?'

Leaping from the trench and taking cover in the tall grass, we began crawling towards the machine gun. At Romanov's signal, one grenade after another flew towards its position. The machine gun abruptly fell silent. A commotion erupted in the trenches, and we heard shouting. Wild firing started up in every direction. The bullets weren't touching us, but we couldn't remain here by the breastworks long – dawn was quickly approaching.

Suddenly a green rocket rose into the sky over our lines, then a second and a third. 'They're signalling us,' I thought. We had already noticed under the light of the German flares a ditch about 30 metres away from us. How were we to reach it?

We weren't aware of how much time passed during our harrowing waiting. Suddenly, several heavy machine guns began working at the same time from our side. Bright lines of tracer rounds passed just over the German trench. At Romanov's signal, we began crawling quickly towards the ditch, but we hadn't managed to reach it when a burst of machine-gun fire caught us. I heard a dull groan next to me. I cautiously crawled over to my comrade. It was Kudryavtsev. Grabbing the Sergeant Major by the right arm, I slung him over my back and began squirming through the tall grass. Bullets here and there snapped through the grass. At the end of my strength, I reached the ditch at last.

I carefully laid Kudryavtsev on the grass. 'Sergey! Sergey! Do you hear me?' I asked.

The Sergeant Major didn't respond. I pressed my ear to his chest – his heart wasn't beating. 'Oh, what a soldier has been killed . . .'

Glancing around, I saw Romanov crawling towards me. The machine-gun fire was intensifying on both sides. It was impossible to return directly to our lines. Staying low and within the ditch, we crawled to the edge of some woods, bringing our dead comrade with us. It was already getting light, when we finally reached our positions by an indirect route.

The battalion commander's bunker, where we arrived to report on our return, was crowded. Major Chistyakov stepped around the table where he had been seated to greet us. He firmly kissed our cheeks in a fatherly fashion.

'Thank you, Comrades, for your service!' The battalion commander removed a flask from his belt and offered it to Romanov. 'It's from Leningrad, saved for a special occasion. Go rest up . . .'

Romanov took the flask, but didn't leave immediately. He pointed at the German officers, who were sitting on the edge of a plank bunk: 'Thanks, Comrade Major, but we'd like to hear what those two have to say.'

'Well then, stay,' Chistyakov said as he reached for his flask.

'No, Comrade Battalion Commander, I won't give up Leningrad vodka!'

The bunker filled with laughter. The Major, smiling, walked back to the table. I was standing by the entrance, scanning those present for Kruglov. He wasn't there. The frightening thought flashed through my mind: 'Perhaps he didn't . . .' But several minutes later, the Senior

Lieutenant noisily entered the bunker and impulsively embraced Romanov and me: 'My friends, time won't forget what you've done . . . You bailed us out of a tough situation . . .'

An interrogation of the prisoners started. Turning to the German seated on his left, Major Chistyakov asked in Russian, 'Your name and rank?' The prisoner stood up. 'I don't understand the Russian language,' he brusquely said in German to the translator.

The Major extended a sheet of paper to the German; on it, there were German and Russian statements written in the same handwriting. The Major asked, 'Did you write this?' The German shot a quick glance at the paper and dropped his head. The Major persisted: 'If you don't want to speak Russian, just tell us everything in German.'

'I am Major Adolf Schultz,' the German answered in accented Russian. 'I am on the staff of Army Group North's commander.'

Romanov leaned over to me and whispered, 'Quite a catch!'

'Why were you visiting the front lines?'

'I was accompanying a battalion.'

'Where will it be operating and who is its commander?'

Schultz pointed at the other German officer: 'He is, Hauptmann Heinrich Kurtz! The battalion will be operating on your sector.'

Romanov rose from behind the table, walked directly up to the German, and asked him in a menacing voice, 'Just what were you doing with that Russian in the bunker?'

The officer's face went pale: 'It wasn't me; it wasn't Kurtz or I . . . The man was a Russian pilot, who'd been shot down over our territory.'

'His name?'

'The Russian didn't answer a single question.'

We glared with hatred at the long face of Adolf Schultz, at his narrow forehead and small, sharp eyes. Kruglov picked up a map case from the table, and walking over to the German, he asked, 'Whose map case is this?'

Adolf Schultz reached for the map case. 'It's mine,' he said.

But Kruglov didn't give him the case. Instead, he slowly opened it and withdrew from it three pairs of women's silk stockings, a pendant on a long gold chain, and a gold watch. Then he asked, 'You prepared a parcel for someone, Mister Nazi?' The officer remained sullenly silent, slowly fingering the buttons on his tunic.

As the prisoners were being led out of the bunker, Major Chistyakov unexpectedly stopped them with a question: 'One minute. I want to clarify one thing.' The Major walked over to Adolf Schultz with a sheet of paper and asked him, 'Can you explain to me what these dates mean?'

With that he started reading from the sheet: '1st of August – Kingisepp; 3rd of August – Volosovo; 5th of August – Ropsha; 7th of August – Krasnoye Selo; 9th of August – Uritsk; 15th of August – Leningrad.'

'It's the Führer's directive . . . It indicates the objectives and the dates by which we should take them,' the German replied.

Through clenched teeth, Major Chistyakov shot back: 'You're late, sir. After all on the Soviet calendar, today is already the 13th.'

They took the prisoners away to the regiment headquarters. We surrounded the battalion commander. He crumpled the sheet of paper and tossed it to the floor, and then pronounced grimly, 'They'll never set foot in Leningrad!'

Chapter Six

My First Wound

At twilight, before the nightly exchange of fire, we emerged from our bunkers and took a seat in the grass behind the trench line. We wanted a breath of fresh air, have a chat with our comrades, and dream a bit about those we'd left at home.

Romanov was sprawled out on the grass beside me. He was dozing. Sergeant Akimov picked up the handle of a mess pot with a bayonet, brought over some porridge, set the pot on the ground, and said, 'Eat; today I've prepared some grub better than our own wives could do it, you'll lick all five fingers and the palm of your hand separately!' We ate with gusto, burning our lips with the metal spoons.

To the left of us, shells began to explode, forcing us to crawl back into the trench. Artillery fire added to the mortar shelling, and we heard planes overhead. We waited for a night attack by the enemy, but no attack came.

Enemy activities on our sector of the front became spasmodic and feverish. Sensing the growing strength of our resistance, the commander of the German Army Group North, von Leeb, despite enormous losses, hurled more and more fresh units into the attack in the effort to take Leningrad. Despite the constant firing and shelling, in the intervals between attacks, many of us managed to sleep soundly while crouched and leaning against the walls of the trench. We normally woke to the shouts of 'Germans!' We would become instantly awake and our eyes would start searching for the enemy.

One day Romanov and I were standing next to a turn in the trench. For the first time, I saw sorrow on my friend's face. Romanov spoke up: 'Buddy, if something happens to me, promise that you won't say anything to my mother; her health is so poor.' I replied, 'And what do you think, my heart is armoured?'

Just then, enemy tanks appeared. Romanov shouted, 'Tanks!' Everyone in the trenches woke up instantly.

The tanks were attacking in formation, advancing at high speed and firing from their cannons and machine guns. The infantry followed in their wake, running and firing on the move, disappearing into the tall rye, falling, rising, and shouting their 'Lia–lia–lia!'

Shells flew overhead with their piercing shriek. We didn't know whose they were. But when the turrets of the enemy's three leading tanks flew into the air, everything became clear. Our heavy artillery had come to our aid, and was firing at the enemy vehicles over open sights. This was the first use of large-calibre artillery in a direct-fire role against tanks on our sector of the front and yielded splendid results.

Now all our attention was concentrated on the enemy infantry. We opened a storm of fire on them and became so focused in the task that we didn't notice the growing rumble of engines behind our trenches. Even now, I remember how one iron behemoth clattered just past my head. Coming to my senses and shaking off the dirt, I took a look: they were our T-34 tanks! They bounded over our trenches and attacked the enemy vehicles head-on. For the first time, I watched a tank battle flare up. It lasted for only ten or fifteen minutes, but left terrible traces behind: the rye, the grass, bushes, even the earth itself was burning, coated with benzene and motor oil.

The highway between Kingisepp and Krikkovo changed hands twelve times during the day. It seemed as if the day would never end. Then once again we hurled ourselves into a counter-attack. The Germans flinched and began a disorderly retreat.

Only a soldier can fully appreciate this turning point in battle. With the sight of the backs of his enemy, his strength multiplies tenfold, his courage knows no limits, and he no longer hears the shell explosions and the whistle of bullets. He sees only the enemy, and fires at him until his target falls to the ground.

Kruglov was running in front of the company with a pistol in his hand. To the left and right, a loud 'Ura!' rang out.

At this climax of the fighting, I suddenly felt as if I'd been scalded with boiling water and I tumbled to the ground. In my battle frenzy I imme-diately jumped back up and ran another 100 metres or so, and then felt a burning pain in my left leg. I suddenly felt nauseous and became weak. I swore loudly, sat down, and automatically began running my hand over my left leg. I felt a sharp shell splinter, still hot to the touch, sticking out of my shin. I tried to pull it out, but the fragment was firmly embedded in the bone. Not far away, I saw a deep shell hole, still smoking from the shell explosion that had created it. I slithered over to it on my belly and slid to the bottom of it. My vision began to grow dark. I took a few gulps of water from my canteen.

'Why have you taken shelter here?'

I looked up; an unfamiliar soldier was standing on the edge of the crater.

'They've hit me in the leg, the vermin.'

The soldier shouted for a medic, and then ran on. Soon an older medic leaped into the crater. Glancing at my wound, he quickly cut the leg of my boot with a knife and vigorously plucked the fragment from my shin. I saw stars from the pain. With skilled hands, the medic bandaged my wound and told me, 'Rest a bit, buddy, and then make your way back to a medical tent.'

When I reached the medical station, they applied some sort of ointment to my wound, gave me some hot tea to drink, and I fell asleep. How much time passed while I slept, I don't know, but when I woke up, it was dark. Someone nearby was moaning loudly.

Suddenly I felt the touch of someone's hands. Thinking that a wounded man wanted a drink, I detached my canteen from my belt and offered it to him, but he didn't take it. Instead, he silently continued to move his hands over my head, face and chest. I found some matches in my pocket and struck one. A fellow with a bandaged face was lying next to me on a stretcher. From his dress, it was difficult to determine who he was. I saw several other wounded with me in the tent.

A nurse entered. In a motherly voice, she said tenderly, 'Just a bit longer, dears. An ambulance will come soon.'

I asked her who this man with the wounded head was, who was persistently resting his hand on my chest. The nurse didn't know. In order to ease the suffering of this fellow, I lightly gripped his hand. He settled down a bit and seemed to fall asleep. However, as soon as I removed his hand from my chest, he began to search for me again. It was clear that my neighbour was afraid to remain alone with his bandaged eyes.

A vehicle roared up, and a doctor and two stretcher-bearers entered the tent. The doctor pulled out a list and began to call out the last names of the wounded. I could feel my neighbour's hand begin to tremble on my chest.

'Pilyushin!' the doctor called out my last name. The wounded man lying next to me crawled off his stretcher, hastily grabbed me with both hands, and said something that I couldn't make out. I carefully placed the wounded man back on the stretcher. He wouldn't let go of me.

Just then I heard, 'Romanov, Petr.' I shuddered, as if from a strong blow, dropped to my knees next to the stretcher, and firmly embraced my combat-friend. The nurse, standing over us, began to cry, and the doctor turned away. The stretcher-bearers silently looked at Romanov's bandaged head and scowled.

I tried to soothe Romanov: 'Petya, friend, get better . . . we'll meet again, and together we will fight again.' The doctor silently shook his head. I thought to myself, 'Has Petr Vladimirovich Romanov really fought his last battle?' Through tears, I watched as Romanov was carried away to the ambulance.

The sun began to set. A light rain was falling. The sounds of combat began to fade into silence, but medics were continuing to bring in the wounded. Several groups of German prisoners were escorted past the medical tent. Sergeant majors and cooks were bustling in the woods, in the clearing, and around the field kitchens – they were rushing to send a hot meal up to the front lines. Artillerymen were changing the position of their guns.

I limped over to the dirt road and took a seat on a stump. There I began to wait for a medical cart. I don't recall whether I fell asleep or just became lost in thought, but I didn't hear it when a two-wheeled medical cart pulled up.

'Hey, brother, are you wounded?' Shaking me gently, an elderly medical attendant was addressing me. I replied that my leg was wounded. The attendant helped me over to the cart. 'It's nothing, friend,' he encouraged me. 'Your wound will heal, but we slaughtered a lot of Germans today.'

'And our brother spilled a lot of blood,' said a Red Army soldier with a weathered face, who'd been wounded in the arm.

The thought of Petr wouldn't leave me: 'Would I really never see him again?'

The Return

I spent two weeks in a field army hospital recovering from my wound. The *politruk*'s news and the summaries from the Information Bureau gave us little comfort. Our forces were still retreating into the depth of the country, towards Moscow and Leningrad.

On 16 August, the enemy cut the Moscow-Leningrad railroad in the area of the town of Budogoshch. The Nazi generals were trying to cut all the lines of communication with Leningrad as quickly as possible, in order to hinder the evacuation of industrial equipment and people into the interior of the country. Savage fighting developed on the ground and in the air on a narrow sector of the front, which extended from Mga Station to the shores of Lake Ladoga. On our sector of the front, in the area of

Volosovo Station, the enemy's advance was almost brought to a complete stop. This revived our spirits, and we were expecting similar news from other sectors. The adversary was still powerful, however. Suffering heavy losses in men and material, the Germans continued to make penetrations into our lines here and there and forced the Soviet forces to retreat. My wounded leg healed and was now almost no longer hurting, but my heart constantly ached, because I knew the danger facing my native city and my family.

During one morning check of the patients, the old, stooped, wrinkled doctor with the kind, fatherly eyes was walking from bed to bed. He was asking each wounded man one and the same question: 'Well, how are you feeling?'

'Discharge me, doctor, I'm fine now.'

'Don't worry, now I'll take a look and I'll tell you whether or not you're well. No, dear fellow, you're not fully healed, but we'll do what we can for you.'

He took a close look at my leg as well. 'Your wound has healed,' said the doctor, 'but you'll still have some pain in the leg.'

A nurse placed a check mark next to my name; this meant that they were going to discharge me. I said goodbye to the other guys in the ward, put on a new uniform, slung my sniper's rifle over my shoulder, and went outside.

It was 27 August. The sun was high in the sky; the leaves on the trees were limp, while the grass was wilted. The air was hot, like inside an oven. Having made my way on foot past the Glukhovo State Farm, I sat down on the side of the road and started to smoke while waiting for a passing vehicle. My shin was hurting, and my toes felt numb. Kneading my leg, I recalled my front-line friend Petr Romanov. Where was he now? How was his treatment going?

I heard the sound of an approaching vehicle. A truck coming from the direction of the forest was kicking up dust. I raised my rifle over my head, the driver slowed, and the truck came to a stop next to me. 'Going to the front?' the driver asked.

'Give me a lift; it's tough for me to walk.'

'Climb into the back and keep an eye on the sky. If you spot any "vultures" [slang reference to German planes], let me know!'

I climbed over the side of the truck, settled down comfortably among some boxes, and the truck set off in a cloud of dust. The driver drove quickly, skilfully manoeuvring around the shell craters. When we reached the outskirts of Gubanitsy, enemy fighters appeared overhead. The driver parked the truck under a spreading maple, hopped out of the cab, and asked, 'Where are you going, brother, to Luga or Volosovo?'

'To Volosovo.'

'Then head straight ahead on foot; I'm going to Khudanki.' He glanced up at the sky, and gestured with his head at the circling planes: 'I don't know if I'll manage to get past them, but I must; the anti-aircraft gunners are waiting for the ammunition.' The driver was silent for a moment, and then gave a sly smile: 'It's nothing; I'll give them the slip. This isn't the first time I've encountered them.' I remembered the sly smile on the broad, sunburned face of this Russian soldier for a long time.

Having thanked the comrade, I set out along a village road leading to Volosovo. Crowds of refugees were streaming in the opposite direction – children, adolescents, women and old men. The people were tired, the children were crying – they were thirsty. The mothers were urging them to hold on just a little longer, trying to get as far away as possible. The people were exhausted, often abandoning their meagre belongings by the side of the road.

On the edge of a ditch, an elderly woman was sitting with two girls. She gave me a friendly look and asked: 'Heading to the front, sonny?'

'To the front-line trenches, mammy!'

'What's with that leg?'

'It was wounded.'

The woman shifted her exhausted gaze to the dusty road, along which refugees were constantly moving. Towheaded girls were sitting on either side of the old woman. One was about 8 to 10 years of age; she was holding a bundle on her lap, and squinting from the bright sun, watching the men, women and children cutting across a field. The other girl, about 5 or 6 years old, having laid her curly-haired head on the lap of her grandmother, was sleeping. I saw her smiling at someone or something in her sleep. But when the smile faded, her face became almost like that of a distressed adult.

The little girl woke up from some artillery explosions, but her eyes were continuing to struggle with sleep. Finally, catching sight of me, an armed man in a uniform, the little girl huddled closely against her grandmother and wrapped her little arms around the old woman's neck. She looked at me frowningly with wide, hate-filled eyes. She thought I was a German.

'Why are you so frightened, Raiska? He's one of ours.'

The girl's gaze softened. She immediately relaxed and again laid her little head on her grandmother's lap, watching me out of the corners of her eyes.

Not far from the road, some boys on horseback were driving a herd of cows across a field.

'You see, sonny, we stay close to the herd,' the old woman spoke up, addressing me. She gave a caress to the head of her granddaughter with her dry, wrinkled hand. 'We have no hot meals. We live on the milk.'

The older girl now and then touched the cover of my sniper's rifle with her little hand and looked at me affectionately. In these moments, it was as if I was seeing the Ukraine, Belorussia, and the lands of Smolensk, enveloped in the flames of war; our wives, children, fathers and mothers, having abandoned their homes, were now resignedly trudging along the dusty roads into the country's interior, in order there to help us with their labour in our struggle against the fascist hordes. Perhaps my own mother was now walking in this same way down a different dusty road?

The old woman looked at me with wise, kind eyes, and as if reading my thoughts, sighed deeply: 'It's hard for you to fight, dears. But it is also difficult for us, oh, how difficult! I'm trying to make my way to Leningrad with my granddaughters. Their father is at the front, and their mother was killed during a bombing.'

Artillery salvoes thundered in the distance. The old woman hastily grabbed the hands of the little girls, gave me a quick nod goodbye, and quickly set off into the woods. On the village road, the people also quickened their pace, glancing backward in fright.

At Volosovo Station I encountered an unusual procession. Two burly old men and several women armed with hatchets and pitchforks were leading four bedraggled, filthy German soldiers. Two carts, loaded with boxes of shells, brought up the rear of this procession. A crowd of women and children, buzzing like agitated bees, were swarming around the little column. Falling in behind this strange procession were Red Army soldiers heading towards the front. I also joined the crowd.

We stopped in a little village. From somewhere an empty box appeared from among the cases of shells. An excited young woman clambered up on the box and looked spitefully at the Germans.

'Comrades!' the woman shouted. 'There they are, Hitler's heroes! He dropped them on us in parachutes [rumours of German paratroop drops were rife among the population in the summer of 1941]. In the daytime, they hid in a haystack like mice, but at night they fired on our villages and roads. They were trying to create panic.'

The Red Army soldiers began talking among themselves: 'A spunky woman!'

'Those old guys – strong like oaks . . .'

'Interesting, how did they catch them?'

Guessing the thoughts of those present, the woman appealed to one of the old men: 'Uncle Mikha, tell the comrades how you tracked down these vipers.'

The thickset – with shoulders as broad as a door – and pale as the moon Uncle Mikha, bewildered by all the attention, was shifting his weight from one foot to the other.

'There's nothing really to say,' he softly said. 'Anyone would have done it . . . It was just before dawn, and the first roosters had only begun to crow. I couldn't sleep; worry was gnawing at my heart: what would our lives be like, if the German comes? I stepped out for some fresh air. The forest was quiet. I walked over to the brook, thinking I'd have a little sit. Just then there was a gunshot. I think, "Who's doing this firing?" I crossed the brook on a board and entered the glade next to the gully. A haystack was standing there, just as it is now. I was about to head back to my forest hut, when suddenly there was a movement in the haystack. Aha, I think, something fishy is going on here; our own guys wouldn't hide in haystacks and fire on places at night. I quickly, or at least as fast as I could manage, ran back to the village and roused the people. At dawn we walked up to the gully and grabbed them.'

Uncle Mikha shot a suspicious glance at the Germans: 'A dastardly people . . . in a word, rats!'

I was just about to leave, when I unexpectedly caught sight of Sergeant Akimov in the crowd. He also noticed me. Akimov ran up to me and almost knocked me off my feet.

'Friend!' He tightly embraced me. 'We meet again! You're alive, well? That's great! We've often been thinking about you.'

Akimov was a young, slender, well-built man, blessed with fine features on his slightly elongated face. The guys all loved the Sergeant, and everyone, even the officers, called him affectionately 'our Akimych'.

By nature, Akimov was a cheerful, clever fellow, but in battle he was a tough and capable fighter. Everyone especially respected him for the fact that wherever Akimych might be, he would never leave behind a comrade in distress.

'Well, what fates have brought you here, so far in the rear?' I asked the Sergeant.

'What "rear"? The bullets might not be whistling, but there are more than enough shell fragments!'

On the edge of the forest, we took a seat on the grass. Akimov propped his rifle between his knees, took off his forage cap, turned it inside out, and wiped his sweaty face with it. Having rested a bit, we went back out onto the road, and by evening we had successfully reached our company area. The reunion with my combat-friends was noisy, with lots of embraces and kisses.

During the war, I more than once had to part from my comrades. The parting was always sad, as if I was losing my dearest friends. But the return to my combat family was always joyful, even though death was always around us.

I reported to my company commander on my return from the hospital. Kruglov, smiling, firmly embraced me: 'I'm very happy that you've come back. After all, there's only a few of us veterans left.'

The Senior Lieutenant remembered something and took me by the arm: 'We're going now to the battalion commander. He has a gift for you.' Kruglov pointed at my left breast.

Chapter Seven

The Fight for the Wooded Hill

Our defensive line in the area of Volosovo Station was separated from the enemy by a dense, mixed forest. At six o'clock one morning, enemy artillery and bombers began to work over the station. Our artillerymen and bomber pilots targeted the enemy's positions in return. This duel continued all morning. The infantry and tanks on both sides took no part in this fighting.

Small groups of enemy scouts were operating in the forest. The enemy was showing particular interest in some wooded knolls lying in front of our positions. This interest was understandable to us. Possession of these low hills would give the Germans a great view of our lines, and would allow them to fire on targets in our rear from machine guns and mortars. The fighting for Volosovo Station indeed began precisely in the area of these wooded hills.

Chistyakov's battalion was ordered to cover all the approaches to these knolls and to hold them for as long as possible. Our company was to make a sweep around one of the hills on its western side and to screen a dirt road.

The company exited its trenches by platoon and quickly crossed some open terrain. When we reached the edge of the forest, we unexpectedly heard a single rifle shot ahead of us, and then everything around us again fell silent: not a rustle, not a shout. We entered the woods at the sound of the shot and soon encountered Petrov, the scout platoon commander.

'Who fired?' asked Kruglov.

'It was the sniper Ulyanov, likely hunting some wood grouse.'

We found the sniper Ulyanov standing by an enormous fir tree with his rifle in the trail position. A body was laying in front of him, dressed in camouflage the same colour as the branches of the fir tree. Kruglov walked up to Ulyanov. The sniper looked guiltily into the eyes of the commander, shifting his weight from one foot to the other, as if he had some heavy burden on his back. Then furrowing his brows and through his teeth, he said: 'Comrade Commander, I know I mustn't make any sounds, but there was no other way around this. I asked him to climb down from the tree properly, but he didn't listen to me and kept shouting, hunched over a radio. So I had to fire once.' Kruglov looked cheerfully at Ulyanov: 'But we were told you were shooting wood grouse.'

The sniper shot a glance over at the platoon commander Petrov. Giving Ulyanov's hand a friendly shake, the Senior Lieutenant thanked the sniper for his vigilance and asked: 'But where's the radio that you took from him?'

Ulyanov handed his rifle over to Private Kotov, and then quickly and agilely climbed the tree. When the radio had been retrieved, Kotov, returning the rifle to Ulyanov, whispered angrily: 'What kind of taiga devil are you, that you couldn't take him alive! Don't you see what's going on around here?'

Ulyanov snarled, 'Why are you pestering me? A taiga man, a taiga man! I had to eliminate him, so I fired!'

The presence of an enemy radio operator in our zone once again confirmed that the Germans had set their sights on these wooded hills. Kruglov called the attention of the platoon commanders to the fact that the German radio operator had undoubtedly reported that the commanding height had been occupied by the Russians, which meant that the adversary would soon begin to bomb it. The company commander ordered Petrov to take his men off the hill and pull them back to the dirt road.

We moved on and reached the western slopes of the hill, where we began to wait for the return of our scout team, which was operating ahead of the company. *Politruk* Vasil'ev asked Ulyanov: 'Is it true that you like to treat yourself to forest creatures?'

Ulyanov's entire face lightly flushed, and his thick, dark eyebrows rose. He didn't hurry with his reply. The political officer's question reminded him of his days before the war, when he would go on hunts in the taiga, and bring back a bountiful bag to his mother. They lived together, just the two of them; his father was killed by kulaks [literally, a prosperous farmer, but the term became extended to anyone who opposed collectivization] during the time of collectivization. The entire burden of the household and care for his mother lay on his shoulders. He loved to hunt and was a crack shot.

'Yes, Comrade *Politruk*, whatever I could get. As it happened, my mother made meals of wood grouse, snipes or partridges – of everything that ranged in our district. But here, look, one has to hunt for other game.' With his eyes, Ulyanov indicated the dead German soldier and continued: 'But you can't make a meal from this creature; it only spoils the appetite.'

The sniper Bodrov ran up to the company commander and hastily reported: 'The Germans in about company strength are moving through a ravine in the direction of the hill.'

At this moment, several German Stukas appeared in the sky; making a steep turn over the hill, they went into their bombing runs. One question was in all our minds: 'Had Petrov had time to move his men off the hill?'

The enemy dive-bombers, their yellow surfaces flashing in the sun, began to release their loads. The whistle of the falling bombs, and the hollow crump of their explosions didn't frighten us – we'd become accustomed to them. The soldiers lay down around tree trunks and hugged the earth, without taking their eyes off the ravine.

Soon after the bombing, Germans began to emerge from the ravine. They were moving in a deployed formation, their guns at the ready. Soon they had drawn quite near to us: their pale, sweating faces were clearly visible. The Germans were swinging their guns from side to side as they advanced.

We opened up, and our rifle volleys merged into a prolonged storm of fire. The Germans, having lost a good half of their soldiers, bolted at a run back into the ravine and followed it back into the forest.

The slopes of the ravine were strewn with corpses. I was firing at a fascist officer, who was walking behind the line of his soldiers. Later, we saw bloodstains from five bullets in his chest. That meant I wasn't the only one shooting at him.

Without wasting any time, we headed for the southern slopes of the hill. Along the route, we bumped into the scout Rumyantsev. He was escorting a German prisoner who was carrying a radio.

'We didn't detect the enemy movement in our direction,' Rumyantsev reported. 'But this guy,' and he pointed at the prisoner, 'we caught in a raspberry patch. The red-headed devil, he wanted to snack on some raspberries. When we took him, he offered no resistance and said he was a communist. He speaks Russian well.'

Prisoners captured in these circumstances were usually sent immediately back to battalion headquarters without any interrogation. But for some reason Kruglov didn't send this prisoner back right away. Turning to Vasil'ev, he asked: 'Doesn't it seem to you that this young fellow could have been operating as a pair with the Fritz Ulyanov shot? Perhaps he lost the connection with him and wanted to check on what was going on. We need to find out.'

The Senior Lieutenant ordered his signalman Viktorov and me to escort the prisoner back to the location of the dead German's body.

The prisoner took one glance at the face of the radio operator, then turning to Viktorov, he asked: 'How did he wind up here? He's a radio operator from our regiment.'

'There's no way for me to know . . . But if you had asked for the circumstances of his death, that's a different matter. Did you serve together with him? Was he also a communist?'

'No, but he was a good young man.'

'Do you have any documents? Prove to us that you're a communist. Do you have even your soldier's booklet?'

'The company commander has the soldier's booklet. I didn't have time to get it, because I was in a big hurry.'

'In order to find out the reason for the sudden silence from this radio operator on your line of advance?'

'Yes, but this was only a pretext; otherwise how could I have crossed over to your side?'

'You grabbed the radio as a cover too?'

We listened to the German and didn't know whether to believe him or not. Perhaps he had called himself a communist just to save his own skin. Later I learned that at division headquarters he was revealed to be a dangerous enemy scout.

Squad commander Akimov returned from reconnaissance. He ran up to the company commander and reported: 'Germans are moving in an extended column to our east. I couldn't establish their strength.'

'Keep them under observation,' ordered the Senior Lieutenant, 'while we decide what to do.' Akimov disappeared into the forest.

'The situation has become complicated,' Kruglov said, turning to the *politruk*. 'You kill some, while others slip away into the woods. The fighting will go on indefinitely, and this is extremely unfavourable for us.' The company commander was perceptibly nervous.

Then Kruglov turned to his platoon commanders: 'The enemy has changed his tactics, so we must now do the same. We'll let the Germans reach the base of the hill – the woods are sparser there – and we'll attack them from the rear. We'll cut off their path of retreat and destroy them before larger German forces come up.'

Our riflemen split into two groups and took cover in the bushes. The Germans were advancing with great caution, stopping frequently to listen to the forest sounds. Again we could see their pale faces and alert eyes.

When the last enemy soldier, bringing up the rear of the German column, had passed us, at the command of the Senior Lieutenant we opened fire. Taking cover behind trees, the Germans resisted furiously, but squeezed by us from two sides, the column was destroyed. This time, though, we didn't get by without our own losses.

As soon as we had finished dealing with this second enemy grouping, Kruglov quickly started to lead the company to the dirt road where we were supposed to meet up with the other companies of our battalion. Just as we were moving out from where we had ambushed the German column, heavy machine guns began to chatter from the hilltop. We couldn't determine their direction of fire, but they weren't firing at us.

Kruglov issued an order to platoon commander Viktorov: 'Immediately send some men to find out who's on top of the hill! If the enemy has got past us, don't engage them and come back.'

The commander dropped to one knee, pulled out a map, and again examined the terrain around these wooded hills. The soldiers sat and lay around on the grass, conversing softly and smoking.

The machine guns on the hill continued their heavy fire. Had the Germans engaged other companies of our battalion? Where were Petrov's scouts? Why had there been no word from them? This uncertainty alarmed not only the commander, but also each soldier. We knew that in a forest, one minute can mean the difference between success and complete failure.

Soon Viktorov reported that our battalion was locked in combat with the Germans on the slopes of the hill. Petrov's platoon was keeping watch over the dirt road. Senior Lieutenant Kruglov seemed to be waiting just for this report. Quickly sticking his map back into its case, he said: 'We're heading for the dirt road.'

A runner from Petrov's platoon came running up. 'Enemy reconnaissance is moving along the edge of the forest in the direction of the dirt road,' he announced. 'What are your orders: open fire or let them pass?'

'Let the reconnaissance element pass and wait for the approach of larger forces. You, *Politruk* Vasil'ev, go to Vladimirov's platoon; Sidorov and Pilyushin will accompany you. If something happens, you can find me with Viktorov's platoon. We'll deal with the German reconnaissance element later.'

Vladimirov's platoon was situated in a large forest clearing, through which ran the dirt road. The platoon commander was located in the centre of his riflemen's positions, several metres from the road. Vasil'ev lay down next to the young, but courageous and experienced sniper Borisov. Borisov's sniper team-mate, Sinitsyn, lay 5 metres away from us.

'Well, tell me, how are things going for you here?' the *politruk* asked the sniper team.

Borisov glanced at his friend Sinitsyn, from whom he never parted, neither in hours of rest nor in combat, before replying: 'Everything's OK, Comrade *Politruk*; if they'll just come a little closer, we'll give them a good thrashing!'

'And if there are a lot of them, what then?'

'We won't retreat, Comrade *Politruk*. Here, in the woods, you can't take shelter behind a tank, but you can find it behind a tree. Something else is troubling us, Comrade *Politruk*: we're now not far from Leningrad.'

There was a long minute of silence. Sinitsyn broke the pause in conversation: 'We have, Comrade *Politruk*, how to say, a militant mindset and a great desire to stop the German advance. Otherwise, wherever the Fritzes have trod, whatever piece of our land they have seized, you see our people there are living under fascist captivity. It's hard, oh, so hard for a man who has lost his freedom to live.'

Borisov's face was flushed and his eyes were burning. He moved a little closer to the *politruk*, as if fearing that the enemy might overhear their conversation: 'Our commander, just like you, Comrade *Politruk*, is demanding that we act decisively. Each shot fired must have a purpose. We riflemen like an order like this and we are carrying it out. But you see to retreat is very hard on us; all sort of thoughts crawl into your head . . .'

I always remembered this friendly conversation between the Red Army soldiers and the *politruk*. Simple men were expressing their innermost thoughts; they were ready to stand to the death against any force, if only to stop the enemy advance as quickly as possible and to hurl him from our land.

The discussion was interrupted by the appearance of the Nazis. Everyone froze. The fascists were moving towards the clearing in a column, confident that there were no Russians here.

Sniper Sinitsyn swore: 'They've finally gone too far, the swine. They're moving at the front in columns.'

Hugging the earth and breathing shallowly, I lay there with my eyes focused on the column. It seemed that if you blinked an eye, the Germans would spot you, and if you took a deeper breath, they'd hear you. Now they were quite near, moving slowly, their heads swivelling as they searched the surrounding woods. Three ambulances at the rear of the column now entered the clearing, one after the other. The German column was not less than battalion strength.

Then suddenly a green rocket soared into the sky. The Nazis momentarily stopped and looked at the slowly falling signal rocket. We opened up, and the fire from our light machine guns and rifles tore into their column. Our attack was so strong and unexpected that the enemy could not immediately organize resistance. Those who remained unharmed started to run back, firing wildly, and soon disappeared into the forest. After about ten to fifteen minutes, they attacked again, this time enveloping the forest clearing on two sides. Field grey uniforms flashed among the trees. In a low crouch, the soldiers were running from cover to cover, hiding behind trees, and firing.

'Look, they know how to cower!' Borisov shouted. 'This looks like something completely different from when they had thought to parade around in columns!' Then the sniper resumed sending bullet after bullet at the Nazis.

A messenger from Kruglov came running up to the *politruk*: 'The company commander is summoning you, Comrade *Politruk*.'

The sniper Sidorov and I were ordered to move to Petrov's platoon in order to strengthen it. Petrov's platoon occupied a position alongside a fire break, about 500 metres from the forest clearing. Once we reached it, the platoon commander ordered us to cross the fire break and watch for the enemy.

My partner crawled in front of me, stopping several times to survey the terrain ahead with the assistance of his telescopic sight. There were no Germans. We looked all around, trying not to miss anything.

Suddenly Sidorov turned his head towards me: 'Take a look, what's there in the spruce grove!' Turning to look in his direction, I caught sight of a line of soldiers. They were advancing with great caution. It was difficult to determine their number through the trees. One thing was clear: they were flanking our company. Without losing a minute, we made our way back, moving in short bounds in some places, slithering along on our bellies in other places. On the fringe of the forest, I spotted Uncle Vasya and his inseparable friend Grisha. Their Maxim machine gun was thoroughly camouflaged.

'Well, fellows, are the Germans close?' Yershov asked.

'You won't have to wait long, look sharp!'

Platoon commander Petrov heard our report and ordered us to move out to the edge of the forest in order to cover the heavy machine gun: 'In case of a German attack on our flank, cover it with your fire.'

Reaching the spot, I passed the commander's order to Yershov and quickly began to dig a shallow foxhole. My partner Sidorov was lying next to me on his back, gazing with widely-opened eyes up at the endless blue of the sky.

I asked him, 'Volodya, why aren't you digging a foxhole?'

'There's lots of cover in a forest.'

Uncle Vasya swallowed several gulps of water from his canteen. He stared angrily at Sidorov, but he didn't say anything.

Vasiliy Yershov was shrewd and fearless in combat. He regarded shift-less soldiers and idle boasters with contempt. He liked to say about such soldiers, 'That man's a cowardly soul.' Yershov always spoke only the truth.

Yershov's inseparable combat-friend, the blue-eyed dancer and cheerful 22-year-old fellow Grisha Strel'tsov was talkative by nature: he even liked to boast a bit on any occasion, which seriously annoyed Uncle Vasya. But in combat Strel'tsov was literally reborn, and became quiet, serious and prudent. In this one could sense the influence of Yershov, who Grisha loved to the point of self-abandonment.

Yershov suddenly propped himself up on his hands, and looked across the fire break: 'Germans! Just look how many of them there are, almost one behind every tree!'

We got ready. Grisha quickly opened the spare case containing a belt of ammunition, and quietly gazed into the eyes of Yershov, waiting for his order. Sidorov quickly crawled away from me and took cover behind a thick stump. Not taking his hand away from the trigger of his Maxim, Yershov looked over towards the platoon commander, waiting for his signal.

Through the telescopic sight of my rifle, I saw a fascist in the branches of a fir tree and took aim at his face. I settled the cross hairs between the eyes of the Nazi. For a certain minute, I choked up, seeing the face of my adversary so closely. His face was pale in the shade of the branches. Several minutes passed in anxious waiting, but they seemed like hours.

Keeping my aim on the Nazi, I thought: 'What if I walked over to him, took him by the scruff and asked him, "Why have you come here? What are you looking for in a different country, in this splendid forest, who did you come for with that machine pistol in your hands? Did you ever give at least a single thought about this? Have you ever asked yourself who and why someone stuck a gun in your hands and sent you to another country to kill, plunder, rape and destroy?"' Then suddenly an unquenchable desire rose in me to kill, to kill the one who had placed his fate in the hands of the Nazi ringleaders and who was vandalizing on our soil.

The cross hairs of my telescopic sight never left the German's face. The foe slowly turned his head and said something to someone. The cross hairs shifted to his ear. At this instant I again felt an immeasurable need to fire

– to kill the Nazi. In order to overcome this desire, I took my eye from the eyepiece and suddenly saw Germans crawling towards us in the middle of the cleared fire break. There were about ten of them, all dressed in camouflage clothing.

'What should we do?' Yershov asked me. 'I can't shoot them and give away my position prematurely.'

'I'll shoot them with my submachine-gun,' Grisha Strel'tsov said, 'while you keep an eye on those hiding in the woods.'

Strel'tsov looked into Yershov's eyes; in his gaze, one could almost read: 'Stay calm, I'll do everything just as you've taught me.'

Grisha crawled towards the fire break on his belly, taking cover behind stumps and bushes. I tore my eyes away from Grisha and looked at the German in my sights. The fascist was still staring at the fire break. Suddenly he disappeared. I began to examine the trunks of other trees with great diligence, but I didn't see anything.

'Look!' shouted Sidorov. 'Grisha is about to open fire on them!' I watched as Grisha raised his submachine-gun, and immediately heard two short bursts, one after the other.

'Good man, Grisha!' Yershov exclaimed. 'You've shot dead two of them, and the others are pinned down!'

Grisha rose just a little higher, in order to see where the other Nazis were hiding. This slight motion cost him his life: a short burst of automatic fire dropped him onto the grass.

'Oh, they've killed him, the swine!' Yershov moaned out loud.

At this moment Nazis began pouring out of the forest, and there were a lot of them. A tall officer was running behind the soldiers. I didn't have time to kill him: Yershov beat me to it; he let loose with his Maxim and gave the officer a full dose. Fascists were dropping dead on the ground, but more and more German soldiers were running into the fire break.

A pile of empty ammunition belts lay next to Yershov's machine gun, and steam from the boiling water in the machine gun's jacket was emitting from the upper vent, but Uncle Vasya kept loading belt after belt of ammunition.

'They're flanking us! Do you hear the firing?' shouted Sidorov.

Yershov didn't move. He was literally deafened. With his fire, he was keeping fascists from reaching Grisha Strel'tsov's body. But Sidorov was right; the sound of gunshots carried from our flank. Several minutes later, furious rifle and machine-gun fire erupted in our rear.

Yershov took his forage cap from his head and violently hurled it to the ground: 'Guys! Once you are fated to die, die like a Russian! Not a step back!' Someone behind us shouted, 'You're right, father, if you're to die, then die a hero's death!'

As if on command, we all turned and looked back. Company commander Kruglov was prone on the ground behind a light machine gun, five or six paces behind us. His face had blackened from soot and dust, and only his familiar large eyes were visible. His right forearm was bandaged.

'Are you wounded, Comrade Commander?' I asked.

'No, that's just a scrape I received as I was crawling towards you.'

'Look! Look!' shouted one Red Army soldier, who was lying next to Yershov. He pointed in the direction of the hill. We saw a German running down the slope. He was not wearing a helmet, his red hair was dishevelled, his face and arms were bloody and his uniform was tattered.

'Just look how he's running!' Sidorov shouted, reloading his rifle. 'They've really been giving it to him!' Vladimir jerked his rifle up to his shoulder. Then unexpectedly for all of us, a woman in a military uniform literally seemed to rise from the ground in front of the German. The enemy soldier stopped, tossed away his gun, and raised his hands. Suddenly he took several steps forward and with a sharp motion of his hands, he tried to knock the woman's rifle to one side and strike her in the face. There was the sound of a gunshot, and the fascist fell dead.

'That's our Zina Stroyeva, what a glorious gal! Attagirl!' Uncle Vasya cried out and then again opened fire from his Maxim. That's how I first learned about the female sniper Zina Stroyeva, who later became one of my closest friends at the front.

Firing suddenly intensified on our right flank. The Germans in front of us were pinned down, and after several minutes they rose and rushed back into the woods. We were suspicious: what was going on, why had the Germans suddenly run off?

Suddenly a loud Russian 'Uraa!' reached our ears. It turned out that a people's militia battalion had come to our assistance. They had attacked the enemy in the flank and had forced him to retreat quickly.

Among the militia men I completely unexpectedly ran into Sergeant Rogov and company commander Khmelev. 'Now we've met again!' Khmelev said, broadly smiling, as he firmly clapped Sidorov on the shoulder. 'Now I see that you don't like to retreat! It wasn't for nothing that you made such an impression on us back then at our first meeting.' Sergeant Rogov tightly embraced Sidorov, saying with a smile, 'I just knew that we'd meet again.' Khmelev and his comrades, who had come into our lines outside of Kingisepp, had been sent to one of the people's militia battalions. Indeed now they had helped us overcome the foe.

Twilight quickly started to settle over the forest. In the sky, the thin silver crescent of the moon appeared. Cawing crows circled overhead. The odour of gunsmoke and human blood was perceptible. The groans of the wounded were audible.

Vasiliy Yershov was on his knees beside the body of his young friend Grisha. Large tears rolled down his stubbly cheeks. He was lamenting, 'Grisha, my friend! What will I say to your mother, when she asks me where her son is? How will I console her in her grief, when she learns of your death?'

The soldiers gathered around the fresh little mound of earth on the edge of the forest. *Politruk* Vasil'ev was holding the bloody forage cap, Order of the Red Star and *Komsomol* card of Grigoriy Stepanovich Strel'tsov. 'We swear, Grisha, that we will take revenge on the enemy for your death!'

Chapter Eight
Behind Enemy Lines

That night, someone gave me a hard jab in the side. I instantly leaped up and grabbed for my rifle. 'Wipe the sleep from your eyes,' Sidorov said with amusement.

'Huh? What, are the Germans coming?'

'No, they're sleeping, but we've been ordered to fall back.'

'What, are you crazy? We just thrashed the Germans.'

'Well, the devil will sort things out . . . the guys are saying we've been outflanked.'

At dawn we took up new positions in the area of the village of Begunitsy. All day we fortified our positions, dug trenches, mined the approaches to them, and patrolled the surrounding terrain.

That evening I was standing in the trench next to the battalion commander's dugout, where I had arrived together with my company commander, and was waiting for the conference to end. Just then a rocket flew into the sky, then a second and a third one. Light and heavy machine guns began to sputter, and short bursts of automatic weapon fire and rifle shots were audible. Our quiet day was over.

Senior Lieutenant Kruglov stepped out of the bunker together with Major Chistyakov. The battalion commander paced back and forth in the narrow trench several times.

'Viktor,' the battalion commander finally said in a tone I had never heard from him before, 'I'm entrusting you with a matter, which could decide the fate of all of us. The Germans are planning something; they're reshuffling their forces. Where do they want to land the main blow? That's what we must find out. Do you understand? It is essential. Perhaps, in this headquarters you'll find some documents.'

The Major against paced off along the trench. He was nervous, and when he walked up to Kruglov, he looked at him fixedly in the eyes and said: 'You yourself know that this is very dangerous business. Watch out and take care . . .' Chistyakov tightly embraced Kruglov and kissed him three times on the cheeks.

Overhearing the conversation between the commanders, I also became worried. To get behind enemy lines was not a particularly difficult task, but to return again, when the front was always changing – that was a very complicated matter.

Parting from the battalion commander, a happy and keen Kruglov walked over to me and asked: 'So, are you tired of waiting? Never mind, anything can happen at the front; let's head home now, for we have a lot to do today.'

These words had been uttered so naturally, that it seemed we really were going to head home along the brightly lit streets of Leningrad. But the rockets and the chattering of the machine guns reminded me of the hard reality.

Entering his dugout, Kruglov took a seat on the edge of a plank bed, pulled a notepad from his map case, tore off a clean sheet and began to write something. *Politruk* Vasil'ev was sitting next to the telephone set and transmitting a daily report. Kruglov quickly stood up and handed the sheet to the Sergeant Major, telling him: 'Quickly bring these people to me, check their weapon and ammunition, and draw two days of rations for each.'

'What's happened? Where are you sending these men and why?' asked Vasil'ev.

'Major Chistyakov has given us an assignment – to make our way into the enemy rear.'

Vasil'ev softly whistled. Kruglov spread out a map on his knees and pointed to a small, red square that had been drawn on it: 'According to aerial reconnaissance, the headquarters of a German unit is located in this area. We need to find it and obtain some documents. I think that the Germans, intoxicated with their successes, won't be very alert.'

'How many men are going?'

'I'll be taking along eighteen men.'

'How many kilometres to the enemy headquarters?'

'As the crow flies, 6 kilometres, but 9 to 10 kilometres indirectly. We have eight hours to carry out this assignment, and not a minute more.'

Sergeant Major Rozov entered the dugout and reported: 'Comrade Commander, I've assembled the men. What are your orders?'

Kruglov folded the map and stuck it into his case. We stepped out into the trench. The company commander greeted the soldiers, and then clearly and succinctly laid out the plan for the upcoming operation.

'Comrade Senior Lieutenant, just how are we going to slip through the German line?' the soldier Ushakov asked Kruglov.

'There is still no continuous front line here. We'll infiltrate the enemy's forward units through the swamp.'

There were no other questions. We turned over our personal documents to Vasil'ev, donned some captured camouflage uniforms, and checked our weapons.

A short time later, we were moving towards the swamp. A group of three led the way: Senior Lieutenant Kruglov, Sidorov and I. Sidorov spoke up as we entered it: 'At least the drought this year is worth something; any other summer there's no way through this swamp.'

We advanced about 2 kilometres into the swamp before emerging in a dense forest of mixed woods. In the woods, everything was deeply slumbering. There was not a single sound: even the birds, frightened by the sounds of the day's fighting, were silent. Kruglov led us onto a forest footpath, and ordered Sidorov and me to go on ahead, while he waited on the path for the other men.

We moved very cautiously, advancing from tree to tree, and maintaining a constant line of sight to those following us. We followed the path to a ravine in the woods, where we stopped to examine its slopes and bottom. We didn't detect anyone's presence. We advanced another kilometre, perhaps a bit more. Everything was quiet.

Suddenly we could hear unintelligible voices ahead of us. The company commander ordered everyone off the path quickly and to lie down, while he took several paces further along the path, fell prone on some grass, and pressed his ear to the ground. Then he sprang up, wiped his face with a kerchief, and said: 'People are coming this way!'

Kruglov quickly took cover behind a birch tree, never taking his eyes off the path ahead. The sounds of approaching people grew: we could clearly hear someone stumble over an exposed root and softly swear.

Sidorov whispered in my ear: 'I don't understand how Germans could make their way to this place. After all, they fear the forest like the devil's lair not only at night, but in the daytime as well.'

'This is the front; you can expect anything.'

'Still, this is strange.'

We fell silent. Kruglov suddenly appeared beside us. 'Let everyone moving down this path pass,' he quickly said. 'If the opportunity presents itself, silently grab the one bringing up the rear, drag him behind this fir tree, and wait for me.'

I dropped down into the grass and shifted a little closer to Sidorov. The silhouettes of people became clearly outlined on the path. The first soldier passed us with a rifle in his hands, then a second and a third. We counted thirty of them as they moved past us before we quit counting. The men were moving slowly, breathing heavily, tripping over tree roots, and some even fell.

'Look at how they're falling all over themselves,' Sidorov whispered to me.

Several more German soldiers passed by us. They were lagging significantly behind the main group. Two of them, bringing up the rear, were moving cautiously, their heads swivelling from side to side.

'Let's take these two,' I alerted Sidorov. 'I'll grab the first, you seize the second, only do it carefully; don't kill him, we need a "tongue" [Red Army slang for a talking prisoner].'

The soldiers approached to within five paces of us, and just as the one in front ducked under an overhanging branch of the fir tree, I struck him on the knee with the butt of my submachine-gun. He dropped his rifle and fell face-first to the ground. I pounced on him, and quickly rolling him over, I shoved a gag in his mouth, grabbed him by the arms, and hauled him off the path. Sidorov dealt with the second one in the same way.

Leaving my comrade to guard the prisoners, I went over to the fir tree, where we had agreed to meet Kruglov. Everything was quiet all around; it seemed as if life itself had died out in the woods.

I stood waiting for several minutes. Something cracked behind me. Turning quickly, I spotted the Senior Lieutenant. Approaching me, he stooped and picked up a forage cap from the ground.

'We've captured "tongues".We've grabbed two of them,' I reported.

'Whose forage cap is this?'

'I don't know, Comrade Commander.'

'Well, we'll try to find out.'

We stopped and listened. The woods were silent, dark, and chilly.

I led Kruglov to the heath thicket, where Sidorov was guarding the prisoners. The commander dropped to his knees, looked the soldiers over carefully, and then pulled the gag out of the mouth of one of them.

'Who are you?' he asked.

'What's it to you?' the prisoner replied in fluent Russian language.

Kruglov ordered us to untie the prisoners and to give them water.

'Our conversation's going to be brief: where were you going?' Kruglov asked sternly.

'Home.'

'What, have you had enough of fighting?'

'Maybe.'

'And what's in that bag?'

'Gifts for the wife.'

With a deft motion, Sidorov opened the bag, pulled a gun sight from it and handed it over to the commander. Kruglov closely examined the artillery device.

'This is a fine gift for the wife!'

'Such as it is.'

'Put this little gift back in the bag for him, and let him lug it in health. But bring him along,' Kruglov said abruptly, before stepping back out onto the forest path. Later I learned that we had taken prisoner cadets from a Leningrad military specialist school, who were escaping enemy encirclement.

When our comrades on the mission came up, Senior Lieutenant Kruglov stretched out on the grass with platoon commander Vladimirov and they began to scrutinize a field map under the light of a torch. We gathered around them, in order to shield the glow of the light.

'You see this area, encircled by red pencil?' Kruglov asked, looking up. We all leaned over for a look at the map. 'Today our pilots discovered some sort of headquarters here. Tonight, possibly, the Germans will change its location.'

The Red Army soldiers were silent. Kruglov checked his compass: 'If I'm not mistaken, there should soon be a clearing with five large oak trees.'

Just as at the beginning of our march, Kruglov, Sidorov and I took the lead of the column. The forest began to grow sparse. Against the backdrop of the night sky, five spreading tree canopies appeared.

'There are the trees,' Kruglov quietly said. 'Somewhere around here there should be the headquarters.' With that he ordered us to scout the clearing and locate the headquarters.

We fanned out and started crawling across the clearing towards the highway. Sidorov was next to me. Our uniforms quickly became soaked with dew, but it was easy to slip through the wet grass.

Sidorov crawled ahead of me. Suddenly he stopped and sniffed the air.

'Do you smell tobacco smoke?'

'No, what of it?'

'Someone nearby is smoking.'

The tall, lush grass interfered with the view of whatever might be ahead. As soon as I raised my head above the grass, I saw the dark silhouettes of vehicles next to a ravine, around which men were scurrying back and forth.

'Well, what?' Sidorov whispered to me.

'Vehicles . . . let's crawl closer.'

Approaching about another 50 metres, we saw one man working on an engine under a raised hood, and another lying on his back underneath the vehicle, doing something with a wrench. A group of soldiers were lying on the grass not far from them, conversing and smoking heavily.

We observed the Germans for several minutes, and then began stealthily crawling back. When we reached the designated spot for reassembly, everyone else was already there. Ulyanov reported to the company commander that several armoured cars equipped with antennas had been detected on the side of the highway. Sentries were guarding the armoured cars, and a patrol was moving along the highway. We also briefly reported on the results of our reconnaissance.

Kruglov and Vladimirov began to discuss a plan of attack. Getting worked up as he spoke, Vladimirov argued that it would be best to launch an immediate attack on the Germans. The company commander grabbed him by the arm, and speaking quite deliberately, asked: 'Yet what if this is a field repair shop, not a headquarters? At night it is easy to make mistakes . . . If we attack, we will disclose ourselves.' Kruglov then rose to his feet and relayed his decision: 'Your plan is risky; we might end up only getting men killed. Take your men around the clearing to the road on the other side. Wait for us there.'

Kruglov took Sidorov and me along with him. The grey ribbon of road passed through the meadow and disappeared into the forest. The silhouettes of sentries appeared on the road. We let them pass and then quickly slipped into a roadside ditch. There we encountered telephone lines.

'Excellent,' whispered Kruglov. 'We'll follow them to the headquarters. If that's our objective, we'll take a look.'

Sidorov pressed my head towards a line: 'Lay your ear on it, maybe you'll hear Hitler.'

I swore softly and elbowed Sidorov strongly in the side. We cautiously made our way along the lines, to a point where they left the ditch and climbed a tree. We crawled another 15 metres or so. It was impossible to follow the lines any further: a patrol appeared on the road. The Germans were conversing as they moved slowly along the side of the highway.

We crawled out of the ditch, concealed ourselves in the tall grass, and began to observe the sentries' every movement. There were two of them.

'Oh, it's a shame Petr Romanov isn't here with us,' I thought. 'He could have had a heart-to-heart talk with them.'

The Germans passed our position, heading towards the woods, but soon came back moving in the opposite direction. At Kruglov's signal we slithered down into the ditch and crawled after the sentries.

We soon again found the telephone lines, which were running from a short post to a vehicle. It was some sort of armoured van. Now and then soldiers were entering it. Two sentries were guarding the entry, holding machine pistols at the ready. A little further down the road, we noticed two more armoured cars, also guarded by sentries, but no one was approaching these vehicles.

We lay there in silence for several minutes. Then Kruglov touched my shoulder and said in a whisper: 'Keep watch; I'll soon return and tell you what to do.' With that, he disappeared into the darkness, slithering quietly on his belly.

The minutes stretched on agonizingly. Sidorov lay gloomily, now and then wiping his forehead with his forage cap, even though the night was cool. Again a patrol passed our position, but didn't return. I leaned over to Sidorov and whispered in his ear, 'Probably our guys have taken them; our commander should be coming up soon.'

Indeed, several seconds later Kruglov materialized next to us and ordered, 'Sneak up on the van.' Lying there, I gave Sidorov a quick embrace. 'Perhaps,' I thought, 'we're seeing each other for the last time.'

It was past one o'clock in the morning; other than the sentries, there was no one else around the van. As we were creeping towards the target, a small car drove up to the van and stopped. The driver switched off the engine and two men stepped out of it. One was tall, the other was pudgy. They lit cigarettes and walked leisurely past the van towards a large armoured vehicle parked to the right of it.

'Officers,' Sidorov whispered to me, 'these are the ones we need to take: see the folders under their arms?'

With the appearance of the officers, the sentries snapped to attention. The tall Nazi opened the door of the vehicle and courteously allowed the pudgy one to enter in front of him. A bright rectangle of light cut through the darkness and fell on a tree, behind which I could see Kruglov, tightly pressed against the trunk. Vladimirov was beside him, holding a sub-machine-gun at the ready.

Just as the pudgy officer was about to climb into the vehicle, a burst of automatic weapons fire shattered the silence. I watched as the plump officer and the lanky Nazi both collapsed to the ground, dropping their folders. At the same instant, there were the abrupt explosions of grenades, and submachine-gun fire. The German sentries were immediately killed, the small car exploded, and the van began to emit smoke. I heard the voice of Kruglov: 'Fall back!'

We hadn't even had time to make 100 metres, when light machine guns and submachine-guns opened up behind us. Bullets whistled over our heads. We dropped to the earth and began to look around. The Germans had quickly overcome their initial confusion. After the initial fusillade, they ceased their wild firing and became quiet. Probably noticing the tracks we had left in the dew-covered grass, they resumed firing and set out in pursuit of us. Crawling was now pointless. We leaped to our feet and started running for the forest. There Vladimirov met us; he was holding thick folders and two map cases.

On the forest path, along which we were retreating, Private Ushakov stopped us and reported to Senior Lieutenant Kruglov: 'Comrade Commander, you can't take this path any further.'

'Why?'

'Germans are in the woods. At first they were shouting, like cattle drivers on a roundup, but now they've fallen silent. They want to block our passage through the swamp . . .'

Once again, we had evidence that our foe was not stupid. Kruglov studied us, and then gave Sidorov a friendly clap on the shoulder: 'Well, I don't think the fascists can block the entire swamp. We'll get through.' Sidorov spat on his hands and wiped them: 'We'll break through, Comrade Commander, and we'll deliver the folders with the papers on time.'

Hurrying through the forest undergrowth, we kept running into dry brush, scratching our faces and hands until they were bloody. Having separated from our pursuers, we entered a patch of dense, tall reeds. The ground began to move beneath our feet like bread dough. Struggling step by step, our feet sinking in the wet bog, we moved deeper and deeper into the tangled vegetation.

We beat the Germans by only a few minutes. We hadn't even managed to get 300 metres through the swamp, when we could hear German voices and the yipping of dogs behind us. But fortunately, further on the swamp was dry. This allowed us to separate from our pursuers quickly.

Sidorov, catching up with the Red Army man we had earlier 'taken prisoner', who was taking a gun sight to his wife as a gift, said, 'You, brother, forgive us: it was dark, and we couldn't make out who you were.' The soldier replied, 'You treated me well, don't say a word about it. Now my ears are ringing, but on the other hand I'm home.'

Chapter Nine

In the Vicinity of Ropsha

The rays of the rising sun were glinting off the stalks of ripened wheat. The rye stalks were drooping under their heavy burden of grain.

I was lying in a foxhole, looking at the waving field of grain and thinking, 'Where is that fellow now, who ploughed this field and then scattered the seed on the fragrant, freshly-turned soil? Perhaps he too is now gazing from a foxhole on a field of grain and yearning for peaceful labour.'

Volodya Sidorov was lying beside me. He was a sharp-witted man with a good memory; he could more quickly and accurately evaluate a complex combat situation than anyone. He always knew how to pick the best position in combat. His small, clever eyes were always smiling on his simple, snub-nosed face. When speaking with a comrade, he loved to clap him on the back. His entire character showed in the sweeping and confident movements of a sniper. Even now, we had dug our position close to the highway at his insistence.

Things had been quiet for two days. We were already thinking that the enemy's advance had at last been stopped. But now on the morning of 7 September, an enemy shell exploded in our battalion's sector. It signalled the start of savage fighting for the city of Ropsha.

With each minute the artillery fire intensified: hundreds of guns on both sides were taking part in it. The air was filled with the thunder of explosions and the screech of metal. Fires were burning furiously all around.

As always during an artillery barrage, a continuous roar filled your head, and your face and hands gradually became blackened with soot. A terrible thirst would develop. It seemed that a single swallow of water would immediately soothe you and reinvigorate you.

This agonizing condition would last until you saw the first helmet of an enemy soldier. As soon as this helmet with its distinctive protective skirt appeared, you immediately forgot about everything else: thirst, fatigue, the noise in your head. You became overwhelmed with one desire – to kill the fascist. You saw a foe – and you rejoiced at his death.

With our faces pressed into the sandy soil, my partner Sidorov and I occasionally exchanged glances. How it happened, I never noticed: but when I took another glance at Volodya, he was sprawled on his side, his face covered with blood. I pressed my ear to his chest – he was dead.

Just a minute before, Sidorov had told me: 'Breathe evenly, and don't open your mouth so widely. Don't let your heart pound, or else you'll spoil your aim.' Volodya, giving me a wink, had added: 'Soon it will be our turn to shoot.' He had noticed that my mouth was wide open, as I was gasping for air from the nearly suffocating smoke of the explosives. Sidorov, smiling, looked away and continued to keep watch over the road. All this had happened just a minute before, and now he was lying there with a bloody face, his skull split open by a large shell fragment.

I didn't want to believe that Vladimir was dead. Over and over again, I pressed my ear against his chest with the hope of catching at least a muffled heartbeat. But the sniper's heart had stopped. He was dead, still tightly clutching his rifle. I lay next to my dead friend, full of resolve to guard his body to my last cartridge. As soon as the artillery firing ceased, Major Chistyakov's order followed: 'Fall back to the ravine!'

I picked up Vladimir's body and placed it on my back, taking one more glance at a grain stalk next to our foxhole, which by some miracle had survived the storm of fire. The head, dusted with soot, continued to rock on its slender stalk. 'Such a life force is in it!' I thought to myself. I began to crawl back to the ravine. It was difficult to crawl across the torn-up field with my comrade's body, but I couldn't leave it behind.

In the ravine, one of our artillerymen ran up to me and asked despairingly, 'You're retreating again?'

'No, we're not retreating; we're taking up new positions.' I took my spade out of its case and began to dig a grave.

'Is that your commander?' the artilleryman enquired.

'No, not the commander – a friend.'

Bodrov and Ulyanov came up to me. Together we silently buried our comrade sniper, the communist Vladimir Andreyevich Sidorov.

The enemy command, despite enormous losses, continued to throw fresh units into the battle, trying to break through to Ropsha. Enemy tanks materialized out of some dense bushes. They started to advance on us at full speed. The German vehicles didn't manage to advance even 300 metres, however, before Captain Stolyarov's battery knocked out a first, then a second tank. Deafening explosions rang out – the shells inside the knocked-out tanks were exploding. Infantry began to leap from the tanks and to take cover in the bushes. Three more enemy tanks stopped and burst into flames. The remaining thirteen tanks took cover in a ravine, sheltered from the direct fire of Stolyarov's battery. The Major's order was passed from mouth to mouth along the foxholes: 'Prepare grenades!'

We quickly bundled several grenades together and tied bottles containing flammable liquid to them. However, none of us really knew how we were going to approach the enemy tanks. Plainly before we could creep close enough to the tanks to hurl our grenade bundles, the Germans would shoot us down from machine guns. Just then as if to spite us, German infantry began to emerge from the bushes, striving to link up with their tanks.

Major Chistyakov was standing in a foxhole not far from us. His face was pale, and there were beads of sweat on his forehead; he was nervously chewing his lips, never once taking his eyes off of the German infantry. Company commanders Zorin, Vorob'ëv and Kruglov were standing together with the battalion commander.

Vorob'ëv looked directly into the Major's eyes: 'How will it be, Comrade Commander? Are we really going to let these bastards break our line?'

'Just what can you advise?'

Heavy silence settled over the little group. I knew that Lieutenant Vorob'ëv would unhesitatingly die before retreating. In this situation, though, this sacrifice would have been senseless. At least a battalion of German infantry had assembled in the ravine, which at any moment might attack us under the cover of their tanks' supporting fire.

However, Vorob'ëv grew increasingly heated and tried to convince the battalion commander that it was better to die in battle, than to remain in the foxhole, waiting for the Germans to shoot you down or grind you to pieces.

Kruglov grew impatient with Vorob'ëv's persistent arguments and swore loudly, then said, 'Calm down, Lieutenant, we need to give this matter a good thinking; possibly, we'll find a way out.' Vorob'ëv shot Kruglov a hostile glance: 'There's only one way out, Comrade Senior Lieutenant – attack and sell our lives as dearly as possible!'

Major Chistyakov gave Vorob'ëv a friendly clap on the shoulder: 'It's a bit too early, friend, to think of dying. We need to know how to fight. We know what war is, but there's no point in spilling our own blood for nothing. To hurl ourselves headlong straight into the barrels of enemy guns and machine guns – that isn't heroism; that's cowardice in the face of enemy strength.'

The Major raised his binoculars to his eyes and carefully examined the slopes of the ravine, which were overgrown with small bushes. Then he continued his interrupted statement: 'You, Comrade Lieutentant, are a commander, and you are proposing not only risking your own life, but also the lives of your men. The Motherland has made you responsible for their wellbeing. Always remember this, or else you will lose that which is most dear: your soldiers' trust.'

German motorcyclists, evidently couriers, emerged from the bushes and drove up to the ravine. One of the motorcyclists passed some order to the infantry, and then the motorcycles quickly sped away.

At this moment, a hatch on one of the German tanks opened. From out of the grey armoured turret, a tanker's head appeared. An infantry officer ran up to him. From our side a single rifle shot rang out, and the tanker, clutching his head with his hands, slowly sank back into the turret. The hatch closed.

Soon the tanks' engines began to roar, and they began to climb the shallow slope of the ravine. Borisov, my new partner after Sidorov's death, whispered through his tightly-compressed lips as he gripped the handle of an anti-tank grenade: 'They're coming . . . Well and good, we'll meet them.'

In front of us now were German tanks and infantry, behind us – a quag-mire. Enemy bombers appeared overhead. But not a single trooper moved from his place. Each one hugged his native soil more tightly.

Everyone waited for a signal. But battalion commander Chistyakov continued to stand calmly in his foxhole. 'What's he waiting for? Why is he silent?' I thought. Then suddenly something happened that was completely unexpected for us all: the tanks turned around, and the enemy infantry showed their backs to us. The firing of light machine guns from beyond the ravine carried to our ears. It was like a miracle. In actuality, as later became clear, a company of submachine-gunners from the regiment reserve, which had been attached to our battalion, had at Major Chistyakov's order cheekily outflanked the enemy's position. As soon as our company had reached the designated place and assaulted the Germans from behind, we attacked the adversary from in front.

Bundles of hand grenades and Molotov cocktails flew at the tanks, as heavy and light machine guns opened fire. The foe, pressed by our fire to the bottom of the ravine, thrashed like a wounded beast. Three tanks burst into flames, and the remainder began to retreat hastily in the direction of the forest. Now once again Captain Stolyarov's battery joined the battle. The Captain was now standing at full height in his foxhole and shouting into his telephone in his thundering voice: 'Fire! Damn it, rapid fire!'

The enemy infantry, deprived of their tank support, began to abandon the ravine and flee, but few made it out alive. When the danger of the enemy attack had passed, Captain Stolyarov ran up to Chistyakov and firmly embraced him.

After the battle, the battalion commander stood above a narrow trench, and with unconcealed pride watched his Red Army troops pass below him. The machine-gunner Yershov was among them. Company commander Kruglov stopped the soldier: 'Well, old boy, well done! But you're probably tired after dragging that Maxim from place to place today?' Yershov, smiling, patted the jacket of the machine gun: 'What are you saying, Comrade Commander, I'm not at all tired! This is a light burden. It is much harder when the enemy is pressing you, and you don't have any way to stop him. But this friend won't let you down! Tak-tak-tak – and it's as if the fascists were never there!'

In the evening, when all was quiet and the day's duties were done, the soldiers gathered in platoon commander Vladimirov's spacious bunker. They felt like having some fun, to spend time with their comrades, and to forget about what they had experienced that day, if at least for a short while. As always, the Russian guitar and accordion cheered us up and delighted us. The cook Katayev carefully kept these instruments in a case with his field kitchen. The platoon favourite Private Vladimir Smirnov could play the accordion like a master, while the sniper Sinitsyn was a superb guitarist. Our musicians comfortably settled on plank beds and began to play at once:

Rise up, enormous country, rise up for the life and death struggle . . .

We deeply loved this song not only for its fine lyrics, but also for its stirring melody. All Soviet people sang it in those years, wherever they might be located. They sang it in the rear and at the front. Soldiers sang it before a battle and workers sang it at their work stations.

Let the noble fury well up like a wave
A national war, a sacred war is going on

A lively Russian dance followed this song. The Siberian Alësha Ulyanov slowly, as if unwillingly, entered the circle of men. A lock of hair fell down over his forehead, and with a toss of his head he flipped it back and immediately began a lively jig. Ulyanov's dance was infectious – the watching soldiers began to tap their feet. From out of the crowd, Zina Stroyeva stepped into the circle. Her khaki-coloured jacket was torn and scorched, but a clean, colourful kerchief was neatly covering her head.

Stroyeva had a beautiful Russian face, tanned by the summer sun, with rosy cheeks. Her large blue eyes looked at us provocatively. Thick curls of chestnut-coloured hair fell around her shoulders. A belt tightly encircled her slender, maidenly waistline.

My, she looked like a treat at this minute! How sweet was her wide, mischievous smile! And how she could dance! Her untrained feet were now tapping out a rhythm, now lightly and beautifully moving across the damp dirt floor on her tiptoes.

Many of the soldiers and officers had an eye for Zina, but she always spurned their advances. Such strictness in the young woman's behaviour under front-line conditions seemed strange and surprising to many.

'Come on, dear fellow, don't rush to declare your love,' Stroyeva would typically cut off a hapless admirer; 'but show me in battle what a hero you are.' She would say this calmly, while at the same time fixing you with a gaze that would leave you tongue-tied.

Gazing at Zina and my dancing comrades, I thought to myself, 'Here it is, the simple soldier's merriment amidst so much death.' At that moment I recalled Stroyeva's entire life story, which she had once briefly told me. Zina's father Vasiliy Aleksandrovich and mother Maria Sergeyevna had been killed in a train wreck in 1922. Her aunt took in the little 2-year-old girl to raise, and she lived with her aunt until the age of 8. In 1928 the aunt passed away. The orphaned Zina was sent to an orphanage. Having successfully completed middle school, Zina enrolled in the Gerzen Pedagogical Institute in Leningrad.

When the war broke out, the fourth-year student of the Institute and *Komsomol* member Zinaida Stroyeva went to see the commissar of the district military enlistment office with an application in her hand. She requested that he accept her into the ranks of the Red Army. To all of the commissar's arguments that she withdraw the petition, Stroyeva firmly responded: 'I'm a sniper, here's the document. I cannot remain on the sidelines.'

In the end, her request was granted. Zina first entered battle in the area of Volosovo Station as a member of our battalion. She endured all the hardships of front-line life together with us without complaint. Stroyeva had mastered the sniper's craft. She had distinguished herself as well in the fighting that day: it was Zina who had struck the tanker with a well-aimed shot.

At the height of our merriment, Major Chistyakov and Senior Lieutenant Kruglov entered the bunker. Our musicians began to play the tune 'Barynya' with enthusiasm. Major Chistyakov happily looked around at the faces of the Red Army soldiers, lit up by the dancing, and broadly smiled. 'Comrade Major, step into the circle . . . Honour us with your presence,' the voices rang out.

'I'm a bad dancer, but with such music, I'm ready to give it another try! Well then, step aside, fellows . . .'

The battalion commander gradually made his way through the circle of men, and then crossing his arms across his chest, he dropped into a squat. Chistyakov, of course, had put one over on us when he had excused himself for his dancing. He was a superb dancer. We awarded him with loud applause and shouts of 'Bravo!' Kruglov also joined Chistyakov in the dance. But the fun was interrupted when platoon commander Petrov came running into the bunker: 'Comrade battalion commander, the Germans are launching flares over no-man's-land!'

'Ahh, flares again . . . Well, that means we must anticipate some trick or another; put an end to the frolicking, comrades,' Chistyakov quickly said.

Without having time to thank the musicians and dancers, we hurried out of the bunker and took up our firing positions. We were expecting a night attack.

Our snipers amused themselves while we waited by shooting at the flares dangling from their parachutes from captured rifles and explosive bullets. When such a bullet struck the flare or the parachute, it would explode, and the flare would drop to the earth, where it would still continue to burn. We spent the night exchanging fire with the Germans, but no night attack came.

The rays of the rising sun illuminated the narrow trench, in which the still standing men had spent an anxious night preparing for battle. To the left of our position extended a swamp, from which a thick morning mist was rising. The tops of alders fancifully rose out of the milky shroud.

The fog thickened with every minute. Soon it had enveloped the trench and the entire no-man's-land. Nothing was visible at five paces. Encountering such a situation for the first time, many of us were at a loss; we stood anxiously in the trench with our weapons, not knowing what to do.

Unexpectedly battalion commander Chistyakov emerged from the fog: 'Comrades, keep alert! Where's the Senior Lieutenant?' Platoon commander Petrov replied, 'Senior Lieutenant Kruglov is checking the listening posts.'

Chistyakov glared at Petrov, as if in reproach: 'Why did Kruglov go out, and not you?' Then the Major walked over to a heavy machine gun and pulled the trigger, firing a long burst. All the enemy's firing positions immediately responded to the sound of the machine gun.

'Aha, they're hunkered down, the scum, fearing our attack!' The Major energetically shrugged his shoulders.

We literally came alive, and our anxieties evaporated. From the direction of the ravine, from which we had driven the Germans the day before, single rifle shots sounded. We perked up our ears. After the single rifle shots, there were bursts of automatic weapons fire, and at this instant a long howl rose from the ravine, like a human voice in the last moments of life. It was drowned out by the chatter of automatic weapons.

What had happened in the ravine? Perhaps, comrades were dying? We didn't know. Platoon commander Petrov forbade us to go out and check what had happened.

At nine o'clock in the morning, the fog finally lifted and dissipated. The machine-gun firing stopped. Together with the battalion commander and Petrov I went to the company command post. There we found Kruglov, Stroyeva, Ulyanov and Bodrov having breakfast. There was also a lanky German officer sitting on a cartridge box in the corner of the bunker, eating some buckwheat kasha slowly and with dignity. The German was holding the mess tin between his knees, and checking his watch from time to time.

Chistyakov asked Kruglov: 'Did you capture him in the ravine? Likely, he was scouting our positions?'

'Yes, he was scouting,' the Senior Lieutenant responded. 'He didn't expect to run into us.'

Politruk Vasil'ev stepped into the dugout; he had just returned from Leningrad. We surrounded him, vying with each other to question him.

'I dropped all your letters into a post box,' he said. 'Excuse me, but I couldn't drop in on your families; I was busy with duties.' Then he continued: 'Leningraders are preparing for the decisive battle. Their lives are hard. They're digging anti-tank ditches on the outskirts of the city, building pillboxes and emplacements, erecting iron barriers on the streets, and mining approaches to the city.'

Complete silence fell over the bunker. Even the captured German had listened tensely to Vasil'ev's words.

The political officer opened a pack of *Belomorkanal* cigarettes, and we all lit one up. The prisoner avidly sniffed the cigarette smoke.

Vasil'ev resumed speaking: 'Yes, the city is at full alarm. The connection between Leningrad and Moscow has been severed . . . There you have it.'

This announcement by the *politruk* struck a deeply painful chord in our hearts. The *politruk* searched me out with his eyes and handed me something heavy, wrapped in tent canvas.

'Here, Yosif, a gift from our factory comrades. It was made in our factory.'

I opened the gift from our own factory and couldn't believe my eyes. Before the war, our factory had produced only civilian items of various types, but now two new, polished submachine-guns were lying in front of me.

'They're for you and me. They asked that we try them out in battle and report on the results.'

The submachine-guns provoked the fervent interest of all those around us. They passed from hand to hand.

During our conversation with Vasil'ev, the German had been fidgeting on the empty case like a magpie on a perch, repeatedly glancing at his watch. Kruglov suddenly walked over to him and asked through an interpreter: 'So you maintain that the attack will begin at ten o'clock?'

The German officer, gazing at the Soviet officer with fixed, empty eyes, dryly replied: 'That was the order.' Major Chistyakov checked his watch: 'Well then, comrades, we'll check what he's saying, that the attack will begin at ten o'clock. As for Leningrad . . .' With those words, the Major shook his fist at the prisoner.

We stepped out into the trench. Soon we heard the throbbing hum of enemy planes overhead. Squadron after squadron was flying towards Ropsha to bomb it. Our anti-aircraft artillery was firing non-stop. The prisoner was led away to regiment headquarters. We scattered to our firing positions and prepared to repulse the attack.

Precisely at 10.00 am, the enemy began the opening barrage. It was particularly heavy. Making use of the heavy fire of their artillery, enemy infantry crept to within 300 metres of our trenches. Enemy machine-gun bullets struck the breastwork of our trench and exploded, spraying us with tiny fragments. Here for the first time I observed the terrifying effect that explosive bullets had on many of our soldiers.

I watched as Orlov rummaged through his pockets and knapsack for a long time, searching for something. Then he ran over to Private Izotov and asked him for a hand grenade. Izotov looked at him and shook his head. Orlov persistently asked, 'Give me just one grenade, I don't need any more.'

'No, a weapon isn't a plug of tobacco. Go look in the trench shelters.'

Orlov walked over to platoon commander Viktorov and asked for a grenade. Viktorov looked at the perplexed face of the private with surprise: 'Have you gone mad? You have five grenades dangling from your belt.'

Orlov dropped his hand to his belt, felt a grenade, and then sighed with relief. Yes, the comrade had lost his head for a moment. But there and then he detached one of the hand grenades from his belt, and propped against the wall of the trench, prepared for battle.

By the end of the third day of constant fighting, the enemy had managed to push our forces back to the city of Ropsha. Street fighting developed. By the onset of darkness, our 105th Rifle Regiment was so heavily reduced in numbers that it was withdrawn from the forward positions for rest and refitting.

We walked through Ropsha. The city was unrecognizable: the streets were filled with the bricks of shattered buildings, blackened chimneys rose from the ashes of burned-down homes, and emaciated dogs were wandering around. Dangling branches of poplars and lindens, broken by bomb and shell fragments, swung in the wind, like the broken bird wings. The city was empty; the civilians had all fled to Leningrad.

On the northern outskirts of the city, I spotted a stooped, grey-haired man wearing an old quilted jacket seated beside a pond, who was holding a fishing rod. We stopped for a minute next to the fisherman. In a metal bucket beside him, half-filled with water, there were three rather large carp. The old man looked at our filthy uniforms and worn-out shoes with his wise eyes, which were filled with sympathy and sorrow.

One of the soldiers, sticking his hand into the water, pulled one of the fish from the bucket. The carp's gills were working furiously, and the fish lashed the soldier's arm with its tail.

'Take the fish, comrades, you'll have a fine fish soup. You won't find such in Leningrad now, and I'll catch a few more for myself before you return; there are a lot of them swimming around in this pond.'

The Red Army man dropped the fish back into the bucket, and then with lowered head he headed back to the road. The fisherman's words: 'Take the fish, comrades, you'll have a fine fish soup. You won't find such in Leningrad now . . .' had pierced the soldier's heart. We were still retreating.

When it began to grow light, we moved some distance off the road, crossed the little Shingarka River and stopped to rest in some woods close to the settlement of Porozhki. It was hard to believe the silence that enveloped us. At this early morning hour, the woods still retained their night-time chill and perfumed the air with the scent of pine needles and resin. The soldiers collapsed on the grass and immediately fell asleep.

Somewhere not far away on the edge of the forest, an accordion was playing and women's voices were loudly singing a song. It was difficult to make out the words, but we all recognized the tune: '*Rise up, enormous country, rise up for the life and death struggle* . . .'

Ulyanov and I settled down close to the company command post, next to some young oak saplings, but we couldn't fall asleep right away. Sergeant Akimov approached us. Ulyanov asked him: 'Where have you been?' Akimov stretched out on the grass next to us, and crossing his arms behind his head, he lay there silently.

'Senya, why are you so gloomy?' Ulyanov tried again.

'You'll be gloomy . . .'

Suddenly Akimov burst out laughing: 'Do you hear that song? That's where I've been, over there. I thought it would be a raspberry patch, but it turned out to be nettles. Eh, I encountered some of our Leningrad ladies. They're digging new lines. When I walked up to them, the girls had gathered for breakfast. They invited me, of course, to have a bite with them. Well, I agreed and pulled out some bread and some canned food and started to share it with them. That's when it all started! Oh, they're furious at us, because we're not fighting well. They were saying, "We women aren't afraid of enemy aircraft; they bomb us and strafe us, but we never stop our work. We're digging trenches and building pillboxes and emplacements for you, but you run away pell-mell, and where are you running? To Leningrad!" They really gave it to me from all sides.'

'What did you do?' Ulyanov asked gloomily.

'What do you mean, "What"? They didn't give me a chance to open my mouth, and yet you're asking how I answered them.'

Chapter Ten

The Decisive Battle

With the sunrise, a light breeze began to whisper through the pines and fir trees, and rustled the leaves on the lacy alders. The forest inhabitants began to stir: across the small meadow, common jays began to sing noisily, and thrush in the willow thickets began to chirp.

Ulyanov and I shaved on the bank of a little stream. Dabs of lather were falling from the razor into the stream and being carried away by the current. We shaved deliberately, for the first time after the hard fighting for Ropsha. Newly-arrived recruits were sitting and reclining on the grass at the feet of fir trees. They were quietly conversing among themselves, sharing items of food from their home kitchens with each other, and listening to each sound in the forest.

Uncle Vasya had just finished cleaning his machine gun and walked up to the recruits. We could hear his deep, smooth and calm voice: 'Our company commander loves for a weapon always to be in good working order. He personally oversees and checks everything, and deploys our forces so that wherever the fascist might stick his ugly snout, he will be defeated. He also keeps a reserve for himself, but – how to say it – not like that which the top commanders keep – a division or two – but only three light machine guns and one heavy machine gun. At a difficult moment in battle, this is a big help.'

Vasiliy Yershov looked over his audience affectionately, wiped his face and greasy hands, and lit up a cigarette. Then he continued: 'All sorts of things happen in battle. Sometimes the Germans will press you so hard that you lack the strength to hold them back. Right then and there, the company commander will rush up with his reserve, and everything turns out all right. Oh, how our company commander hates to retreat! It puts him in a nasty mood.'

'You say that you're thrashing the Germans. Then why are our guys retreating?' one of the newcomers asked.'There are all sorts of retreats, my dear fellow,' Uncle Vasya responded in an authoritative tone. 'To run away out of fear is one thing, but a fighting withdrawal is something else entirely. It is true, guys, that we smash them, but we're yielding in the face of their equipment. They have a hell of a lot of tanks, self-propelled guns, transports and aircraft. There's no need to try to convince you; you yourselves have arrived at the front, and you'll see it with your own eyes. It would be better if you told us how life is in Leningrad.'

'Life is bad,' an older Red Army soldier in a new uniform spoke up quietly. 'At first they evacuated the factories, the children, the women . . . But now the Germans have cut all the roads.' Yershov replied sharply, 'Have they really cut them?'

'Yes, they've cut them. That's so.'

'And where were you born? Are you a Leningrader?'

'Born and grew up there, this is the second time I'm defending it.'

Everyone fell silent at once and gazed in the direction of Leningrad. There was so much pain and alarm in their eyes, but also a firm determination to defend their city!

After breakfast, Ulyanov and I returned to the company command post. Kruglov was sitting at the foot of a low, branching oak tree, with a greatcoat flung over his shoulders. Hugging his knees, he was pensively chewing a dry blade of grass and looking in the direction of Leningrad, which was now visible to the naked eye. Next to Kruglov, *Politruk* Vasil'ev was lying on his back on the dewy grass, his hands under his head. He was keeping his eyes on a narrow crevice in the trunk of the tree, around which bees were bustling.

'Viktor, look at the bees. Do you like honey?'

'No, thank you, I feel sickly enough without honey: it is galling to see how close the Germans are to Leningrad.'

The officers fell silent. A simple, sometimes gruff, but solid front-line friendship connected these two men. I thought of the death of my own front-line friend Volodya Sidorov. His friendly eyes, rapid speech and confident step were still vivid in my mind. Where now was his family, had his wife returned to Leningrad? How he would have suffered through these days, when the fate of the great city was being decided.

Abruptly Kruglov tossed the greatcoat from his shoulders and pulled a cigarette case out of his pocket. He spat out the blade of grass, stuck a cigarette into his mouth, and tossed another one to Vasil'ev. 'That's enough of this misery. This won't help anything. Have a smoke and drop by the new recruits; have a chat with them,' Kruglov said with a toss of his head in the direction of the woods. 'The guys are worried . . .'

Vasil'ev straightened out both arms above his head, and then swung them in a way so that he instantly sprang to his feet. 'Gymnasts,' Ulyanov whispered to me, 'only they know how to get up like that.'

The *politruk* left to visit with the new recruits. The ceaseless sound of fighting carried to us from the direction of Krasnogvardeysk.

. . . At dawn we took up new positions. A wide valley stretched in front of us, from the shores of the Gulf of Finland towards Novyi Petergof. It was mostly covered with scrub brush, with grain fields scattered here and there. Leningrad was now quite close behind us.

On the enemy side, things were quiet. A damp wind was blowing in from the Gulf of Finland, carrying with it the faint sound of crashing waves. Ulyanov and I were standing guard by battalion commander Chistyakov's dugout. Now and then, company commanders and political officers came and went. The entire day was full of bustle: our unit was preparing to attack.

A machine-gunner, mortar men and we riflemen were standing in an open trench. Here and there you could see the glowing tips of cigarettes as men inhaled, and you could catch the sound of restrained conversation. Though everyone's minds were preoccupied with the coming attack, people were talking about anything else. Many men were inquiring about when and how I had received my new boots. Even as I satisfied all their curiosities, I never stopped thinking about my wife and children.

At seven o'clock in the morning on 15 September, the word was given to our artillery. The ground began to quake beneath our feet. It seemed that the earth had risen and was suspended in the air, swinging from side to side like a hammock.

Major Chistyakov was standing next to Kruglov and Vasil'ev. I watched as the eyes of the battalion commander never for a second left the face of his watch, which he was holding in his left hand. He was watching the minute hand, which slowly moved around the face from the number '6' to the number '7'. In his right hand, Chistyakov was holding a loaded flare gun, and as soon as the minute hand indicated 7.35 am, green signal flares streaked into the sky.

It was our first attack, for which we had meticulously prepared. Company commander Kruglov had split up the snipers, assigning one pair to each platoon. Ulyanov and I joined Vladimirov's platoon in the attack.

As we approached the German trench, our artillery shifted its fire more deeply into the enemy's positions. Senior Lieutenant Kruglov was leading the company on the attack quickly and decisively, in short bounds. With insignificant losses, we reached a railroad embankment, behind which the Germans were taking cover.

At the platoon commander's order, Ulyanov and I changed our

position and flopped down directly next to the company commander. Soon, the commander of the 1st Rifle Company, Lieutenant Vorob'ëv, came running up to Kruglov and shouted: 'Comrade Kruglov, the enemy has been shaken! Why are you lying there? We must keep the pressure on them! You understand? One step, one minute can decide the outcome of the battle!'

Kruglov looked with surprise at the Lieutenant and asked: 'Clamber up onto the embankment, without artillery cover?'

Vorob'ëv wanted to offer a retort, but couldn't get it out: an enemy shell exploded next to us. Dirt rained down upon us, and there was the nauseating smell of explosives. Vorob'ëv lay next to Kruglov, tightly hugging the earth. Kruglov seemingly didn't even notice the shell burst.

He replaced the drum on his light machine gun and resumed fire. Then he stopped firing and looked at Vorob'ëv. Their eyes met. Kruglov shook his head: 'What, a bit frightened? And you wanted to force me to run across an open field to catch the Germans. Wise up, brother . . .'

The Lieutenant loudly swore and crawled away in the direction of his company. Kruglov glanced at us, and tossed his head towards the departing Vorob'ëv: 'A fine commander, but also quite hot-headed, particularly on the attack.'

The snipers Sinitsyn and Borisov were inseparable friends, fellow natives from the Smolensk area. They were not only the same height, but even in their mannerisms they resembled each other. During a conversation, each man liked to scratch the tip of his nose. They were both courageous, experienced fighters. The friends were now keeping watch on a reinforced concrete culvert, through which the Nazis with light machine guns had twice tried to penetrate our side of the embankment. The snipers had picked them off one after the other. Then Borisov held position, while Sinitsyn quickly crawled to the dead Germans and took possession of their machine guns. Borisov immediately rushed up to his partner, and together they concealed themselves in the culvert. A minute later, we heard light machine guns begin to operate from that direction. Rifle shots and hand grenade explosions joined the machine-gun fire. It was riflemen from Viktorov's platoon who had passed through the culvert and engaged the Nazis in battle. Other platoons of our company rushed to exploit this tiny gap, torn into the enemy's position by the two Russian snipers. The Germans took to their heels in the direction of a swamp, but many were cut down, while others were taken prisoner.

We forced our way into Novyi Petergof. On the southern outskirts of the city, the enemy put up fierce resistance, firing from windows and attics. Our battalion surrounded the foes and killed the majority of them, but those that remained alive fought to the last cartridge. Soon even these began to emerge from their cover with raised hands, crying 'We give up, Hitler kaput!'

'The vermin, they've run out of ammunition, so now they recall "kaput",' said Stroyeva as she dragged an enemy machine-gunner from a cellar.

We pushed on towards Staryi Petergof. But soon we were forced to take cover. The Germans had received reinforcements. Our battalion fought off enemy counter-attacks all day. Only with the onset of complete darkness did the fighting subside.

The company command post was located on the edge of the city in a badly-damaged school building. Ulyanov and I took a seat on the edge of a plank bed, while Senior Lieutenant Kruglov and Captain Ushakov, the commander of a newly-arrived naval infantry battalion, were standing at a table and leaning over a map. They were carefully studying alternative approaches to Staryi Petergof. Our company and Ushakov's battalion had received an order to conduct a night-time reconnaissance-in-force to determine the enemy strength in this sector of the front.

Captain Ushakov was about 35 years old. Of average height and compact build, Ushakov was deliberate in his movements and always smiling in conversations. His large grey eyes looked at us trustingly. As he began to picture the looming combat, he paid even greater attention to each of Kruglov's words. The Captain's naval uniform was brand new and well-pressed, just as it should have been. This was going to be his first time to go into combat on land.

Kruglov folded up the map, and sensing the Captain's close gaze at his cotton jacket, from which tufts of cotton were sticking out, he quickly ran his hand across his unshaven face and said, 'We'll attend to these matters after the operation, but if I get killed, you won't remember me kindly.'

Then Kruglov looked at his watch: 'Let's get started, Comrade Captain; there will be no artillery preparation. We've been ordered to launch a surprise attack.'

We went out into the trench. It was raining heavily. The soldiers and officers, huddled under shelter halves, were straining their eyes to peer through the darkness of the night, trying to make out the enemy's trenches. But the darkness concealed the Germans' positions. Everyone knew that they were going on the attack, and they were ready for it, waiting for the command.

In the light of lightning flashes and flares, I looked at Ushakov. His face had changed dramatically from the one I had seen in the dugout: his smile had vanished, and he was perceptibly worried. I understood this transformation. For the first time in his life, Ushakov was going to lead his battalion on the attack, moreover at night, when each soldier must operate with the precision of a watch mechanism. He apparently hadn't had the time yet to familiarize himself with the men of his battalion in any real way.

Kruglov appeared calm. He was giving final instructions to the platoon commanders. Then he strolled over to a young sailor, armed with a light machine gun, and asked: 'Is this your first time to go into an attack?'

'Yes, Comrade Commander.'

'Keep close to our riflemen: they've been in combat a dozen times, and they've learned how to fight the German swine both day and night.'

I noticed that some of our new recruits were paying close attention to the friendly words of the commander. Then they turned to us: 'Comrades, advise us where and how to act, or else we'll ruin the entire operation.'

The calm voice of Ulyanov sounded from beneath a shelter half: 'Don't rush. You've been told to stay close to us, and we don't need to teach you how to shoot. Just don't stop to worry about your new combat blouses and jackets; hug the earth even more tightly. But if you hear the order "Forward!" get up and run without a glance back. That's all my advice for you.'

Just then a red rocket soared into the sky, followed by another one. Our company and the naval infantry battalion silently rushed towards the enemy lines. Our lunge was so impetuous that the Nazis couldn't resist it and started to run. We burst into the enemy trench. Having finished off anyone who tried to resist, our soldiers pushed ahead. Soon, however, we ran into heavy machine-gun and mortar fire. We had bumped into the enemy's main line of resistance. It was impossible to drive the enemy from it with a frontal attack: the defending German force was much too strong.

Kruglov ordered me to find the naval captain and tell him to withdraw his men out from under the enemy fire back towards the railroad embankment, and then to launch a flank attack on the Germans. I quickly located Ushakov and passed him Kruglov's order. Ushakov, however, acted as if he hadn't heard me, and continued to attack directly into the teeth of the enemy fire. Kruglov, taking advantage of the darkness of night, pulled his company back to the railroad embankment, where we moved under its concealment to outflank the enemy on the right. In a brief clash we overran the enemy's forward outposts, and with a loud 'Ura!' we plunged into the Germans' trench.

Firing broke out also in the streets of the settlement. The Germans were firing machine guns and machine pistols from doorways and windows. They were firing in every direction, apparently believing that the Russians were attacking not only from the front, but the rear as well.

The most agonizing thing in battle is when you see two men locked in hand-to-hand combat, but in the darkness of the night, you can't make out which one is yours, and which one is the enemy. They might be rolling around in the muck, trying to strangle each other, and you don't hear cries, only a muffled wheeze. You might have only seconds to save the life of a comrade.

I experienced just such an incident on this night. With great effort I separated the men locked in mortal combat and pointed the barrel of my submachine-gun at both of them. One of them began rubbing his neck with his hands and turning his head from side to side, while the other with a sudden motion tried to kick my submachine-gun out of my hands, and babbled something in a foreign tongue. I jumped to one side and gave the adversary a short burst from my weapon. Then I helped my comrade to his feet. He amiably offered me his hand: 'Thanks for the help, brother, or else that swine might have had a death grip around my neck.'

Together, the two of us started moving towards a heavy machine gun, which was still firing. But someone on our side beat us to it: a grenade explosion rang out, followed by a long burst of automatic weapon fire. The machine gun was silenced.

German corpses were sprawled on the street. We had carried out our assignment, though the ranks of our company and Captain Ushakov's naval infantry battalion were noticeably thinner. All the same we celebrated our small victory. It served notice that we also could attack. Each one of us secretly dreamed of a new offensive, in order to drive the Germans from the walls of Leningrad. But we still lacked sufficient strength.

The next morning we were forced to defend against furious German infantry and tank counter-attacks. For the next five days, fighting didn't subside day or night. The Nazis were making every effort to preserve the wedge that they had driven into our lines, and to prevent us from linking up with the Lomonosov [Oranienbaum] grouping of Soviet forces. We were separated from the Lomonosov [Oranienbaum] grouping by only 2 or 3 kilometres, but we couldn't close that gap. We had to fall back to Novyi Petergof.

At seven o'clock in the morning on 21 September, the enemy launched a new attack with large infantry forces, supported by self-propelled guns, tanks and aircraft. Our forces could not withstand this heavy attack and began to retreat to Zavodskaya Station. We couldn't hold there, however, and by the end of the day, we were compelled to make a further retreat to Strel'na, where we finally dug in.

The enemy resumed the attack the next day at sunrise, but now we were fighting to the death. After some time, we heard the thunder of a cannonade to the left of us, in the area of Krasnoye Selo, which approached us as time wore on. As I later learned, it was the 2nd Naval Infantry Brigade and troops of the people's militia, which had gone on the attack against the Nazis, aiming their blow towards Novyi Petergof. The hostile forces were split into two pieces, one of which was pressed against the shore of the Gulf of Finland and destroyed, while the other hastily retreated.

We entered Novyi Petergof for the second time, but couldn't keep our grip on the city. The enemy introduced fresh tank units into the battle, and we were forced to retreat once again. The Germans managed to drive our forces back to Gorelovo Station and simultaneously resume attacks on Strel'na. Fighting on the shores of the Gulf of Finland flared up with renewed intensity. Our forces were in an extremely unfavourable position: the narrow strip of land that we occupied was subjected to constant bombing from the air and heavy artillery barrages. In order to save our forces, we were ordered to abandon Strel'na and fall back to Uritsk. Here, the 6th Naval Infantry Brigade and people's militia battalions came to our aid.

Thousands of Leningraders day and night were marching to the front. Among them were workers, engineers, professors, doctors, teachers – men and women from every profession. The front and Leningrad had become indistinguishable from each other.

In the first days of October, the enemy succeeded once again in driving us back and took possession of Uritsk and Ligovo Station. Now there remained only 8 kilometres to Leningrad. A mortal danger now hung over the cradle of the proletarian revolution – the city of Lenin.

The front line in our sector passed 500 metres away from some distinctive concrete V–shaped buildings. No-man's-land was a gully, which skirted the east side of Uritsk and ran in the direction of Gorelovo.

The engines of tanks and self-propelled artillery constantly rumbled on the enemy side. The Germans were bringing up fresh forces, preparing for the final assault on Leningrad. Infantry on both sides were poised on lines of departure, but remained quiet. Ships of the Baltic Fleet and our ground artillery constantly fired on enemy troop concentrations.

Then the date 13 October 1941 arrived. This day has entered into the history of the heroic defence of Leningrad.

Signalmen were finishing stringing telephone lines to the command posts. Artillerymen were checking the latest results of aerial reconnaissance on the enemy's firing positions around Sheremet'ev's former dacha.

The enemy's infantry units were showing no signs of life. It seemed that the Germans had abandoned their lines. But I knew that they were standing in their trenches with their rifles and machine guns, just as ready for battle as we were. All my efforts to catch a fascist in my telescopic sight on that memorable morning failed.

The enemy artillery remained completely silent. Our ground artillery was also quiet, although the artillerymen were poised to open fire at any second. There was something both sublime and alarming in this solemn yet menacing silence on both sides of the line.

Then suddenly the earth shook. The air was filled with the howl of shells, followed by the hollow crump of explosions, and then the shots and shell explosions merged into a continuous roar, which was accompanied by the dull and extended moan of the earth itself. This was the initiation of the great, decisive battle at the walls of Leningrad.

A savage battle went on for two hours, with neither side yielding an inch of ground. However, in the third hour of fighting the German resistance started to crumble and they started to give ground grudgingly. They lashed back at every step, clinging to each clump of earth.

From a fork in the road, our battalion attacked along the left side of the highway directly in the direction of Uritsk. To the left of us, naval infantry and volunteer units of Leningrad workers went on the attack.

Retreating, the Germans continued a withering fire from heavy and light machine guns, which had been set up in the basements of the concrete, V-shaped buildings and the brick buildings on the outskirts of the city. Hugging the earth, we crept forward, taking cover in folds of the ground and behind the corpses of fallen soldiers. It was impermissible to stop: the Germans might dig-in on intermediate lines and counter-attack us.

Major Chistyakov ordered Senior Lieutenant Kruglov to send forward a group of snipers, in order to pick off enemy machine-gunners ensconced in the buildings. Six snipers – Ulyanov, Borisov, Sokolov, Sinitsyn, Stroyeva and I – started off at a crawl towards the ravine. The enemy machine-gunners noticed our movement across the open ground and shifted their fire onto us. In order to continue our way forward, we were forced to crawl into a pond, and make our way closer to the Germans while up to our necks in water.

We still found the range too far – at a range of 1,500 metres, which still separated us from the buildings in which the machine-gunners were sheltering, we could not count upon any accuracy. We had to close within at least 800 metres of the buildings.

At last we reached a ravine. Stroyeva and Sokolov were moving in front. Soon they dropped to the ground and signalled for us to halt. Stroyeva turned and reported that German infantry was massing in the ravine: 'We need to warn our side. But how?' Our battalion had already joined battle over by the highway.

As the senior of the group, everyone was waiting for my decision. To turn back was impossible, but we also couldn't sit idly by in cover and watch as the enemy prepared a counter-attack. I ordered to open fire on the enemy infantry, which was about 500 metres away from us. For the first five to ten minutes, the Germans were unable to locate the source of our fire. They were engaged in fighting with Chistyakov's battalion. Over the next ten minutes, each of us fired a minimum of fifty aimed shots. The Germans grew suspicious and tried to find our position, but we kept firing with the same precision and speed.

Zina Stroyeva inserted a new clip and said, 'Our senior made the correct decision; look, guys, they're wavering.' With that, she again nestled in behind the telescopic sight.

The Germans set up machine guns on the opposite slope of the ravine, intending to fire on the attacking Soviet naval infantrymen from that vantage point. But the machine-gunners managed to fire only one burst, before Stroyeva and Sokolov picked them off. No one seemed willing to take their place at the guns.

Suddenly German helmets emerged from the ravine in front of us, about 300 metres away. We instantly shifted our fire to the new targets. Nevertheless, one of the fascists managed to fire a burst. Sniper Sokolov's head dropped onto his arms. Stroyeva, clutching a hand to her left shoulder, slid to the bottom of the gully. Borisov's telescopic sight was shattered, but he immediately picked up Sokolov's rifle and continued to fire. Ulyanov hurried down to Stroyeva's position and bandaged her arm.

Returning to our position at the top of the ravine, Ulyanov said, 'The wound isn't dangerous, but we must nevertheless get Zina to some medics.'

As soon as the bandage had been applied, Stroyeva crawled off to one side, clambered to the top of the ravine, sighted in on a German light machine gun somewhere, and opened fire. Germans, who had been working their way along the slope of the ravine, dropped out of sight. We thought the naval infantry had rushed to our help, but it was Zina. I shook a finger at her: 'Sit down and don't even think about getting involved in the battle. We'll manage without you!'

Stroyeva, as if she hadn't heard me, kept firing. Ulyanov grabbed the young woman and carried her off to cover.

'You damned bear,' Zina shouted, trying to beat him off, 'you're hurting my shoulder!'

From the direction of the highway we could hear grenade explosions, short bursts of automatic weapons fire, and shouts of 'Ura!' It was our comrades firing at point-blank range on the German soldiers fleeing in the direction of Uritsk. The naval infantry and Chistyakov's battalion pursued the Germans.

In a rage, Zina picked up a handful of gravel and hurled it in the direction of the fleeing fascists. 'Ooo, vermin, run!' the young woman shouted. She was inflamed. Her combat fervour was muffling the pain of her wound. When our comrades took control of the V-shaped buildings and continued to pursue the enemy towards Uritsk, Zina's face suddenly became covered with large drops of sweat. Only now did she sense the sharp pain in her shoulder.

More and more fresh elements of naval infantry were running past our position, continuing to press the attack. Soon we turned Stroyeva over to some medics, and then we returned to our company.

Kruglov immediately asked: 'Has everyone returned?' 'No, Comrade Commander,' Ulyanov replied. 'Sokolov has been killed, and Zina wounded.' 'Oh!' groaned Kruglov. 'Today has cost us dearly!' The commander made a chopping motion with his fist in the air, and started to walk away down the trench line.

At that moment, an enemy shell exploded not far from us. I watched as Major Chistyakov, who was walking towards us, collapsed in the trench. When we ran over to him, he was already dead: a shell fragment had severed his carotid artery a little below his left ear.

This day had brought us so much grief. The company's *politruk* Vasil'ev had also been killed. I couldn't even look at his dead face, so anguishing was the pain. I recalled his entire life, our work together at the factory, and the hard path of our retreat from the bank of the Narva River to the walls of Leningrad.

The fighting subsided with the setting sun. We carried away the body of the dead battalion commander and laid it at the foot of a mound, next to *Politruk* Vasil'ev's body and those of our other fallen combat-friends. Kruglov took the Party card of Georgiy Sergeyevich Chistyakov out of his pocket and placed it on his chest. He pulled a photograph of Chistyakov's wife and daughter from the battalion commander's billfold. Kruglov gazed at the photo for a long time – at the luxuriant hair of the Major's wife, at her unblemished high forehead, at her large, tender eyes, at her smiling lips. Chistyakov's daughter, a girl about 11 or 12 years old, was standing next to his wife. The girl's face was a copy of her father's: lively, dark eyes were looking at us. We didn't want to believe that our beloved commander would not open his wise hazel eyes, smile at us, and tell us: 'Well, fellows, another precious day has fallen to our soldier's lot.' But the battalion commander's lips were compressed, and his eyes were closed forever. We buried our combat-friends on the mound just outside the city of Uritsk, where the foe had finally been stopped.

The day was nearing an end, and it was getting much colder. The front had literally lapsed into slumber: there was not a single rifle shot. Only the sound of axes and the scrape of spades carried from the German trenches.

Ulyanov, Borisov and I stopped next to Uncle Vasya's machine-gun nest. Yershov handed us a tobacco pouch: 'Have a smoke, fellows. Now you can take your time and enjoy it. You see what the Germans are doing? They're digging in their spiffy uniforms.'

Yershov glared angrily at the Nazis' breastwork, from which clumps of dirt were flying from time to time. 'Yes, they're digging in . . . But do you remember how they used to go around the front in columns? Indeed they were awfully nimble.' Yershov strolled over to his Maxim and fired a long burst. 'Just so the fascists don't stick their heads up and gape at Leningrad.'

I was thinking: 'Every soldier and resident of the city knows that the foe didn't come this far just to stand 12 kilometres from the city and stare at the golden dome of St. Isaak's Cathedral. The enemy was still strong, and he had tried to take Leningrad more than once. Sensing the mortal danger hanging over the beloved city, Leningrad's defenders never forgot for a minute their duty before the Motherland. Every civilian resident of Leningrad believed that he or she was now a front-line fighter, and each soldier considered himself a Leningrader.'

Senior Lieutenant Kruglov and Sergeant Akimov walked up to us. 'Are you resting comrades?' the company commander asked. 'Taking a smoke break,' Yershov answered, 'and I'll let you know what we're thinking.

We've accomplished one thing: we didn't let the Germans into Leningrad. But where are we going to find the strength now to turn them around and give them such a shove that they smack their foreheads against the walls of Berlin?'

'Give it some time, guys,' Kruglov said amicably. 'Our wounded comrades will return, and the Motherland will help us, and we'll give it a go. We've now learned how to beat the fascists. That's the important thing!'

Chapter Eleven

Ulyanov's Death

In the first days of November 1941, after the heavy and prolonged battles for Uritsk, the remnants of our battalion were pulled out of the fighting. Now we were seeing Leningrad . . .

How the beautiful city had been transformed! How it had changed in the four and a half months of the war! Barricades blocked the streets. Deep trenches had been dug into the gardens and parks. Long gun barrels poked around previously peaceful corners. People in civilian dress were marching around with rifles in their hands, learning to fight. Shop windows had been nailed over with boards. The streetlamps had been extinguished: the city was in darkness.

The muffled sound of airplane engines was in the air. Anti-aircraft shells streaked into the sky and exploded in bursts of golden light; shell fragments rattled on the rooftops. Observing the stern beauty of a front-line night, I strained to look into the distance around me and saw a wounded city plunged into darkness, but also a living and proud Leningrad.

The three days of rest flashed past. Our battalion was disbanded, and I was sent to the 21st NKVD Rifle Division. Happily, here I ran into some old comrades from Chistyakov's battalion and Kruglov's company.

A new stage in the war began – trench warfare. The command of Army Group North decided to besiege Leningrad and wait for it to die. Things were tough for us too. It required a lot of blood and lives to stop the fascists, who were armed to the teeth with first-class equipment and still intoxicated by their successes, and force them to dig in to the earth.

We snipers weren't held long in the headquarters of the 14th Regiment: Ulyanov and I were ordered to join the 1st Battalion, which was occupying a sector of the defence in front of Uritsk. Along the road to the battalion, we bumped into our old friend: machine-gunner Vasiliy Yershov. Uncle Vasya rejoiced at the meeting: 'Where is the road taking you, fellows?'

'We're going to the 1st Battalion, Uncle Vasya, and once there, to wherever we're ordered.'

'Where else, but to Kruglov's company! He, brother, has been pestering the battalion: "Give me back my snipers – and I won't say a word more!" But we don't have enough work for you, friends.'

Yershov placed the zinc cartridge case on the ground. 'Truly, the Germans in the winter aren't like those in the summer. They've become quiet fellows. But it happens sometimes a drunken voice will call out to our side: "Rus, give up, you're surrounded and starving!"'

We had a smoke. We recalled our combat-friends and comrades who were no longer with us. In parting, Uncle Vasya warned us: 'Look sharp, guys, and take care of yourselves: the German marksmen also don't miss. They shoot to kill. And indeed, they know how to conceal themselves well.'

We continued on our way. They didn't hold us long at battalion headquarters either. The chief of staff, smiling, handed Ulyanov a note and said: 'I have to suppose that you'll find the road to Kruglov's company. The area is familiar to you.' Ulyanov left immediately.

Kruglov's company was holding the battalion's most difficult sector of defence. They hadn't managed to dig communication trenches. In order to reach any platoon, you had to creep across open ground, and indeed only at night.

Sergeant Major Kapustin greeted us. I knew him: he was a capable manager and a good comrade. The soldiers jokingly called him 'our night owl' (Kapustin preferred to perform his duties as sergeant major at night).

Several days passed. I was lying on an upper bunk, when Senior Lieutenant Kruglov stepped into the bunker: 'Greetings, fellows!'

The commander was suffering from a heavy cold. His voice was hoarse and he was coughing heavily. His eyes were reddened and seemed angry. Kapustin began to report on company matters. I watched the commander carefully. Things had been grim lately. The *politruk* had been wounded, and they hadn't yet sent a replacement. The day before during a mortar barrage, the sniper Nazarchuk had been killed, and three other men had been wounded. Kruglov was silent. Loudly crackling, some brushwood was burning in the iron stove.

Kapustin broke the silence: 'Two snipers – Ulyanov and Pilyushin – have been sent to the company, and a little earlier, the female sniper Zina Stroyeva. She knows you. I sent her to Nesterov's 2nd Platoon.'

The wrinkles on Kruglov's forehead relaxed. Kapustin continued: 'On the sector of Ol'khov's platoon, enemy leaflets have begun to appear recently. Some swine must have infiltrated our ranks with the last batch of replacements.'

The commander sharply raised his head. 'Have you taken measures to find the sneak?' he dryly asked.

'No, we were waiting for you.'

'And you haven't reported this to anyone?'

'No, not to anyone.'

'Such cases must be reported immediately. But send Pilyushin to Ol'khov's platoon.'

With that, Kruglov picked up his submachine-gun and stepped out into the trench. My drowsiness had vanished. I hopped down, tightened the belt around my cotton jacket and set out for Ol'khov's platoon, where Aleksey Ulyanov had been sent at the order from the sergeant major three days before.

I found Ulyanov in one of the 1st Squad's bunkers. He was hunkered down by a metal stove and stirring some kasha in a pot with a spoon. An unfamiliar sergeant was seated on an empty cartridge box next to Ulyanov. They had been discussing something; my entry interrupted their conversation.

'The "Night Owl" has sent you to this platoon as well. That's great!' Ulyanov rejoiced to see me. Then he introduced me to the squad commander, Sergeant Andreyev, a fellow Leningrader who had already been decorated with two Orders.

Ulyanov proposed that at dawn I take a shift to keep an eye on the Germans. I asked him to come out into the trench with me. There I told him that a traitor or an enemy scout was operating within our platoon sector. Ulyanov heard me out and then said:

Here's something else to ponder. Various people are walking around here . . . You know, they received me in Ol'khov's platoon like a brother. But one messenger said spitefully: 'We were expecting twenty, and you've arrived alone. Well, what of it; as the saying goes: *A bird in the hand is worth two in the bush.*' I remained silent, but the platoon's assistant commander Nikolayev seemed to be seething. The messenger continued: 'You've come to boost our defences, just when the same thing repeats itself day after day: we have few men, and are forced to stand in the trench for days on end without any rest, while the Germans live so much better than our guys do. They stand at their posts, I've heard, for only two hours a day, and they bring them three-course meals.' I told him, 'I don't know where you're getting all this information. According to you, the Germans in their trenches and bunkers are living just like in a hotel.' The messenger snapped back: 'Who do you think I am? A provocateur, perhaps? I'm fighting side by side with you. I'm only saying what I've heard from prisoners.'

But Nikolayev answered him: 'That was at the start of the war; you should take a better look at the Fritzes now. You saw the prisoners recently. One was wrapped in so many rags over his uniform that we wore ourselves out trying to peel them off of him. What didn't he have on him: women's scarves, pieces of quilts, and over his thighs, the son of a bitch, he'd managed to pull a sheepskin sleeve. And you're babbling about their comfort, some hotel, and three-course meals.' Nikolayev even spat. But the runner, just like nothing had happened, looked around at everyone and then turned to me: 'There you see, sniper, how we live – arguments every day. There are few of us left, we're exhausted, and they aren't sending replacements.' I didn't answer him. The orderly stomped around the stove, had a smoke, and went out into the trench. I haven't seen him since.

Ulyanov finished his tale. 'Do you think he . . .?' I didn't finish my question. 'I don't think so,' Aleksey interrupted me. 'I was about to tip off Andreyev about this conversation, but he says that he has served together with him and really knows the messenger.'

Ulyanov and I spent all day preparing materials for our sniper hole, which we had to rebuild in the railroad embankment. With the sunset, we donned camouflage suits and crawled towards the embankment. A north wind was blowing. Sleet painfully lashed my face. The enemy trenches were quite close. In order to leave no trace of our work in the snow, we carried away the dirt in bags back to the trench, and spread it out on a ruined segment that had been smashed by a shell.

From the machine-gunners' bunker, the sound of a guitar playing carried to us. One of the guys was singing. Ulyanov laid his spade on the breastwork, wiped the sweat from his forehead with a sleeve, and stood motionlessly for a minute, listening to the singing: 'He sings with real feeling . . .'

Our work was nearing its end, when Sergeant Andreyev crawled up to us with a light machine gun. It was apparent that he was agitated about something.

He quickly told us: 'Guys, Nikolayev is searching for you. He dropped by our bunker several times and asked, "Where have our snipers gone?" I told him that I didn't know. When he went back out into the trench, I followed him unnoticed. He went around all the firing positions and bunkers, searching for you.'

'Perhaps the platoon commander has ordered him?' Ulyanov asked.

'Absolutely not; I saw Ol'khov, and he wasn't asking about you. Something else is going on . . .'

We were silent a bit. Then Lesha [diminutive nickname of Aleksey] blurted out: 'I'm even suspicious about a crow now; perhaps she's scattering the leaflets.'

Someone opened the door of the machine-gunners' bunker back in the trench. The sounds of the guitar again spilled out of the bunker into the snowy landscape.

'Our machine-gunners are fine singers!' the Sergeant interrupted the silence. 'They're Ukrainians and really love to sing.' Ulyanov replied, 'Just who doesn't love to sing?' Then deeply sighing, he picked up the spade again.

Andreyev took a seat on the bottom of the future sniper pit, and concealing the burning cigarette with his hands, smoked. Tossing away the butt, he rose: 'Well, fellows, I'll stay out of your way. I'm going.'

The Sergeant grabbed the machine gun, released the safety, and crawled back to the trench. A few minutes later, we heard Andreyev's machine gun begin to work. 'A fine fellow,' Ulyanov said, listening to the chattering machine gun.

Andreyev and I finished our work just before dawn and we slipped back into our trench. We went back to our bunker, and had just picked up our spoons, when suddenly Nikolayev ran in, out of breath. In his hands he was holding a German leaflet.

'Brothers! More leaflets! Listen to what they've written: "A pass for Russians. We, Germans, guarantee safety and freedom to Russian soldiers and commanders, who wish voluntarily to come over to us. They will be given the possibility to return home and live together with their families and dear ones."'

Andreyev stuck his hands into his pockets, walked up to the assistant platoon commander, and shifting on his feet from side to side, asked: 'Why are you reading this shit? We know how the fascists "guarantee safety and freedom". Someone is scattering these leaflets, and you're reading them.'

I watched as Nikolayev's face instantly went pale, and his sharply chiselled chin slightly began to quiver. The assistant platoon commander thrust the leaflet into the burning stove, and stepping out of the bunker, cried: 'Mind your own business, Sergeant Andreyev!'

Andreyev silently stretched out on a plank bed, propping himself up on the hard mattress on his elbows. The Sergeant's eyes watched the narrow ribbon of flame, which was flickering in a tin can, licking at its oily rim. In the semi-darkness of the bunker, his swarthy, coarse face looked focused and thoughtful.

It began to grow light. 'Time to get to work,' Aleksey said. Together, Ulyanov and I went out into the trench. The frosty dawn sky was particularly beautiful; stars still twinkled as it began to become light in the east.

We crawled out to our sniper pit. Just 100 metres separated us from the German trench. After a few minutes, Ulyanov tugged my sleeve and handed me the periscope, saying 'Osip [Editor's note: variant of Josef], take a look at that Fritz over there, crouching behind a tank track. That's very strange.'

The Nazi was wearing a camouflage cape; only his face, reddened by the frost, was visible. Several times in a row, he flashed a torch on and off, and was looking intently in the direction of our defences. We looked back over the line of our platoon with great thoroughness, but didn't see a single person, though the German continued to flash a signal.

Ulyanov took aim and fired at the fascist. The torch went out.

After the first few shots from our lair, we could hear some hasty footsteps. I quickly crawled back to the trench to meet the approaching person, while Ulyanov remained behind. As soon as I dropped into the trench, the platoon commander's messenger came running up to me, loudly shouting: 'Who's shooting?'

'What's it to you?' I asked.

'The assistant commander ordered me to find out and report back to him.'

'Tell him that we only put out one torch.'

I returned to our sniper's nest and we continued to scan the German trenches. Then suddenly, three Nazis stepped out of the ruins of one of Ligovo Station's brick buildings. They were also wearing camouflage suits. Two of them were carrying kettles suspended from a long pole, while the third was wearing a backpack and holding a bundle of sausage and a bottle.

'Do you see?' Ulyanov asked me. 'They're carrying breakfast; steam is still rising from the kettles. Shall we add something sweet to their breakfast?'

Aleksey fired at the German walking at the rear, and his target fell to his knees and collapsed to the ground. I managed to shoot a second

German, but the third dropped into the snow and disappeared from view. When we returned to our bunker, our comrades congratulated us on our first success.

After midnight that night, Vasiliy Yershov dropped by to see us. 'Uncle Vasya!' Ulyanov exclaimed. 'What fates have brought you to us?'

'We share the same fate, Lesha,' the machine-gunner answered, smiling, as he warmed his hands at the stove. 'We both serve. We go wherever we are ordered. Say, I was just with the company commander, and on my way back I glanced in on you at Zina's request. She instructed me to find out where and how you set up your sniper's nest here, which allowed you to pick off the Fritzes so cleverly.'

'Zina's returned!' Ulyanov exclaimed. 'Which platoon is she in?'

'In our platoon.'

We treated our friend to as much food as we could offer. I gave him my vodka ration. Lesha crumbled his ration of tallow onto the lid of the kettle and lit it. We drank the tea without hurry, again reminiscing about our friends to our hearts' content.

'Uncle Vasya, have you received a letter from home?' I asked.

'Somehow, I got one. I'm no longer troubled about my family: they're not at the front, they'll live. My wife is a tenacious lady; she's taking care of the kids, or those still with her. But my eldest son is at the front, fighting somewhere. I'm waiting for a letter from him.'

Yershov lapsed into silence. I regretted that my curiosity had touched a painful spot in him. I knew full well that Yershov wasn't the type to succumb to his inner sufferings for very long, but this time Vasiliy Dmitriyevich was melancholy. He tipped his head onto his left shoulder and, it seemed, was listening to the beat of his own heart. Without changing position, he fell asleep.

Before sunrise, we had breakfast with Uncle Vasya. Then Ulyanov and Andreyev went out into the trench, while I lingered in the bunker with Yershov for some time.

'Well, show me where your nest is, I've got to get going back to my platoon,' said Uncle Vasya.

The night was cold and icy. A north wind was blowing. The darkness, as if unwillingly, was yielding its place to the illusive light of the coming dawn.

We entered the sniper's nest and froze in shock: on the ground, with his arms outspread, Ulyanov lay in a pool of blood. I rushed to him. His heart had stopped; he was dead. Uncle Vasya picked up Lesha's fur cap, and squeezing it in his large palms, moaned: 'Alesha, friend, how did this happen, huh?' Tears glistened in Yershov's eyes, and there was a catch in his voice.

I quickly went to the embrasure: there were no holes in the armoured shield. Yershov handed me an empty shell casing from a submachine-gun. His hands were shaking. He raised the cap to catch the light and called me over: 'The matter's clear. Aleksey was shot from behind. Look at his cap.' I wanted to take the body of my friend into my arms, but Yershov stopped me: 'Don't move Aleksey from his spot. Let's go.'

We hadn't even passed two turns in the trench, when we saw Andreyev running to meet us. 'Where's Aleksey?' asked the Sergeant, choking with agitation. 'Ulyanov is no more,' the machine-gunner replied in a shaking voice.

I couldn't say a single word. My throat was tight, and it had become difficult to breathe.

Andreyev rocked back, as if struck by a knife, and leaning with his back against the wall of the trench, shouted: 'Lesha! Buddy, I'm guilty for everything!'

The Sergeant quietly motioned with his hand towards no-man's-land. I saw a man in a camouflage cape lying on the snow. His left leg was bent at the knee, while his right leg was straight.

It seemed to me that we were silent for a long time. I looked at Andreyev. He was distraught. Tears flowed down his pale face.

'Who is that? How did all this happen?' Yershov finally asked.

Anatoliy wiped his face with his hand, and in a halting voice, told us: 'Aleksey left for the sniper's nest, while I stayed behind with the machine-gunners, to have a smoke. After a short time, we heard a shot. I thought that it was Ulyanov shooting. But when I went out into the trench, I saw a man crawling back from the sniper's nest. He was crawling quickly, glancing all around. I thought that Lesha had spotted something important and was hurrying back to inform us. I clambered out of the trench to run and meet him, but he had vanished. I headed towards where I last saw him, when suddenly the man I had taken for Ulyanov appeared about 30 metres away from me and fired at me with a pistol, but missed: the bullet hit my sleeve. I ran back to the trench.'

'Did you see his face?' I asked.

'No, it was covered with camouflage netting. I began to wait for him to reappear. At this time I heard a rifle shot from somewhere else in our position. In order to find out what was going on, I ran over to the machine-gunners. There I learned that someone had tried to cross no-man's-land, but he had been killed . . . That's all I know . . .'

I hurried to a telephone, in order to inform Kruglov about what had happened, but I hadn't managed to leave the trench when enemy mortar rounds started to fall on us. 'Do you see what they're up to?' Yershov said. 'They're trying to keep our heads down with the mortar fire while they recover the body. No, we won't give up that creature to them so simply.'

From the enemy's side, heavy and light machine guns began to chatter. An intense fire-fight flared up. When everything had quieted down, fresh German corpses were visible beside the body of the fugitive.

'That's better,' said Uncle Vasya, pulling a tobacco pouch out of the inside pocket of his quilted jacket. 'The time has passed when you could parade around the front in columns.'

We started smoking. We were all uneasy inside. All the comrades were gloomily standing in their positions. Once it was completely light, Kruglov arrived with an unfamiliar lieutenant. The commander was pale.

Kruglov didn't say a word about Ulyanov's fate, but it was clear that this death had shaken him. Ol'khov was sitting at a table with his head lowered, his fingers now and then fingering a flap on his greatcoat. His assistant platoon commander Nikolayev was nowhere to be seen.

Once darkness fell, we brought in Ulyanov's body and carried it to the rear, where we buried him with full military honours. After the service, Kruglov asked Yershov and me to take him to the place where the fugitive had exited the trench.

One of our soldiers was firing on the German front line in short bursts from a light machine gun. It was Sergeant Andreyev. Approaching him, Kruglov laid a hand on his shoulder.

'It's dark, Comrade Commander, and hard to see, but I keep firing on the spot where he's laying . . . Comrade Senior Lieutenant,' Andreyev continued, 'permit me to drag him into our trench. After all, I'm guilty for Aleksey's death.'

'We'll get to the bottom of this . . . But how do you plan to bring in his body?'

'In my opinion, it's better not to wait for deep night. I'll crawl up to him in a minute and carry him off.'

'Fine. Only not alone, and not a word about this to anyone.'

Kruglov took the machine gun from Andreyev's hands, and then ordered us to don camouflage cloaks and come back quickly. When we returned, the company commander said: 'I'm assigning an important job to you. Andreyev and Yershov will go lead, while you' . . . he turned to me . . . 'stop not far from where the body is laying, and keep watch from that position. It's possible that the Germans will make an attempt for it.

Do only what Yershov tells you to do. I'll direct covering fire from here if you need it.'

Yershov and Andreyev jumped over the breastwork and quickly crawled away. I checked my submachine-gun, made certain that I had grenades, and then set out in the wake of my comrades. I crawled quickly, scraping my hands on the icy crust on the snow. I strained my eyes to see through the darkness, but nothing was visible beyond five paces. I knew that the enemy maintained close watch over no-man's-land, and if they spotted us or heard our movements, we wouldn't get away alive. Swallowing my fears, I stubbornly made my way to my assigned place. It is hard to describe in words, that which we experienced during this half-hour in no-man's-land. Both sides were still exchanging fire, and bullets were humming angrily through the air.

Nearing the position of the dead man's body, I saw that my comrades were already lying next to it. Now Uncle Vasya pulled a sheet out of his sleeve and covered the body. Andreyev hoisted the body onto his back and quickly started to crawl back. Yershov remained lying where he was. I didn't know what else he might have been ordered to do, so I waited for his signal, and listened to some moaning coming from somewhere nearby.

Yershov wasn't moving. I started to wonder if he had been killed. 'But if he had been hit by a bullet, he would have moved,' I thought to calm myself, continuing to wait for his signal.

Suddenly somewhere quite close to me, I heard a sound: someone was crawling across the field. Tensely peering into the white shroud of snow, I was thinking what to do if a German showed up. My knife! Clenching it in my hand, I waited for the foe's appearance. A minute later I saw the German. He was crawling on his hands and knees. A submachine-gun was swinging from his neck.

At first I thought that he might be making his way out to the wounded man who was moaning. However, he wasn't heading in the direction of the moans, but instead towards the spot where Yershov was lying. 'What if Uncle Vasya is really dead?' the thought flashed through my mind, 'then what?' I didn't take the barrel of my submachine-gun off the German. When he reached Yershov, he took him by the collar, and started to drag him back to his own trenches.

Yershov gave no sign of life. At this moment, I didn't notice either the cold or the bullets as they whistled past. All my thoughts were concentrated on one thing: the straining, heavily-breathing German who was dragging Yershov.

Suddenly tracer rounds streaked over my head, and for a moment, the moon emerged from behind the clouds and illuminated the ground. The German stopped and lay next to Yershov, sheltering his body from the bullets and the moonlight. As soon as the moon disappeared again behind a cloud, the German hoisted Uncle Vasya onto his back and began crawling again. I aimed my submachine-gun at the German and was just about to fire, when suddenly I froze. Vasya's hand was moving: I saw a knife in it, which he placed against the throat of the enemy. I almost cried out in joy.

Uncle Vasya instantly shoved the head of the fascist into the snow, and keeping the knife to his throat, with the other hand he removed the machine pistol from his neck and pointed him in our direction. The Nazi obeyed, knowing that the least sign of resistance would mean his death. In this fashion, Vasiliy Yershov rode back to our trench on the back of the German. I crawled in behind them.

In the trench, the German stood up and wiped his sweaty face with his sleeve. He was a tall, husky lad, with overgrown hair. He sullenly looked around him. The body of Nikolayev, traitor to the Motherland, was sprawled on the bottom of the trench. Zina Stroyeva was standing over it. It was she who had spotted the turncoat fleeing to the Germans and had shot him.

Chapter Twelve

Home

The severe winter days of the blockade . . . The glow of fires never died down over Leningrad. The soldiers and officers glared at the enemy's trenches with fierce bitterness.

After the death of Lesha Ulyanov, I began to work as a pair with Zina. Once early in the morning we were observing the adversary's first line of trenches; plumes of smoke rose from their bunkers, and we could hear the ring of an axe somewhere. Suddenly one of the Germans ran out into the trench to tend to some need. Stroyeva spotted the Nazi and fired, then turned her head and spat.

When we returned to our bunker, Sergeant Andreyev jokingly greeted us with the words: 'Akh, you snipers didn't even take pity on a man who'd been sent out in this weather.' The Sergeant pulled a blue envelope out of the pocket of his short fur coat and flapped it in front of my nose: 'For the killed fascist, thank you. So here's your reward!'

It was a letter from my wife:

Greetings, my dear! Yesterday I received your letter. You can't imagine how happy we were to learn that you are alive, healthy, and in good spirits. Don't worry about us. We're all alive and well. But our separation is hard on me. There are such questions in life, dear, that can't be resolved in letters. If you could only know how much I need to meet with you, if only for just an hour! There's an important matter we must discuss!

I was lost in speculation: what could have happened? I stretched out on my plank bed, and I don't recall if I dozed off or imagined it, but I could clearly see my wife's face. She was standing over Volodya's bed. Her chestnut-coloured hair cascaded down around her pale neck. My wife was saying something to our son. Her large, dark-blue eyes were laughing. Volodya, stretching out both of his little arms, was babbling something.

I lay there, holding my breath, afraid to move. What could have happened with them?

Senior Lieutenant Kruglov walked up to me. Looking at me closely, he asked, 'What's the news from Leningrad?' I handed my commander the letter. Its contents, of course, reminded him of his own family, which remained in Leningrad. However, he kept his own feelings concealed. Returning the letter to me, he quietly said, 'Yes. It is hard for them without us.'

Then he stretched out on a plank couch and folded his arms under his head. His thick eyebrows were twitching. At times, his forehead wrinkled in concentration before relaxing again. I had seen this many times before – it was a sign of deep worry.

A runner entered the bunker and handed Senior Lieutenant Kruglov a letter addressed to the deceased Ulyanov. The commander opened it and read the letter out loud:

Greetings, my precious son Aleshen'ka. Yesterday I received your long-awaited message. I can't express my joy. My son, write me more often and don't forget Naden'ka. The poor girl is waiting for you and is very worried. Aleshen'ka, you're my dear; I pray for you every day and believe that you will return. Don't worry about me; I have everything I need except for you here beside me. Write, my son, as soon as you drive this fascist scum from our land. Greet your comrades for me, my son, I'm praying for them too, so that enemy bullets will always miss them. A deep bow from Uncle Prokhor and Aunt Anastasia. Naden'ka herself will write you about everyone. Farewell, my dear.

I am tightly hugging you.

Mama
3 November 1941

Kruglov bowed his head. We were also silent.

Uncle Vasya, tossing and turning, was coughing on the upper bunk. Andreyev quickly walked over to the stacked guns, grabbed his machine gun, and stepped out into the trench. Zina was sitting next to the burning stove, her lips tightly compressed. Now and then she wiped her eyes.

The company commander quietly lit a cigarette, neatly folded the letter, and stuck it into the breast pocket of his combat blouse. 'Viktor Vladimirovich,' Zina spoke up, 'don't write Lesha's mother now, wait a little bit.' Kruglov started to reply, 'It'll have to wait. Why it's . . .' His voice trailed off as he left the bunker.

Soon I received a pass for a three-day leave in Leningrad. My joy was boundless. Three whole days with my family! Three days, three years, three centuries!

It was four o'clock in the morning. I reached the fork in the road from Leningrad, one leading to Strel'na and the other to Ligovo. I looked around. Behind me, over the front lines, flares were going up. In front of me lay a straight, paved road, covered with a thin icy crust. Little wisps of snow were writhing and twisting across it. 'I step out alone onto the road . . .' – for some reason I recalled this childhood verse.

I travelled the 8 kilometres in an hour. I stopped on Prospekt Stachek to rest a bit. The war had changed everything around. The façades of buildings were peppered with shell and bomb fragments; instead of windows, yawning black cavities looked out onto the snow-covered streets. A long, tightly-packed line of people stretched along a wall on Narva Prospekt. Spotting me, my face totally reddened by the frosty air and my rapid gait, the people turned their pale faces in my direction for a second. But only for a second, and then the heads turned back again and the gazes of the famished eyes returned to the shop door. Many were sitting; hunkered over with their hands between their knees, they seemed dead. A brief German barrage fell, but no one headed for a shelter. The people were patiently waiting for the bakery to open, in order to obtain their blockade ration of bread.

Fatigue and sleep were overcoming people. Some of them sat down on the frozen ground by the wall in order to rest a bit and died on the spot.

At the corner of Raz'ezhaya and Ligovka Streets, an enormous five-storey building was burning. Nobody was trying to save their belongings. People were standing outside the building, stretching their hands towards the fire, and using the heat to warm their backs and sides.

Two women along Nakhimson Prospekt were labouring to pull sleds, which were bearing tightly-shrouded corpses. A group of Red Army soldiers was moving towards the front. One could hear shells constantly exploding.

I approached the street, where my family lived. My heart was pounding. Here was Mikhailov Street and my apartment building.

I ran up to the third floor and stopped before the door of my apartment, not daring to knock. 'The children are probably sleeping,' I thought. All the same I cautiously knocked on the door and began to listen. It was quiet . . . I knocked again, this time more strongly, but nobody came to the door. I took a seat on a staircase step and lit up a cigarette. My hands were shaking. Fear was crawling up my spine: 'Where are they? Why didn't anyone answer the door? What might have happened over the four days since I had received Vera's last letter?'

Suddenly I heard footsteps on the staircase. I rushed down the stairs. It was Katya Pashkova, our building's janitor. She had changed so much it was hard to recognize her.

'Aunt Katy, where are my wife and children?'

She didn't answer, but quietly embraced me. Without looking me in the eye, she finally said: 'Vera Mikhailovna left home day before yesterday and she hasn't returned.'

'Where did she go? Were they evacuated?'

'No, she left without her things, together with her older boy, but where they went, I don't know.'

Barely moving her feet, Aunt Katya descended the staircase, not responding to my further inquiries. I stopped outside in the middle of the yard. Where to go? Where to look for them? It was an early morning hour. I started to wander the empty streets of the city; patrols kept stopping me to check my papers, and then I walked further without any particular destination in mind. I reached Kondrat'ev Prospekt. An air-raid warning started up. The sirens howled piercingly, joined by alarm whistles from factories and locomotives. In the sky one could hear the heart-rending hum of enemy aircraft engines. Our anti-aircraft artillery opened fire. Shell bursts appeared in the night sky.

For some reason only now did a thought occur to me: I should ask the residents of our building whether they knew anything about my wife. Returning to my building, I began to ask neighbours where my wife went. No one knew anything.

'Perhaps she got caught in a barrage and was wounded,' I thought. I visited all the hospitals. No. She was nowhere to be found.

Not far from our building, on Nizhegorodskaya Street, I saw people gathered in front of a shattered building. Here, I was destined to experience the strongest grief in my life. The people were watching as recovery teams dug the dead out of the rubble. One elderly woman recognized her daughter among the dead. They led the stunned, grieving mother away. Several hours of waiting passed on Nizhegorodskaya Street. Two young women emerged from the ruins with the mutilated body of a child on a stretcher. I immediately recognized my 7-year-old son Vitya. I took my son into my arms and pressed my ear against his chest, but my fragile shred of hope was in vain: he was dead.

Without releasing my dead son, I took a seat on the street kerb; how long I sat there – an hour or two, or days – I don't recall.

Passers-by gathered around me. They were saying something, women were crying, and some were arguing with the police that were there. I didn't pay them any attention. I sat there, my head lowered, tightly clutching my child in my embrace. I was afraid to lift my eyes, knowing that I might see them carry out my dead wife.

Someone touched my shoulder. It was a policeman – he asked me to take my son's body to a nearby truck. Here, beside the truck, I saw the mother of my children Vera Mikhailovna, lying on a stretcher on the ground. She was also dead. I dropped to my knees in front of her and laid Vitya beside her. Then I picked up first my wife, next my son, pressing each one to my chest, kissing their dead faces. Then I laid them back down side by side, not really understanding what I was doing.

Aid workers took my wife and put her on the truck together with my son. The next morning I buried them together in one grave in the Bogoslovsky cemetery. I sat for a long time by the fresh gravesite. While I was there, trucks transporting the bodies of Leningraders kept pulling up to the wood shed by the gates of the cemetery. I dragged myself over to the shed, into which they were carrying the mutilated bodies of adults and children, searching for my infant – my son Volodya – among them. Not finding him, I again returned to the gravesite.

Somewhere in the city, shell explosions were audible, aircraft motors hummed in the sky, and little snowflakes whirled in the air, as if fearing to fall on a ground so soaked with human blood. I couldn't stop thinking of my second son, Volodya. Where was he? How could I find him? I decided to head back to my apartment and begin my search there.

Another air-raid alarm caught me on my way back. I stepped under the archway of a building and wanted to stay outside, but two young female civilian patrol workers persistently demanded that I go to a shelter.

Cribs and baby carriages stood in the spacious air-raid shelter, which was lit by a kerosene lamp. The small children were sleeping. Those a bit older were playing hide-and-seek. The adults were sitting quietly, their heads bowed. One of the girls went up to her mother and began to tug on her sleeve: 'Mama, I want something to eat, give me a piece of bread, give me.'

The mother caressed her daughter's head: 'No, my precious daughter, we have no bread.' The girl buried her face into her mother's lap, her thin little shoulders convulsively shaking. The mother, biting her bluish lips, caressed the child's blonde head with a withered, lifeless hand.

I took my knapsack off my back and pulled some bread and a chunk of dried meat out of it. I cut off a piece of the stale bread, laid a slice of meat on it, and handed it to the girl. The other children stopped playing and looked at me silently and expectantly. Like a machine, I cut slices of bread and meat. I gave them to the children, continuing to think of Volodya.

An old woman walked up to me: 'Dear comrade, don't feed us with your own ration. Keep it for yourself, you must fight.'

The air-raid sirens stopped . . .

Aunt Katya greeted me in our building's courtyard. My appearance must have been terrible. I hadn't closed my eyes for the last forty-eight hours, and I had forgotten entirely about food. The janitor didn't ask me about anything. She already knew everything. She silently took me by the hand, and led me up to her room like I was a blind person.

There I heard her say: 'Forgive me, an old fool, for not saying anything upon meeting you downstairs. We're all living for the moment now . . . He's alive, your son Volodya is alive; I have him.'

I rushed over to the crib standing in the corner and saw my sleeping son. Alive! Unharmed! My son, my heart. My heart was overflowing with happiness, and I kissed the emaciated, wrinkled hands of Aunt Katya.

We cautiously went to the common kitchen and closed the door behind us. This kind, simple Russian woman, holding me by the hand like I was a child, tried to comfort me: 'You mustn't despair, Yosif Yosifovich. You have a son, and you must take care of him.'

I took my knapsack off my back, pulled the remnants of my rations out of it and spread them out on the table. As soon as I took a seat on a sofa, however, I fell fast asleep, and I didn't hear Katya approach me, lay me down on it, remove my boots, and cover me with a blanket. When I woke up, it was already seven o'clock in the morning. There was no one else in the kitchen. I quietly opened the door to Katya's room and glanced in on the sleeping Volodya. After a short time had passed, Katya returned. She was carrying two buckets of water from the Neva. Little pieces of ice were floating around in it.

Aunt Katya sat down on a stool. Her hands were trembling. She was winded and breathing heavily through an opened mouth. Silvery flecks of frost glistened on her eyebrows. Her head slowly nodded. She dozed for a few minutes. I was afraid to move, so as not to disturb her peace.

Giving a jolt, just as if from a blow, Aunt Katya stood up with difficulty, and headed over to the table where the bread was sitting. She tore off a little piece of the crust with her fingers, placed it in her mouth, and began to fire up the makeshift heater.

When Volodya woke up, he didn't recognize me, and reached for Aunt

Katya. 'What's wrong with you, Voloden'ka,' she said tenderly, 'don't you recognize your father? It's your Papa; Papa has come.'

Volodya turned his head. Knitting his brows, he glanced at my face, but continued to cling tightly with both arms to the neck of the unfamiliar woman. The word 'Papa' soothed him – apparently he had heard this word many times from his mother. Then at last Volodya was sitting on my lap and fingering my Orders and medals.

That evening I went to the district health department and obtained a referral for my son to an orphanage. When I started to say goodbye to Aunt Katya, she picked Volodya up into her arms, pressed him to her breast, and asked me to leave Volodya with her for a short time.

'That's not possible, Aunt Katya, that's not possible.'

I left her the address of the orphanage and asked that she visit Volodya, time permitting. I opened the door of my apartment and stepped into it with my son, in order to say goodbye to my orphaned home. The rooms were dark and cold. I found a lamp – the base still had some kerosene – and lit it. Volodya toddled over to the play corner, where toys were lying on the rug. He began to move them from place to place, saying something, and waving his little arms.

Everything was in its place. A photograph of my wife and eldest son Vitya in a leather frame was standing on the chest of drawers. Only now, looking at the photo, did I feel the full depth of my grief. I don't recall how many times I laid my face on the sofa, where the skiing outfit of my eldest son had been casually tossed. Someone touched me on the leg. I didn't immediately understand who. It was Volodya, who was holding a toy pistol in his little hand. Pointing with his finger to the window, the toddler firmly repeated: 'Bu-Bu-Bu.' I embraced him, and gathering him up, squeezed him against my chest.

An hour later, I took him to the Children's Home. Volodya didn't want to go to the unfamiliar woman in the white gown. He started to cry loudly and kept insisting: 'Papochka, I want to go home. I want Mama, I want Mama!'

I kissed the most precious one that remained of my family, and silently went outside. The voice of my son continued to ring loudly in my ears for a long time: 'Mama, Mama!'

Chapter Thirteen
'A Mistake'

The trench warfare had become even more difficult. We had no auxiliary communication trenches connecting the front lines with the rear areas: we crossed the open ground at a run at night, under enemy machine-gun fire. Life had become difficult to the extreme. We didn't have enough firewood and water, and there were no kettles. We ate dried foods. People became weakened. We stood at our posts for an hour – it was very hard to stand any longer in the subzero temperatures in only a greatcoat. The Germans kept shelling us.

The soldiers and officers courageously suffered all these hardships. The Germans liked to stick entire loaves of bread onto bayonets, hoist them above the breastwork of their trenches, and loudly shout: 'Rus! Have some bread!' Then they would fling the loaves into no-man's-land.

Once, the following scenario unfolded after another such demonstration by the Germans: 'They're mocking us, the swine . . .' Anatoliy Grigor'ev or someone else picked up a torn cotton jacket on the point of a bayonet, and waving it above the trench, shouted: 'Hey, Hanses and Fritzes, take it, it's suitable for a parade!' Then he hurled it into no-man's-land. A voice rose from the German trenches: 'Listen up, Ivan! We don't need gear; give up; you're dying anyway, while it's time for me to go home. The wife is writing that she's become bored!' Grigor'ev replied, 'Take a run through the nippy air, share your lice with it, I'll let you.' The verbal exchange continued for quite some time.

On one of these frigid days, Zina and I were scanning the enemy's positions, but without any luck. The Germans were being very cautious, and refused to stick their heads above the trenches. That evening, when I returned to my bunker, a real joy was waiting for me: Petr Romanov, my old front-line friend, was standing there in front of me.

'What, Yosif, you don't recognize me?' he jokingly asked. We tightly embraced each other. Petya had become noticeably thinner. A deep scar marred his left cheek. 'I have a lot I need to talk about with you,' Romanov quietly said.

At that moment, Sergeant Andreyev came running into the bunker and hastily reported to the company commander, who was squatting beside the stove, warming his frozen hands: 'Comrade Senior Lieutenant, fresh forces have moved up into the German trenches: they're preparing something. They're bawling enthusiastically. It doesn't even sound like German.'

Kruglov glanced at his watch. Then he said: 'The fascists are still trying repeatedly to break into Leningrad. They see how hard things are for us, so they're intensifying their barrages and not sparing any of the residential quarters of the city, thinking that we might lay down our weapons and raise our hands.'

Kruglov looked around at the subdued soldiers and officers before continuing: 'You, friends, see how the Germans mock us with bread? In war, however, the strong doesn't mock the weak; he beats him. The strong man is the one who goes into battle and knows what he is fighting for. Soon help will arrive from the rest of the country. That's when we'll settle accounts with our foes.'

I recall everything that I experienced with this man on our front-line journey. What a commander! He became a genuine friend to us, though he was a demanding, strict officer.

Kruglov walked over to Andreyev and gave him a friendly embrace: 'There you are, dear Sergeant. We need to grab a prisoner. That's what we need!' Andreyev answered simply, 'That can be done, Comrade Senior Lieutenant, just give us the order.'

'There's no particular need for hurry. Wait a bit, fellows, we'll take a look on another day and see what they're intending to do. Then we'll see where it might be best to slip through their lines and pay them a visit!'

'Oh! If the night was just a little darker, we'd pass the Nazis a little gift from the Leningraders!' Andreyev said, turning an anti-tank grenade in his hands.

For the next several days we prepared for the operation. Only Leonid Sobinov was silently glum and tried to keep to himself. Our comrade's reticence worried us. Leonid didn't respond to our questions.

'Speak up, what are you thinking about?' Andreyev asked him.

'I just feel a bit poorly. It's nothing; it will pass.' With that, Sobinov headed out into the trench.

We knew that such a melancholy mood settles upon even the most hard-bitten soldiers before a serious operation. Having troubled the soldier a bit, though, the mood would usually pass when the moment for action arrived. That is what happened on this occasion as well.

With the sunrise, Stroyeva and I were ordered to keep the enemy's positions under constant observation, but not to shoot. This is real torture for the sniper: to see a target and not be able to shoot at it. Just as if to mock us, two Nazi officers stepped out of one bunker and into the trench while we watched. They were conversing, and shooting occasional glances in our direction.

'No, I can't sit and watch them,' Stroyeva said, 'I'm going to shoot.' I restrained her.

'In that case, admire them all you want; I'm leaving.'

At the end of the day, Romanov crawled up to our observation post. He looked very worried. 'Guys,' Petr said, 'I've spent all day listening to their voices. There are not just Germans there, you know. There are some French men and Magyars among them. I've reported about this to the company commander; he's promised to come take a look tonight.'

During dinner, Romanov asked Andreyev, 'Have the passages to the enemy's trench been checked?'

'Everything's in order, Comrade Junior Lieutenant.'

Kruglov arrived at 3.00 am. Romanov and Andreyev reported that we were ready for the forthcoming mission.

I picked up a submachine-gun and some grenades. Zina firmly shook my hand, and then walked up to Kruglov: 'Comrade Commander, allow me to go along with the guys on the scouting mission. I'm afraid of nothing.'

'I know, Zinochka, but it's not allowed. A scout must be more than brave; he must also be physically strong and agile. Grab a light machine gun and cover your comrades with your fire.'

At night the fire-fight intensified. Illumination flares soared into the sky. The whine of bullets passed over our heads. The company commander personally checked our weapons and before sending us out, told us: 'It's time, comrades; I wish you success; be careful, and don't take any risks.' It wasn't easy to say goodbye to friends, when you didn't know if you would return.

Orlov, Sobinov and I started crawling along the railroad embankment. Romanov, Grigor'ev and two sappers were a little behind us. Sharp bits of ice tore our greatcoats and scraped our hands to the point of bleeding. Each rustle of sound made us cock up our ears. The passage through the barbed wire turned out to be clogged with snow. We had to dig more deeply into it in order to crawl through the breach that Orlov had made the night before. Bullets were striking the wire. The prickly iron barrier rang and sprinkled us with icy dust each time it was hit.

We overcame the four rows of barbed wire successfully and crawled up directly to the enemy trench embankment. The wide mouth of an embrasure was looking down on us. It was an enormous pillbox with three embrasures. There was no sound coming from it.

'It's secured,' Romanov whispered to me. Stealthily he clambered up to the German trench, rose up on his hands to peer over the edge, and immediately dropped back into the snow.

'We have to wait, guys; three are standing at the turn,' Romanov whispered down to us. A minute later, the commander again rose to look into the trench and again flattened himself on the ground.

'They're still standing there.' The commander glanced at the illuminated face of his watch. 'It's risky to make a rush at them; we'll wait a bit more.'

Our sappers placed a demolition charge next to one of the pillbox's gun slits. They tossed the ends of the fuse to the side. 'Everything's ready, Comrade Commander,' one of them said in a barely audible voice, 'we only need to touch a light to the fuse, and there will be nothing left of the pillbox.' While they were placing the demolition charges, the rest of us crept to the top of the breastwork.

To the right of us somewhere quite nearby, there was the sound of the Germans' conversation and laughter. In the enemy rear, from behind a shattered brick building of the Ligovo Station, different coloured flares were soaring into the sky one after the other.

'They're having some fun, the vermin,' Sobinov whispered through his clenched teeth. 'Oh, if only we could reach them! No doubt there are only officers there.'

'Hey, Lenya, just climb into the trench and take a look at what the ones at hand are doing. You're not at home here, brother – you're a visitor,' the older sapper joked, covering his mouth with the palm of his hand.

Several more long minutes of waiting passed. The frigid night air bit at our faces and hands. From time to time I glanced at the dark silhouettes of the Germans and listened in. One of them, a lanky lad with some sort of white rag wrapped around his head, abruptly turned, tossed his cigarette to one side, and strode over to the pillbox. After sharply kicking the door with his foot, he said something to his colleagues and disappeared inside.

I saw how nervously Sobinov, lying next to me, was chewing his lips. My submachine-gun was aimed at the Germans still standing in the trench. Suddenly an enemy heavy machine gun started up. Romanov took advantage of its loud fire and dropped the Germans with two well-aimed pistol shots. Without losing a second, we rolled over onto our backs and into the trench. Orlov and Sobinov tossed the dead Germans over the breastwork, while Romanov and the remaining comrades sealed off the pillbox. We waited for the appearance of enemy soldiers.

Romanov whispered to me, 'We'll wait for the third one to come back out.' The machine gun kept firing and firing, emptying one belt of ammunition after another.

'What are we waiting for?' Orlov hissed. 'Finish it off and let's go!'

'No, we'll wait,' answered Romanov.

Now to the left of us quite nearby, German voices were audible. I looked around. A hundred metres away, I saw smoke rising from a metal pipe that was sticking up out of a mound. Plainly, it was the bunker where they rested and slept.

The door of the pillbox swung open. The blond-haired German appeared at the threshold. He gasped, seeing a pistol barrel pointed at his nose, and raised his hands. Romanov took his machine pistol and pulled the knife from its sheath. Sobinov stuffed a gag into the German's mouth. The fascist never managed to shout, and only blinked his pale, bulging eyes.

Romanov ordered the two sappers to take the prisoner, crawl off into no-man's-land with him, and to wait for our return. The sappers carried away the prisoner. We swept away their traces left in the snow on the breastwork, and began to make our way into the German rear.

All was quiet. We were heading for the sleeping quarters along a connecting trench. Suddenly Orlov yanked hard on the sleeve of my jacket. We took cover.

'Do you see? Over there.'

'No.'

'Look this way.' Kolya pointed towards a living scarecrow, wrapped in rags, over which hung a machine pistol. It was a sentry. We counted the German's paces: he made exactly twenty steps in our direction, turned, and made twenty in the reverse direction. 'Where is he hiding his hands?' Orlov whispered to me. 'He's all in rags. I don't know how to take him.'

The Nazi stopped at the door of the bunker, took a listen to something, and then started walking towards us again. As soon as he turned his back to us, we were on him in several bounds. Orlov struck the sentry's head with force with the butt of his gun. The German collapsed at our feet. We picked him up and tossed him out of the trench, before moving on to the bunker's half-opened door. A bright rectangle of light fell on the rear wall of the trench. We gave a sign to our comrades.

'Grenades!' Romanov blurted out the command. Anti-tank grenades flew into the opened door of the enemy bunker with a hissing sound.

Romanov, Sidorov, Grigor'ev and I scattered before the explosion, but Orlov didn't manage to get away. The enemy's bunker collapsed. Nikolay, clinging to the side of the trench with one hand and clutching his chest with the other, made several steps towards us and reeled. Sobinov managed to catch him. Orlov was gasping, and blood was pouring from his mouth.

'Something struck me in the chest,' he managed to mumble before losing consciousness.

After the explosions ended, we stood in place for several moments, anticipating the appearance of Germans, but none came. Then we set out back to our trenches. Romanov and Grigor'ev led our small column, while Sobinov carried Orlov in his arms and I brought up the rear, watching so that the Germans didn't surprise us from behind.

Not far from the place where we had entered the German trench, a sapper met us. In an agitated whisper, he reported:'Five Germans came to the pillbox; they made quite a racket for a long time. They have a telephone in the pillbox. I heard them as they wound the handset. After the explosion, two left the bunker and headed towards the railroad embankment; the other three stayed in the pillbox, making no noise. They're just sitting there, waiting for something.'

'How did you wind up here?' Romanov asked.

'After you left, I moved down the breastwork a bit and waited there until I heard you coming back. Then I came here to intercept you and warn you.'

'Where's the prisoner?'

'We've taken care of him, Comrade Commander. Alekseyev carried him back to our trenches.'

'Fine. The guys are carrying a wounded comrade. You wait for us by the pillbox, where you placed the demolition charge.'

'How are they going to get past the pillbox?' the sapper answered back. 'There are Germans in there, you know. We must wait, Comrade Commander.'

'Do what I've ordered.'

In one motion the sapper leaped onto the breastwork. Sobinov and Grigor'ev hoisted Orlov, who was still unconscious, over it, and they soon disappeared as well. Petr and I remained alone in the enemy trench.

'We have one way out,' Romanov said. 'Go to the pillbox. I'll try to summon the Germans out into the trench; otherwise they'll notice our guys and mow them down with machine-gun fire.'

We cautiously crept up to the enemy pillbox. Petr cracked open the door and shouted in German: 'Guys, come quickly, there are Russians in the trench!'

I could hear hasty footsteps. Soon three Germans spilled out into the trench one after the other. Romanov cut them down with a burst from his submachine-gun, and we made our way out of the enemy trench. Beyond the breastwork, the sapper was holding the end of the fuse at the ready, waiting for us.

Romanov ordered, 'Light it!' The sapper replied, 'It's burning.' The little flame flickered and sparked. We crawled to the barbed wire. A geyser of earth and smoke shot high into the air behind us. We felt the blast wave.

… In our bunker, the prisoner was warming himself beside the stove. He was repeating over and over again, tapping his chest with a finger: 'I am a Frenchman, I am a Frenchman.'

'Brothers!' Grigor'ev shouted. 'A mistake! You went after a German, but you pinched a Frenchman.'[2]

'I said after all,' the older sapper grumbled, 'you're a guest here, and whatever you're given, be satisfied. The commander shot a fascist, and hurled him over the breastwork. The dead fascist had such a load on him as you've never seen.' The sapper pulled a whole loaf of bread out of a bag. 'You see, he, the son of a bitch, had prepared this in order to mock us again.'

We didn't want to believe that we had Frenchmen in front of us, but a fact is a stubborn thing. This one was one of those who had donned the uniform of a Nazi soldier in return for money, and betrayed his own country and honour.

2. There are several possibilities to explain the presence of this Frenchman. Given the time (November-December 1941) and location (the Leningrad front), it is possible that this French-speaking prisoner may have been a member of the *Freiwilligen Legion Flandern*, which in November 1941 was sent to the Leningrad front to become part of the 2nd SS Motorized Infantry Brigade. Though this unit was recruited from the Flemish region of Belgium, it is likely that at least some of the officers and soldiers spoke French. However, it is also possible that this prisoner was a French-speaking Alsatian recruited into the German Army. Finally, he may have just been a French volunteer.

Chapter Fourteen

At the Front and in the Rear

I woke up from a sharp jolt. The bunker was shaking. My ears were ringing, and sand was raining down on me from the bunker's ceiling. I leaped out of my bunk. Comrades were already standing with weapons in their hands.

'Get out quickly!' a voice shouted out of the darkness. 'Or else we'll suffocate.' 'Why leave?' Romanov retorted. 'You want to leave the shelter and face the shell fragments? We'll wait right here for the barrage to end.'

There was another muffled explosion. Our mess kits fell from the shelf to the floor with a ringing clatter.

'They've been finding the range. Now they'll hammer us . . .'

Holding my breath, I waited for the next blow. My knees were shaking. Several explosions, following in quick succession, were audible, but now much further away. The bunker gave one last shake and then remained standing firmly.

'That's it, it seems. But it gave us quite a shake,' Andreyev said. A voice responded, 'Don't celebrate; more will be on the way.'

'In the future, but today it passed us by.'

'Get out!' Romanov ordered.

I ran out into the pre-dawn darkness, hungrily gulping the dry frosty air. Dust and smoke from the explosions obscured my vision. Running about 200 metres along the trench to my sniper position, I stopped to catch my breath beside an open Maxim machine-gun position. Two unfamiliar soldiers were bustling around the gun. They were cleaning the sand and snow from the machine gun.

'Andrey, this means the Fritzes will be attacking, eh?' a rather scrawny, narrow-shouldered soldier asked his comrade. The other one was a head shorter than me, but a sturdy guy – like a short Hercules.

'It's in revenge for our scouts' work yesterday. No doubt they didn't like it. Just look what they've done: one end of the beam is sticking up into the air. So you see they're angry . . . I tried their bread yesterday – it was a piece of shit. That's all they have . . . They call it "ersatz" or something.'

'You think the Germans won't attack? Then why did they fire on us so heavily?'

'I've just told you – out of spite.'

The stout strongman carried boxes with full ammunition belts to the machine gun. At the time I didn't know that he would be the one to save my life, but simply out of curiosity I listened in on their conversation.

'Andrey, our new platoon leader is a fine man! He himself lately led a reconnaissance behind enemy lines.'

'Yeah, he's an experienced fellow. He was on a snatch operation, and you can't make a mistake in that business.'

The scrawny fighter, catching sight of me, began to smile with embarrassment, glancing sideways at Andrey, who was sitting on a cartridge case.

'Look, Fedor, you immediately noticed another guy's courage, but you yourself tremble, and you're afraid to attack.'

'You're a real comic, Andrey, you're really laying it on . . . I'm not the one who cowers, you understand, I'm not the one. Did you hear what the company commander said?'

'I heard him.'

'So why cower? "He who knows how to defend well and how to carry out an order, that's the brave one." All the rest, if you will, is just bullshit.'

'That's right, so there's also no point in cowering.'

The machine-gunners had prepared their machine gun for battle, and were now crouching in expectation of an enemy attack. I left for my lair, took a seat on the dirt bench I had fashioned, opened the gun port, and began to scan the enemy's trench.

At first, other than clumps of snow and chunks of ice, I didn't see anything. Even in their own trenches, the Nazis were acting very cautiously.

After a while, Sergey Naydenov, a strong, fair-haired young soldier who had recently arrived in the company, crawled up to my nest with a light machine gun. His handsome face with its fine features and calm, heavily-lidded eyes made a good first impression. He didn't smile often, but he had a fine smile. His every movement conveyed confidence. Naydenov behaved calmly and circumspectly in battle.

Naydenov tugged the sleeve of my jacket and gestured at the enemy breastworks: 'Take a look there. An officer is sketching something on the wall of the trench with a stick.'

I caught the Nazi officer in my telescopic sight. He was standing with his back to us, his helmet slightly askew. A slender twig stuck out of the sleeve of his camouflage cloak, and was slightly moving in the wind.

'Seryozha, have you ever been to a puppet show?'

'What of it?'

'I can boil it down to a word: "dummy"! They often set one out, trying to catch our marksmen out with the bait.'

'Catch how?'

'Very simply; you, spotting a German like that one, fire on the spur of the moment, and then you'll stick your head up to see if you hit the target. That's when one of their snipers will pop you.'

'Take a better look,' Naydenov insisted, 'his head is turning.'

'We'll leave the dummy alone and search for a live target.'

Naydenov put his eye up to the eyepiece of the periscope: 'You're right, it's a dummy! All the same, the rogues had a clever idea.'

I stubbornly continued to search for the German sniper that had to be lurking somewhere, but for a long time I didn't see anything. A beam, lying behind the rear parapet of the German trench with its butt end sticking in our direction, helped me. Right in line with the butt end of the beam, from time to time a white hump appeared, sometimes growing in size, sometimes diminishing, or else disappearing entirely.

Focusing in on the hump more attentively, I discerned that it was the head of a German, covered with white camouflage netting. I directed Naydenov's attention to it.

'That's a sniper?' Sergey asked, not taking his eyes from the periscope.

'No, that's their observer. You see, he's not holding a gun. Keep your eye on him, while I search for the one who set up the dummy.'

A short time later Naydenov alerted me: 'Comrade Commander, that German disappeared, and another one has taken his place. But this one has a rifle in his hands, do you see?'

The enemy sniper was lying right up against the beam. I could see the barrel of his rifle and the top of his helmet. The German was holding his weapon at the ready. I cautioned Naydenov not to open the embrasure of the gun port under any circumstance, while I then crawled away into the trench, in order to shoot the fascist from a reserve position.

From my new position I could see the upper part of the helmet, but the beam was concealing the German's body. I waited for him to raise his head, holding the cross hairs of the sight on his helmet. Time passed slowly, ponderously. My hands were growing numb, tears were interfering with my vision, and the blood was pounding in my temples like the blows of a hammer. I began to count, reached the number 1,000, lost count, and started again. But my adversary continued to lay there without moving. In our trench someone began to cough loudly and the fascist slightly raised his head, exposing his entire helmet. I fired and quickly moved to rejoin Naydenov.

'Got him!' Sergey exclaimed. 'He's lying there motionlessly.'

Everything that had happened in front of Naydenov's eyes dazzled him. 'Ye-es. A snii-per,' he thoughtfully drawled. 'I learned to shoot in the people's militia. If only they had taught me to shoot like that . . .'

Naydenov tossed a few twigs into the little trench stove. The fire immediately flared to life. We had a smoke. Sergey started to think aloud: 'In open combat at some other time, you can lie under a torrent of bullets and shell fragments and not get harmed. But here . . . one careless motion and you're done for. Can someone learn all this?'

'It's possible. He who wants to learn, learns.'

Naydenov was silent for a bit. Moving back from the periscope, he took a seat right on the ground. Having thought for a moment, he told me: 'There was mail today, but again no letters for me . . .'

'Who are you expecting one from?'

'From my family, of course, and also . . . from a girl and some childhood friends.'

'You must have a girlfriend. Who is she?'

'Here, read this letter. Only I ask you – don't blab about it, or the guys will start to laugh.' Naydenov pulled a pair of warm mittens from a pocket – and a blue envelope.

'Can I read it all?'

'Go ahead, but she sent it to me back before the war began. I sometimes re-read it.'

I took the letter from him and read it out loud:

Greetings, my friend and our future Zakrechensky agronomist. Seryozha! Today I passed my final state exam. Now I can help you finish your final course. Seryozha, beloved! My dream has come true! I'm now a doctor! I'm saying goodbye to Moscow, and I'm travelling to our Zakrechensky. My dear, I will be waiting for you on the banks of the Volga, by those two cottonwood trees, where we once swore eternal friendship to each other. I will never forget our vow or your curly blond forelock. Seryozha, how happy we will be together, although a bit silly too. How much I long to have you with me now, right now; do you recall our times on the bank of the Volga?

I can't get enough of you. How I also wish that you could see my happiness and be the first to congratulate me on my diploma.

Seryozha! My friend! There are blotches on the letter. Tears have made these blotches. I'm laughing and crying from happiness. How lucky we were, to be born and to grow up in our time.

Dear! Don't dally after the exams in Leningrad. I'm not waiting for letters, but for you . . . Hugs and firm kisses. Yours eternally,

Svetlana

My eyes teared up as I read the last lines of this carefully-preserved letter from a beloved girlfriend. They reminded me of so much. I wanted to know how these two people, who sincerely loved each other, had met. I didn't have time to ask for more information about their meetings, before enemy shells began to fall on our defences. Naydenov quickly ducked into the trench. I opened the gun port. I spotted little white figures crawling on the snow towards our lines. From our side, to my right and left light and heavy machine guns opened fire, submachine-guns chattered in short bursts, and single rifle shots rang out. I fired without ceasing.

My head was ringing from the frequency of my shooting and the nearby explosions. The Germans crossed the 100-metre registration mark and approached to within hand-grenade range of our trenches. One of them, propping himself up on his left hand, rose and tried to fling a grenade. I shot him in the chest. The grenade dropped from his hand and exploded beside him.

Suddenly everything around me abruptly fell silent. A ball of fire rose into the sky. I felt as if some enormous hand was rubbing my right eye with sandpaper. Dancing flames spread in front of me. Colours in it, playing fancifully, disappeared and then reappeared again. I saw these patterns in a fiery ring, beyond which yawned a bottomless abyss, into which I was swiftly falling. Throwing my arms apart to the sides, I am trying to catch the edge of the abyss, but I cannot; my hands slip . . . Then everything disappears.

Later, having returned from the hospital, I found out that the little Hercules, Andrey, had dug me out of my sniper's lair and handed me over to medics. But I didn't manage to thank the comrade, who saved my life: several days before my return to the front from the hospital, he was killed by an enemy bullet.

* * *

I woke up in a hospital. My right eye was bandaged. A gnawing pain was in my legs. A little home-made heater was burning with a low flame in the corner of a spacious room. Along the walls stood beds with high and low backrests, upon which lay piles of striped mattresses, grey greatcoats and khaki-coloured cotton jackets.

A woman in a quilted jacket was sitting at a table, covered with a multitude of flasks and piles of paper. Her head lowered over her work, she was slowly rolling up a narrow gauze bandage. It was the duty nurse, Aleksandra Sergeyevna Voronina.

I stirred. The nurse immediately raised her head, opened her large blue eyes, adjusted the scarf on her head, and strode over to me: 'You've been sleeping for a long time, esteemed comrade. Now though I'll ask you to look at me.' The nurse raised a hand above her head. 'Do you see it?'

'I see it.'

'That's great. Now it's time to have a bite to eat, no doubt you're hungry?'

'Thank you, I don't want to eat.'

'How can that be? For five days, you've taken nothing into your mouth but a little sugar water – and you don't want to eat?'

Aleksandra Sergeyevna walked out of the room between the beds and disappeared behind a wide door. Next to me on my left, one of the striped mattresses stirred, a grey soldier's greatcoat rose, and out from under it emerged a bandaged human head: 'Brother, from which sector of the front have you arrived?'

'From Ligovo.'

'What's going on there?'

'The Germans came creeping towards us. I was wounded at the start of the battle, and I don't know how it concluded.'

'Where are you from?'

'I'm a Belorussian, but since childhood I've been living in Leningrad.'

'Well, that means you can be regarded as a Leningrader. I'm from Vologda, but I was hit at Tikhvin, when we were drubbing the Spanish Blue Division on the outskirts of Tikhvin.'

The stranger paused, pulled a mug out of his bedside nightstand, took a few gulps of water, and wiped off his closely-trimmed brown moustache: 'Well, see here, I've been a poor host; you've been unconscious for some time. Bread, sugar and cigarettes are kept in the nightstand, they've been bringing soup and kasha, and a teacher comes to teach us to read.'

The nurse brought me breakfast. My neighbour's head instantly disappeared under his greatcoat. The nurse left, and the head re-emerged: 'I can see, brother, you're poorly dressed; you're freezing, and it is like ice in this ward. Why don't you ask the nurse for another blanket? Our nurse is a good one. Oh, and eat, before it gets cold.'

The head withdrew under the greatcoat and didn't reappear until lunch. The breakfast consisted of a mug of tea, two lumps of sugar, two spoonfuls of kasha, and two thin slices of black bread.

As soon as I picked up a slice of bread, the hungry eyes of my neighbour on my right were following my hand. He was completely emaciated and was constantly shivering from the cold, despite the fact that he was laying beneath two wool blankets. As soon as the sound of dishes came from the corridor, he would rise, look at the door with famished eyes, and lick his chapped lips. His Adam's apple bobbed up and down, like a door latch.

With each day he became more weak and irritable. For several days, he never once said a word to anyone, and he never once smiled. The hunger had altered his face terribly. His withered long fingers were constantly moving, although he never tried to grab or pick up anything. His large, angular, and closely-shaved head turned from side to side with difficulty. He ate breakfast, lunch and dinner with lightning speed, but from his eyes it was clear that hunger was increasingly tormenting him.

After several days he died; they covered him with a sheet and carried him with his bed out into the corridor. That same day, around evening, two hospital attendants rolled a trolley into the ward and stopped at the bed of the soldier from Vologda.

'Well, Ponurin, it's your turn now,' the nurse said, pulling the greatcoat off his head.

'What are you saying, little nurse, I haven't yet re-learned how to walk; please, give me a hand and we'll take a stroll together.'

'No, Aleksandr Zakharovich, that's not permitted. Some other time I'll be glad to take a walk with you, but today I ask you to lie down.'

The Red Army man gave a wave with his hand, gathered together the rear of his gown, and took a seat sideways on the trolley, like peasants do when transporting grain to a mill.

'Now, Zakharych, don't be embarrassed; lie down. Sitting is not permitted,' said one of the attendants.

Awkwardly, like a drunken man, the wounded man fell onto his side on the trolley. An hour and a half later, they brought him back.

'How's it going, Zakharych?' I asked my neighbour.

'This time I couldn't resist, and they cut it out.'

'But how, without your agreement?' I asked in surprise.

'You're an odd one! No one even asked me. They did everything like this question had been settled long ago. They didn't even say much while they did it. "Well, shall we get started?" the surgeon Natalya Petrovna asked, and that was all. A moment or two, and everything was ready. Two nurses took position on the sides of the table and grabbed my arms. A grey-haired man, I don't know who, stood at the head. I say: "Natalya Petrovna, I don't want to lose my eye, is there really no way to save it?" She answered, "No, dear comrade. This is necessary, do you understand? Necessary or not, you'll lose the eye. Whatever's mutilated must be removed, in order not to prevent you from living a normal, healthy life."'

Ponurin tentatively touched the gauze patch with his fingers and pensively shook his head: 'They cut it out. I'm not joking, forty-five minutes on the operating table! I recalled my entire life. I didn't feel pain. I was suffering inside.'

Aleksandr Zakharovich, pressing his palms to his bandaged head, sat motionlessly for several minutes on the edge of his bed. I sensed that it was difficult for him to speak, and I didn't want to distress him further.

The severe January days of 1942 passed slowly . . . Someone asked a nurse what was happening in Leningrad.

'There no way I can comfort you, dears. Each morning, when I come to the hospital, I meet passing trucks, loaded with corpses. Starvation is laying low everyone in succession. My eyes have grown tired of seeing them.'

The nurse stopped. She had caught the groan of a patient, and quickly jogged over to his bed.

At ten o'clock in the morning on 28 January, I was lying on the operating table. Everything that Ponurin said about his operation, I experienced myself.

For several days after the operation, I was totally out of sorts. The loud first reading of literature, the political discussions, and the debates about the *Sovinformburo* communiqués – I had no interest in any of it.

Then suddenly there was the loud voice of Aleksandr Zakharovich Ponurin: 'You, brother, enough of your moping, you aren't the only one to lose an eye; we'll live and fight with the remaining eye!' With that he tugged back the blanket that was covering my head.

'I'm a sniper, without my right eye it's impossible for me. Do you understand?'

'Of course I've considered that! They don't only need soldiers at the front. The entire nation is involved in this war. Yet you're saying there's no place for you.'

'Hey you, Zakharych, leave him alone,' a severely wounded officer, a new neighbour in our ward, said in a calm voice. 'Give him a chance to come around. It's no laughing matter, the right eye!'

'I've lost my eye too, Comrade Commander. He's thoroughly confounding me. It's a fine thing – the guy hasn't said a single word in three days!'

A nurse appeared. She quietly took Zakharych by the hand, led him out of the ward, and wagged a threatening finger at the badly wounded officer. He had been told not only not to speak, but also not even to move his head.

Six days after the operation, I felt relatively well and started to spend time in the smoking room with comrades. Wounded men of every rank gathered there. We took turns warming ourselves by the little stove, and exchanged the latest news.

Some of the wounded were gathered at the window. Two of them were heatedly arguing about something. The remaining men were quietly smoking.

'You say that you're ready, on crutches, to lug bags of flour on your back across Lake Ladoga for the Leningraders? You're talking out of your hat, brother; they'll take care of this business without you, while we front-line soldiers must drive the fascists from the walls of Leningrad as quickly as possible.'

'I told you that I'm ready to do it at any minute,' said the pale-faced patient with high cheekbones, turning on his crutches.

'Ready, but this now is the sixth month you've been lolling in the hospital.'

The pale patient tossed a hostile glance at his neighbour, turned away, and hastily started to clump down the corridor on his crutches.

I asked Zakharych: 'Do you know who he is?'

'Of course I know. You're the one who has buried his head under the blankets, like a hibernating bear in its den. That guy on crutches is some sort of fake. Everyone knows this. They address him in no other way than "Good God, a head case!"'

'That's how they greet him?'

'Why are you surprised? I'm telling you the truth, brother. It isn't the first time I've encountered him in this hospital. Last time, the Fritzes slashed my ass with a shell fragment – oh, you have your work cut out for you with such a wound, devil take it: you can't sit, you can't lie down like a human, you hang around here for two weeks on a bed with your butt in the air! I was lying in the surgical ward with him. Pereletov is his name. He had a flesh wound from a bullet, an entirely trifling wound. I was discharged, but he remained loafing around here. In November, I again happened to be here – for the third time now – and he was still here, still recovering.'

Zakharych affably took me by the arm. We returned to our ward. Ponurin glanced at the severely wounded officer. Lowering his voice, he continued his story: 'The guys say that as soon as Pereletov's wound heals, he goes and thinks up some new complaint. He'll collapse on the ground like a plague-stricken cow. Once the doctors figured out that he's dogging it, Pereletov goes and falls down a staircase. He scratched his snout and contrived to break his own leg, so now he's on crutches.'

Zakharych spat, gave a dismissive wave of his hand, climbed onto his bed, burrowed under the covers, and fell asleep.

In February 1942, eleven of us, some without their left eye, some without their right eye, were sent to the prosthetic institute on Rastannaya Street. After our long stay in the hospital, our heads were spinning once outside on the street! The wounded men were hushed. The city was on alert in the gloom of a grey winter day. The building façades were pockmarked with shell fragments, the windows were nailed over with boards and plywood. There were enormous mountains of ice and snow in the yards, like at the North Pole.

My city! How little attention I had paid to your former beauty, when you were resplendent with the blooming gardens and verdant parks . . . How little I knew the preoccupied and happy faces of the Leningraders I passed on the sidewalks, who were now dead, so that the name of their beloved city above the train stations would never be written in German letters.

We passed the Pushkin Baths. Zakharych stopped and looked at the empty cavities of the windows: 'Eh! If only we could spend a little time in the sauna! With a bundle of birch branches, huh? Wouldn't that be grand, guys?' He placed his fingers on the collar of his combat blouse and ran them around his neck from ear to ear.

'You're a dreamer, Zakharych,' one soldier with a bandage over his left eye said, 'you take such fancies!'

'No, not at all, but a quick wash in a bath-house wouldn't be a problem, that's a fact.'

'And how! But first we'll arrange a bath for Hitler!'

At the Novokamenny Bridge, we were met by a woman with a boy about 10 to 12 years of age. Both could hardly shuffle their feet. They were staggering from side to side. Ponurin pulled out a piece of hardtack and a lump of sugar, and offered them to the boy.

'And how will you get by, uncle?' the boy asked.

'Never mind, sonny, I'm a little older, I'll manage.'

We continued on. I kept glancing back at the boy, and saw that his eyes followed us for a long time.

Now, many years later, whenever I cross this bridge and see a happy, red-cheeked scamp, my mind recalls the famished eyes of that boy. Yes, I'll never forget this emaciated, starving Leningrad boy with his upturned head.

We walked down a long corridor of the prosthetic institute. The hall was dark and musty, and smelled of charring. On the walls, covered with hoar frost, there were the repeated words 'Bomb Shelter' and arrows. There was a sheet of paper attached to a board: 'Comrades! Today during the lunch break, there will be a lecture on the international situation in the Red Corner. The docent Yashina will deliver the lecture. The Party Committee.'

We gathered before the entrance to the office. On the other side of the hall, a door slowly opened and a tall, gaunt woman appeared with a folded newspaper tucked under her arm. Approaching us, she hungrily scented the smell of tobacco and, frequently blinking her irritated eyes, asked for a smoke. She wasn't in a condition to roll her own cigarette; her hands were shaking and tobacco spilled onto the floor. The woman, holding onto one wall with her hand, tried to gather the particles of spilled tobacco. Aleksandr gently hoisted her by the elbow.

'I feel somewhat unwell,' the woman said.

I quickly fashioned a cigarette. The woman took a deep puff and dryly coughed. Suddenly, clutching onto my shoulder, she slowly began to drop to the floor. When we raised her, she was dead. It was in fact the docent Yashina. In the severe winter days of early 1942, this was a common occurrence in besieged Leningrad.

A nurse called out my family name. I entered the room, which had a number of low cabinets. The office was gloomy. A sheet of plywood covered the window. A small pane of glass had been cut into the centre of the plywood. Opposite the door was a jury-rigged stove, from which an iron flue stretched across the entire room to the plywood sheet.

The elderly female doctor was wearing a fur coat. Curls of grey hair fell from beneath the scarf on her head. She was sipping hot water from a mug and examining my medical records. I pulled two lumps of sugar and a piece of hardtack from my bag and set them on the table. The doctor glanced up at me and took a piece of sugar: 'Thank you. I haven't seen any in a long time. We're Leningraders, you know . . .'

She couldn't finish her statement, and propping herself on the table with both hands, rose to her feet with difficulty. Lurching, she went over to a cabinet and pulled out a drawer full of little cardboard containers. The woman, glancing at my left eye, opened and closed one container after another. Finding what she needed, she said, 'It's not quite right, but it's all we have. After the war, you'll find and pick out a new one, but for now, there's nothing better than this.'

That's how I received a new, beautiful glass eye. I travelled the rest of my combat journey with it, and I haven't parted with it even now.

On 23 March 1942, Ponurin and I were discharged from the hospital. It was a warm, sunny day. Walking as far as the Neva, we stopped – we had to part ways. He was heading to Nevskaya Dubrovka, and I – to Uritsk.

'Eh, if now we could just work a little,' he said on parting. 'What's there to tell you that you don't already know? A peasant is a willing worker. It is spring, my hands are itching to feel the soil, and a home without its master at this time is like a rotten tooth in the mouth.' Ponurin gave a wave of his hand, adjusted his kit bag on his shoulder, and loped off along the quay towards the Finland Station.

I lingered by the granite quay of the Neva. It was spring . . . a narrow ribbon of water, enveloped in heavy mist, was lapping against a sharp clump of ice. On the bare branches of the trees, sparrows were chirping and preening their feathers. An icicle broke off a nearby roof and crashed to the ground.

Sailors on a ship were cleaning its anti-aircraft guns. One of the sailors, straddling an anchor as if it was a winged steed and squeezing a balalaika between his knees, began to play 'Saratov's Shanties'. Women were dragging a block of dirty ice on a sheet of plywood to the Neva, in order to dump it into the river.

Suddenly the ground rumbled from heavy explosions. Angry clouds of smoke and dirt rose above Mars Field. The women stopped, looked at the shell explosions, and then resumed their work while swearing: 'The vermin, they're ruining the fraternal graves.'

'Frosya, what are you looking at, drag that sheet more quickly!' a woman by some gates shouted.

I approached them. 'Butterflies, just let me lend you a hand, take me into your team,' I proposed.

In the yard, there were mountains of ice mixed with trash and filth. This entire, horrible waste dump, warmed by the March sun, was emitting an acrid, nauseating odour. The emaciated women, old women and adolescents as thin as reeds, were stubbornly attacking these mountains with crowbars and axes, loading the rubble and blocks of ice onto plywood sheets, and dragging them to the Neva. Some were simply carrying pieces of the ice by hand and dropping them into the river.

One small, gaunt woman, leaning on her shovel, asked me: 'From the hospital, sonny?'

'Yes, Mamochka.'

'Heading to the front?'

'That's where I'm going.'

'We're cleaning up the city, though we're still a bit weak.'

A husky grey-haired man casually pulled a tobacco pouch out of his pocket and handed it to me: 'Comrade, here, smoke some real tobacco. You, Pasha, quit complaining. We didn't yield the city to the fascists in the winter, and they won't take it this summer. Meanwhile, what we created ourselves, we'll tidy up ourselves. We'll greet May as it should be greeted.'

After his minute of rest, the old man struck at the ice again with his pickaxe. Looking at him, I pictured him labouring over an anvil. Now he's tossing an ingot of hot iron onto the anvil and forcefully striking it with a hammer. He's pounding it so hard, that fiery sparks spray a dozen metres from the anvil with every stroke of his 16-kilogram hammer as he turns the ingot with his other hand. Even now, his broad shoulders stood out amid the backs of the other working people.

Two young women, who were dragging a plywood sheet, drew even with me and stopped: 'Why have you become sad, Sergeant? Lend us a hand here! Don't be afraid that we're bony; we can give as good as we get.' Then without waiting for my reply, laughing impudently, they resumed dragging their load to the Neva.

On every street I saw people with pry bars, shovels, and plywood sheets. With their last remaining strength, they were striving to restore order to their city.

On this day, dozens of enemy bombers dropped their loads on the Admiralty Shipyard. The bombs exploded on the territory of the Yard, and on the neighbouring streets. I stood there, pressed up against a building. Some people ran past me. Their mouths were opened wide, terror was in their eyes, they were shouting, but I didn't hear them.

On the Staro-Kalinsky Bridge I saw a woman. She was standing, pressed against one of the granite columns, sheltering her child with her body. I stopped next to her and shouted: 'You'll be better protected in a bomb shelter!' The woman, not answering me, was looking somewhere off to one side with unblinking eyes. I helped her reach the nearest bomb shelter on Gaza Prospekt.

Emerging on the outskirts of the city, I sighed with relief. I slapped the brick-dust from my greatcoat and looked back at the city, where flames were still raging, sending brown plumes of smoke into the sky. I could hear explosions. It was already evening when I reached division headquarters.

Chapter Fifteen

In the Administrative Platoon

The headquarters of the 14th Red Banner Rifle Regiment was located on the northern slope of a ravine, not far from Sheremet'ev's former dacha. Mounds with enormous trees on them surrounded it. Through the branches you could see a partly demolished stone church with a wooden cupola.

I entered a quite spacious bunker, which was illuminated by an electric light. The space smelled of tobacco and dampness.

Behind a long writing table, a young senior lieutenant was sitting. A female typist was working in the corner. Two majors were standing in front of a map, festooned with little black and red flags, and were scribbling something down onto notepads. The man sitting at the table took my documents: 'Take a seat and tell me, what's new in Leningrad? Which district were they bombing?'

I briefly reported on everything I had seen in the city. The senior lieutenant listened to me attentively, drumming his fingertips on the table. His light eyelashes and brows blended with the colour of his skin; it seemed that his large blue eyes had been set into their sockets without any eyelids.

After my tale about life in the city, he rose, and seemingly pondering something, walked over to a desk and moved some papers around.

'You'll have to wait a bit for the return of the chief of staff from the front lines. I'm at a loss as to how to handle your case. I request that you go to the signalmen's dugout, we'll summon you.'

In the dugout, two soldiers were loafing around a jerry-built stove; they were smoking and exchanging short phrases from time to time. The older one of the two, a short and stocky man with a weathered face, tenderly caressing a mug of tea with one calloused hand, looked up at me and asked: 'Where are you from, brother?'

'From the hospital.'

'Where are you going now?'

'I don't know.'

'Yes, that happens . . .'

138

A telephone rang.

'Answer it, Senya, who's calling?'

'They're summoning some Pilyushin to the chief of staff.'

In the course of several minutes, my future stay at the front was decided. Now my path lay with the 1st Administrative Platoon.

In the yard of a house, lying on his back in a two-horse carriage, a man wearing a short leather jacket was firing shots into the air. An unharnessed grey mare with a canvas feedbag on its muzzle was chewing some oats, calmly watching the man doing the shooting. Striped mats and piles of smashed wine glasses and dinner dishes lay scattered around on the house's small wooden porch. Tattered soldiers' foot wraps, stained by time and use, were hanging on a line stretched across the yard. Against the walls of the house were stacks of cartridge and grenade cases.

Two soldiers were fast asleep on the lower bunks inside the house. Neither the rifle shots nor my knocks on the door were waking them up.

Only now did I understand the type of service for which I was considered still suitable in the ranks of the Red Army. I let myself into the home.

A few minutes later, a young, solidly-built junior lieutenant wearing the uniform of the Border Guards entered the room. A smile never left his dark face with its handsome features. Yellowish dimples – the traces of smallpox – were visible on his small, slightly-humped nose. He first looked at the sleeping men, then at me, and asked, 'Are you the master target-shooter Yosif Pilyushin?'

'Yes, I am. I've arrived in your command for the term of my rear service.'

'We'll get acquainted. I'm the commander of the administrative platoon, Vladimir Yerkin. Come along with me.'

We walked into a room, stuffed with cases and bottles, large and small; strewn with horse collars and saddles; and piled with packs of summer uniforms. A thin grey cat was sunning itself at the window.

Yerkin spent a long time looking for something, shifting things around as he searched, then at last handed me a spanking new sniper's rifle: 'Here, a relic from our regimental school. I trust that I'm placing it in reliable hands.'

I glanced at the junior lieutenant with surprise.

'Take it, you're braver. Or have your hands become unaccustomed to holding a sniper's rifle?'

I tentatively took the rifle and thought to myself, 'Will I become adjusted to sighting with my left eye and firing with my left hand?'

Yerkin noticed my discomfiture: 'You shouldn't worry, friend, give it a try . . . You'll have decent results even from the left side.'

All this was said so simply, so affably, that a spark of hope appeared in me. I understood well that it wouldn't be easy to reacquire the skill of the sniper's shot. It would require a long period of training – with uncertain results.

We stood there quietly. Yerkin had a good heart; he understood my anxiety. Laying a hand on my shoulder, he again tried to convince me: 'Just give it a try. If you can't do it, no one will find out about it, I give you my word.'

I held the rifle, making out the number '838' that had been stamped into it, and trying to hide my rising agitation. I had to calm myself inside and regain my strength before I could begin my rifle training. My half-starving rations since my wounding had clearly affected me: my hands shook, and I was experiencing some double vision in my eye.

From that very day, I began to train vigorously: I dragged cases with cartridges and grenades to the front and hauled beams for constructing pillboxes and bunkers. Each morning I spent time crawling on my belly and leaping ditches. When leaping, I couldn't always judge the distance correctly and I often didn't reach the other side of the ditch. Sometimes I fell painfully to the ground flat on my face. Exhausted, I would sit on the edge of the ditch and gulp down salted water, but my training never ceased.

Once even before sunrise, I grabbed my rifle and left unnoticed for the shores of the Gulf of Finland. I set up a target at precisely 100 metres range, but as soon as I sighted in on it through the rifle's scope, everything in my vision began to jump around. I dropped my head into my hands. The same thing repeated itself several times. At last I calmed myself down, and fired five shots at the target one after the other. I was so certain that I had missed, that without even checking the target, I returned to the platoon. But the question – had I hit or missed? – gave me no peace. I didn't manage to check the results: the next morning, the target wasn't there when I returned to inspect it. I set up a new one, the profile of a human head, and perched upon a green knoll, began to train myself to chamber a new round with my left hand.

On the shore of the gulf itself, a single starling was sitting on a branch of a tall, budding willow tree. I watched the bird for a long time. It sang, slightly fluttering its wings. Spring was claiming its right to arrive.

Orioles flew low above the ground with cries of 'Ki-gik, ki-gik'. Buds were swelling on the branches of the alders and birches, and it seemed as if they were lightly powdered with yellow and green dust. Birds were chirping and hopping around on the lower branches of a shrub, peering at me with curious eyes, and plucking at their little tails. At the front, one could rarely catch sight of a bird. Something stirred in my heart.

'I won't touch you, don't be afraid.'

On this day I took a lot of shots and successfully so: the shots were all on target, although the bullet holes were scattered. Despite all the difficulty of firing with my left eye, I had achieved my main objective: I could defend myself in combat. With each shot, the bullet pattern in the target became tighter and tighter. But it still required a lot to calculate each shot accurately from any distance.

At night I listened to the quiet conversation of the two soldiers – they were sitting on a bench in the yard right beneath the window.

'The other day, the guys were cursing our sniper,' one said, whose silhouette in the moonlight was taller. 'He has come to the front, even though his papers clearly indicate: "Rear service".'

'He's a Russian, Senya, understand? A Russian,' said the other, whose silhouette was shorter. 'That he's left-handed now isn't a bad thing, and he'll be firing from the left side. He really despises the Fritzes. They've painfully wounded his heart.'

'That may be,' the first one said with a sigh, 'but having only one eye is totally inconvenient at the front: you're a little closer to death.'

They both lit up cigarettes, and without resuming the conversation, walked out to the road, gleaming white under the moonlight.

One morning Vladimir Yerkin woke me up. He was holding my target in his hand, and broadly smiling, extended his hand to me: 'I congratulate you with all my heart! I'm happy for your success, though I knew that's how it would turn out. You're a strong-willed man, Pilyushin.'

On a peaceful June morning, returning from the gulf shore after a training session, I unexpectedly bumped into a comrade from Kruglov's company – Anatoliy Bodrov.

'Tolya, friend, no way; are you heading to Leningrad?' I exclaimed to the sniper. Bodrov stopped on the side of the road, and looked at me with surprise: 'Osip, is it really you?' I extracted myself from his firm embraces with difficulty.

'It's me, of course, who else?'

Bodrov clapped me on the shoulder: 'You're alive! That means it was all a lie.'

'What are you talking about, Tolya? What was a lie?'

'What else, but that you were killed four months ago? Do you understand?'

'Who came up with this?'

'Romanov, that's who. He said after the battle you couldn't be found. OK, I'll tell everyone about everything when I get back, but now I'm hurrying; they've invited me to the Gor'ky House of Culture.' Bodrov proudly jabbed a finger into his chest: 'I'm getting my sixth medal. I'm a famous guy!'

'And how are the guys in the company?'

'I'll drop by – I'll tell everyone about everything.'

I observed that Anatoliy kept glancing at my prosthetic eye, but he acted as if he hadn't noticed anything. He gave me a friendly wave of the hand and set off towards Leningrad.

That night, I was urgently summoned to regiment headquarters. There was a new order waiting for me there. Captain Polevoy told me: 'By order of the regiment commander, you have been put in charge of a training programme, where you will train young snipers for the front. But first, there must be a decision about where and when to begin, so the chief of staff wants to discuss this with you in person.' The Captain amicably tapped my shoulder, and then added in an unofficial tone: 'You, Senior Sergeant, don't worry. Your experience is needed. You'll manage. Teach our youth how to use a telescopic sight correctly when firing. Show them how to handle the rifle and how to shoot at targets. Most importantly – teach them the sniper's craft.'

I didn't answer Polevoy and quietly followed him to the headquarters. In the headquarters bunker, when I entered it, I found a major of around 35 years of age sitting behind a writing desk, leaning over a field map. He had a somewhat lean, energetic-looking face, with a full head of dark hair touched with grey at the temples, without which his manly face may have seemed somewhat craggy. He was Major Ragozin, our regiment's chief of staff.

Emerging from behind the desk, he offered me a handshake like we were bosom buddies, although this was only our second meeting. 'I've summoned you, Pilyushin, on a very important matter,' the chief of staff said softly, calmly and with assurance. 'Since you are not a line officer, I don't have the right to give you an order – the doctors have taken away that right. But I'm obliged to make this request to a communist and master target-shooter.'

I tried to say something in response, but he stopped me and continued in a jocular tone: 'I know what you've been doing all this time. As you know, the front needs snipers, and you are the only specialist in the regiment. To teach a soldier to shoot precisely is not an easy task. So we in fact have decided to organize classes for fledgling snipers. You will indeed head this "university of the trenches".'

'What length of instruction can I count upon?' I asked the Major.

'Fifteen days.'

'Fifteen days! That's impossible: after all, it's the first time for a good half of these soldiers to hold a rifle. Over such a short interval, it is impossible to teach a person how to handle a rifle properly, much less to fire it accurately from any distance.'

'You're surprised that I, a regular officer, am expecting you to generate first-class marksmen for the front in such a short period of time?'

'I simply cannot teach a soldier to fire accurately in fifteen days.'

'Never mind that, they'll take some shots at targets, and they'll polish their shooting skills with live targets at the front. Isn't that so?'

From this day on, the sniper classes became a continually operating link in the regiment.

One day, Petr Romanov came to visit me at the sniper school. Every soldier knows how dear every encounter is with a comrade and friend at the front. Petya asked me about my son Volodya, whether I had dropped by the factory, and how my training of the young snipers was going; but the main reason he had stopped by to see me was to find out how I was doing with my vision. He brought it up as if he had forgotten to ask.

'How's Uncle Vasya?' I asked Romanov.

'He dropped by to see me yesterday. I informed him of your return from the hospital. He said, "As soon as I finish my work on the bunker for my Maxim, I'll go to see Yosif." If only you could see what a structure he's constructed for his machine gun; it's a genuine blockhouse – and all with his own hands!'

Two or three days later, Vasiliy Yershov actually came to see me. 'Damn it, you're a hard man to find!' Yershov started the conversation. 'So, you're teaching the guys how to fire accurately. That's a good thing. Only how are you managing to do this with one eye?'

Having second thoughts, Uncle Vasya stopped and waved his hand with annoyance: 'Forgive me, Osipych, I blurted out something I really didn't mean to say; after all, there's a lot of good things one can do with just one eye. That's right, isn't it?'

'That's right, old man,' the future snipers that had gathered around us answered in a chorus.

We took a seat beside a railroad bridge support. Yershov pulled an envelope from the breast pocket of his combat blouse and handed it to me:

'Read it, it's a letter from my wife. Together we'll discuss the best way to answer her.' I replied, 'Has your elder son been writing?'

'You mean Lenka? He's already been in a hospital once, but everything turned out OK. Now he's writing from the front again.'

I read the entire letter aloud:

Greetings, our dear, your entire family is bowing deeply before you. Our thoughts of you never leave us. How you are doing? No doubt you are tired, having tussled with these cursed fascists, and may they be damned three times by us women. Don't worry about your kids, Vasya, they'll be OK, only you come home unharmed. Vasya, I wanted to hide our needs from you, but I'm painfully tired, managing these kids alone. Nina, Yuliya and Serafim go to school, but Volodya and Lyusya knock about all through the house all day, while in the evening we all gather together and each blessed day ask one and the same thing: 'Will you, dear, come home to us soon?' Vasya, how should I deal with the older kids? I do everything alone – I've worked myself to a complete frazzle. We don't have nearly enough firewood, but I'm afraid to send the kids alone into the woods, while I don't have enough hands to do everything that needs to be done, and our situation with bread is no better. Tell me how to act, and that's what I will do.

'Vasiliy Dmitriyevich, what do you yourself think?'

'I've given it a lot of thought, but everything boils down to one thing, the most difficult thing – the firewood. I wanted to ask my father to help, but his health is a bit poor, and he's already past 80 years old. If I send my girls out to procure needed things, they'll remain illiterate, but the boys are still too young to help their mother manage the house. I don't see any way out of this mess.'

'Vasiliy, let's write a request to the Secretary of the Party district committee to help your family with the heating,' I proposed. 'What are you saying?!' Uncle Vasya waved his hands at me. 'Write the Party Secretary? After all, I'm not a Party member.'

'That doesn't matter.'

Yershov was silent. I didn't try to persuade him, but took a seat and wrote out a request in his name to the Party Secretary of Gor'ky Oblast's Murashka District.

Once the letter was written, I asked Uncle Vasya what the Germans had been doing. Yershov told me a story in reply: 'They've come to life with the arrival of spring, just like flies . . . "Ivan, do you want to live? We will be assaulting Leningrad!" they shout from every direction in the evenings. But Akimych handles the conversations from our side. He shouts back: "Hey, Fritzes! Don't forget to spend time at a bathing and delousing station, or else they won't let you into Leningrad with lice!" The Germans reply: "We will storm Leningrad!" Again our response: "You're dreaming, your paws are too short!" That's when the exchange of curses and firing begins. That's how we're living.'

Chapter Sixteen

A Trench Stage

After one gloomy day, the evening sky was clear and the weather was warm. The soldiers and officers emerged from their damp dugouts into the fresh air. Quite nearby, beyond a turn in the trench, someone was quickly running his fingers over the strings of a guitar. The sounds pierced the silence. Someone's young, velvet voice began singing in accompaniment to the guitar. Several more voices joined in:

In a meadow among the birch trees
Under a red snowball tree
A young woman gave birth to a fine son.

From somewhere beyond the breastwork came the chopping sounds of axes and the rasp of saws. The singing suddenly stopped. But its sounds seemingly still circled above us, dying away slowly.

On the German side, there was the sound of clapping and voices rose: 'Rus, Rus! Play! There's no need to shoot! Rus! More songs!'

'Bah, we've found an audience,' the guitarist told me, gesturing with his head in the enemy's direction. 'I wish I could play them a song to make the devils sick, while we prepare the firewood we need.'

'Fedya! Play some more,' someone's voice called out.

'This isn't an opera, you know, but the laying-in of firewood. It's a long way to haul it from the ravine, but there's firewood close by, just beyond the breastwork. We can't get it there; the enemy will kill us. So we've devised a scheme to procure the firewood while we lull the enemy with music. The Germans love our Russian singing with a passion. So they don't shoot. For how long, I don't know.'

Right next to the very trench was a massive, blackened poplar. Its intact trunk was standing like a sentry at his post. Three musicians had taken position on its roots: Sergeant Major Nesterov, Sergeant Nazarenko and Private Petukhov. Nesterov picked up the guitar and gave its strings a boisterous strum: 'Well, fellows, let's sing "When I was a Driver for the Postal Service".'

Once again, song began to flow in a lively stream. Again, axes began to chop and saws began to rasp.

'Rus!' a German voice was heard. 'There's no need for noise, we don't need all that racket, let us hear the songs!'

I strained my eyes peering through the darkness, but other than a cloud of tobacco smoke above the German trench, nothing else was visible. However, the German voices were clearly audible.

The performers completed the final couplet of song, the music stopped, and again we could hear the sound of applause: 'Bravo, Rus! Another song, no shooting! Play on, Rus!'

'Bite me, fascist scum! They're deeply touched, the lousy devils, by our music and song,' Nesterov swore furiously.

On the right, around the V-shaped buildings, a machine gun began to chatter, rifles began to bang away, and within an hour, the entire front was seething and roaring with thunder. The bright flashes of artillery salvoes now and then lit up the dark sky. Flickering flashes of rifle shots and machine guns lit up the trenches from one end to the other. Tracer rounds streaked through the darkness and ricocheted wildly into the air. A typical night at the front had begun.

We knew precisely the Germans' night-time rules of gunnery: each of their machine guns fired within an assigned sector at a specified range, and changed the range only when urgently necessary. Even on this night, two of their machine guns were raking no-man's-land, but without using tracer bullets. Stroyeva and I spent the entire night searching for the location of one of these machine guns, but it was hard to see the gun flashes when your face is pressed into the ground by the bullets whistling over your head.

All night long, we observed the enemy pillbox locations. At dawn Zina, hugging the damp breastwork, again and again tried to locate a suspected enemy machine-gun emplacement by checking the line between a reference stake we had placed the night before and the position of some chevaux de frise, upon which a rifle was lying. We examined every centimetre of ground. Finding nothing, we again checked the direction of the reference stake. Everything was in its place, but the enemy emplacement had literally disappeared into the earth.

Suddenly an enemy signalman appeared. He was making his way towards a brick building on the outskirts of Uritsk. The building's cellar had been turned into a centre of resistance.

'Yosif,' Stroyeva hailed me, 'come take a look, I can't understand whether our aiming stake was bumped last night or whether the Germans were firing from an open position.'

'Can you wait a minute, Zina?'

'Why?'

'Because some fool is now unrolling telephone line to a brick building. There he is; do you see him?'

'Finish him off and get over here quickly; we have more important business here.'

Zina had evidently forgotten what had happened to me; she still considered me a good shot. But this was going to be my first shot at a living target since losing my right eye.

'Check it once more, Zina, I'll be right there.'

Just as the signalman rose up on his left hand, and gave a tug on the telephone line with his right hand, I fired – the signalman dropped face first on the ground. I did it! That meant I could do it! An enemy soldier I had just killed was lying in front of me!

Returning to Stroyeva's position, I asked: 'Well, what do you think?'

'You just finished him off in fine style; his legs didn't even twitch,' the young woman offered in praise as she blushed from ear to ear: she had recalled my eye wound.

For the next three hours, without changing our position or moving a muscle, we monitored a narrow strip of ground along the Germans' breastworks, where we assumed the embrasure of the enemy emplacement was located.

The Germans didn't do a bad job hiding their embrasures from the sniper's eye. The armoured shields were painted on both sides with camouflage patterns; in the summer, the colours of earth and sand; in the winter, white. It was impossible for the naked eye to discern such an embrasure from a distance of 200 metres.

It was the wind that helped us spot it. There was a narrow strip of ground, where tall blades of grass were waving in the wind on either end. But the grass in the middle wasn't moving.

'Aha, that's where you are! At last! Tonight we'll take care of you!' Zina exclaimed as she rubbed her hands in anticipation, not taking her eye away from the eyepiece of the periscope.

We finished all the necessary preparations for exchanging fire with enemy machine guns that night while it was still light. Stroyeva departed for the company command post, while I dropped by the machine-gunners' bunker.

These quarters had been calculated for ten people. The light passed through a small piece of glass that had been set into the massive plank door. Stacked rifles stood in a pyramid at the entrance, next to covered spare machine-gun barrels with their ribbed barrel jackets. Boxes of full ammunition belts were sitting next to the wall of the bunker a short distance away. It was warm and comfortable inside the bunker; the soldiers, half-dressed, were lying on their plank beds and listening to a reading of *Dead Souls*. The first spring blossoms were propped in a tin can atop a box of cartridges. A young, red-cheeked fellow with a striking pair of eyes and a closely-shaved head was reading the book expressively.

'Andryusha,' someone's familiar voice sounded from the upper tier of bunks. The reader stopped. A sly smile formed dimples in his ruddy cheeks. 'You know we have our own Plyushkin [a memorable character from Gogol's *Dead Souls*] – Sergey Bogdanov. He walks hunched over, always unshaven, in a filthy combat blouse. He last washed at home, likely, before he left for the front. There is absolutely nothing in his kit bag, except for a live hedgehog, that's all it contains!'

'Don't listen to him, Andrey, he's just drunk and yapping at me,' Bogdanov responded. 'We really do though have someone with a likeness to that Plyushkin. Just take Prokhor . . .'

'Sergey,' an older soldier with a prominent nose interrupted, 'you've taken leave of your senses. Take a look at how clean I am.'

I couldn't fight my fatigue any longer and started to snooze on the edge of a bunk. How long I slept, I don't know. But someone suddenly grabbed me by the arm. I reached for my rifle.

'Don't be afraid, it's me.'

I rubbed my eyes and saw Zina Stroyeva. She was holding a mess tin in her hands.

'You see, while you've been snoring, I've made my dinner. Surely you're hungry. Our guys are already giving a concert for the Fritzes.'

We went out into the trench. In the quiet twilight of the coming white night, somewhere in the sky, late swans were honking. A heavy fog was rolling in from the Gulf of Finland, slowly creeping through the ravines and drawing ever nearer to the front lines.

'Hey, Sergeant Major, what will we be doing this evening to your music?' Stroyeva asked Nesterov as she came up to him. 'Zina, wait just a bit to shoot; today we're building one little earth and timber emplacement,' Nesterov answered as he absent-mindedly strummed his guitar.

'Fedor!' an unfamiliar sergeant called out. 'Play our Saratov dance!' Then, having lowered his voice, he added: 'Now, guys, let's start carrying our framing for the emplacement.'

The sergeant tossed two boards onto the bottom of the trench. Nesterov affirmatively nodded his head and from the song switched to a playful *chastushka* [a quickly-devised rhyming quatrain, often with racy themes, which was a favourite form of entertainment in the Red Army]:

Hey! Well, just think!
I'll get your attention with a flirty wink.
I'll knit my brows together, that's what I'll do
And come to spend the night with you!

'Ah, oh!' the guys all voiced their approval.

A sergeant in enormous canvas-topped boots was stamping out an intricate rhythm on the boards. He approvingly smiled at the comrades, who were carrying the beams for the emplacement. The soldiers, passing the musicians and dancer on their way to get another beam, wiped their sweating faces with their sleeves and smiled back. But not one of them stopped to take a rest, listen a bit to the music, or watch the boisterous dance. They were hurrying to pass the dangerous locations, knowing how short the Leningrad white nights are.

The sergeant with all his effort tried to distract the Germans' attention away from his labouring comrades. He raised his hands high above his head and danced, waving his arms in the air, pouring sweat, with no thought to the fact that he was placing himself under potential enemy fire.

Two guys from the same village were standing next to me in the trench. I often encountered them together, even though they served in different platoons.

'Why are those Germans shouting?' asked the taller one of the pair.

'They love our Russian songs. So they're asking us to keep singing.'

'Hell, no, brother,' the tall one erupted, 'that serves no purpose. Let them amuse themselves in their own Germany; we'll soon have something other than songs for them. They must be killed, the vermin, and not entertained with singing and dancing.'

'Matvey Il'ich, you're wrong. We're being clever here. Sometimes a song strikes the heart better than a bullet or a shell fragment.'

'Well, brother, maybe you think that it's better to grab them by the heart, but I've had enough. I'm leaving, so long.' The soldier angrily slapped his forage cap on his head. Tossing a surly glance in the direction of the enemy, he walked away.

Watching the dancing and focusing on the soldiers' conversation, I didn't notice that Stroyeva had come up to me: 'Enough dreaming, let's go, or else the Germans will start shooting, and we'll never reach our position.' Zina was holding a rifle in her hands. She checked whether or not she had forgotten to grab some grenades, and then started off down the trench.

Following her, I thought about the cruel battles that Zina had fought together with us. She never once flinched in the face of danger, but courageously met it head-on. Even today she was taking the lead towards a terrible risk – to crawl out into no-man's-land and engage a well-protected German machine gun.

The night-time fire-fight, like a fire in the wind, flared up around us. We lay in an old shell crater for several hours, keeping vigilant watch on the enemy's firing positions. Suddenly Stroyeva jabbed me in the ribs: 'The Germans are creeping towards our trenches. Look, there they are . . . they're crawling.'

About 30 metres away from us, I spotted the silhouettes of crawling men in a thin shroud of mist. It was difficult to count their number because of the fog. Obviously, enemy scouts were intending to probe our lines: their backs sometimes submerged into and re-emerged from the fog, bobbing on the low layer of fog like rubber pouches.

'What should we do?' Zina asked as she quickly began to shift grenades from her grenade sack to the pocket of her camouflage cloak. 'Let's toss grenades at the Fritzes.'

'More likely their own grenades will find us in this depression, and what's worse, they'll drag us away to their own trenches.'

'Like hell,' the young woman hissed, 'I'll leave one grenade for myself.'

'Why take a chance, we have a way out: when they crawl nearer, we'll shove a pair of "pineapples" [hand grenades] under their noses. The ones trailing will think the advance has bumped into a minefield. Our guys will also hear it.'

Stroyeva approved of my proposal. We prepared for the encounter.

Three Germans were crawling in front. Now they had closed to within 15 metres of us. Tightly hugging the earth, I flipped a grenade backhanded at them. There was an explosion, followed by another one. That one was Stroyeva's grenade.

From our side, a light machine gun opened up with short bursts; then there was a rattle of several rifle shots. The bullets ploughed up the earth next to the crater we were in. I cautiously raised my head above the rim to try to see what had become of the German scouts. They had literally dissolved into the fog.

Zina leaned towards my ear and asked: 'What shall we do? Leave or wait for when their machine guns start up?'

'We'll wait a few. Perhaps they're lying in no-man's-land; they might notice us.'

From our side, several heavy and light machine guns were now firing:

their tracer bullets were chewing up the edge of our crater; it was impossible even to stick our heads up.

'Quite a hunt today!' Stroyeva said as she wiped sand from her eyes.

That night we were unable to snuff out the fire of the enemy machine gun. It was destroyed the next night.

The only available wartime portrait of Yosif Pilyushin (right) and Pilyushin's commendation for the Order of the Red Star (below) which reads: 'After volunteering for the Red Army during the first days of the war, comrade Pilyushin showed heroism and bravery in battles against the German fascist invaders. Disregarding the danger to his life in every battle, under artillery and machine-gun fire, he went into the front line in order to hunt for and exterminate the Germans. After being gravely wounded and disabled (he lost his right eye and was wounded by shell fragment in the legs on 21 January 1942) comrade Pilyushin, motivated by hatred of the fascists, returned to his unit and continued to take revenge on the aggressors. As a sniper he killed 55 fascists, and as a sniping instructor he trained 380 snipers. He now serves in a divisional training company and continues to pass on his knowledge and experience. For bravery and heroism shown in the fight against the German invaders and his self-sacrificing labour in training snipers, comrade Pilyushin deserves to be decorated with the Order of the Red Star.'

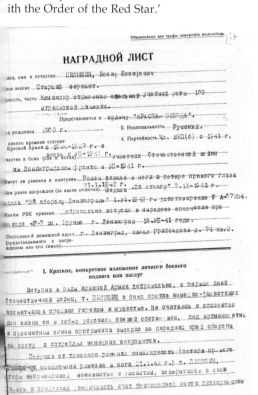

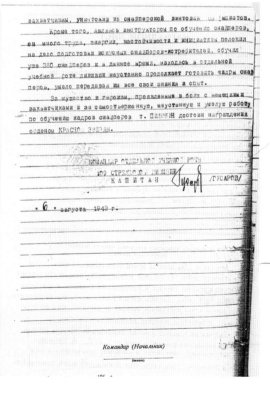

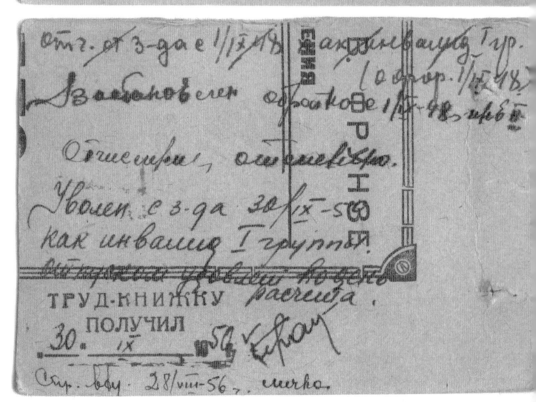

Registration card of Yosif Pilyushin at the Frunze plant where he worked from 1945 till 1950.

Sniper training. A portrait of Hitler is used as a target. The soldier is holding a Mosin rifle model 1898/1930 equipped with a sniper's PE telescopic sight.

A pre-1943 photograph of a sniper-instructor who has been decorated with the Medal for Bravery.

Snipers of the 32nd Army after receiving their decorations. They are wearing summer overalls in order to indicate their profession. In the front line they would never wear such conspicuous medals All of them are armed with a Mosin rifle with a telescopic sight.

Snipers of the 104th Rifle Division on 15 March 1943. The sniper on the left is dressed in a pre-war style of winter overalls. The other sniper is dressed in two-part overalls dating from 1941 and Finnish-style hat.

Snipers on the Karelian front.

A sniper in the firing position.

Two photographs, taken in different conditions, showing snipers in the firing position.

A sniper of the 104th Rifle Division of the 19th Army posing with his rifle. The photograph was taken in the spring of 1943 soon after introduction of the new uniform. The Order of the Red Star shows on the left side of the soldier's chest, and shoulder bars have been sewn onto his 1935-style tunic. He is also wearing the Medal for Bravery.

A sniper decorated with the Order of the Red Star posing for the camera.

Chapter Seventeen
In Ceiling Rubble

With the sunrise I stepped out of a shattered two-storey brick building on the outskirts of Uritsk in battalion commander Major Ogurtsov's sector of the defence. Here on the second floor in some ceiling rubble we had set up a sniper's nest for observing the enemy's trench line. We only fired from this location when it was extremely necessary.

Emerging from the trench, I quickly scurried towards the crossroads, when suddenly a machine-gun burst rang out. The machine gun's stream of bullets set up a barrier along the edge of the ravine, blocking my way. I hopped into a shell crater to wait out the fire, or more accurately, hide from the eyes of the German observer.

I was forced to huddle here in the crater for more than an hour. The sun was warm and I nodded off; when I awoke, the sun was at its zenith. The firing had stopped. From somewhere, seeming from beneath the ground itself, I could hear the sound of a woman's singing. A gossamer thread was slowly spinning in the air.

Cautiously peering over the edge of the crater, I saw someone's freshly-washed army-issue underwear hung out to dry on the branch of a bush beside a brook at the bottom of the ravine. A woman in a combat blouse was sitting on the bank of the stream with her feet dangling in the water. The Germans couldn't see her here. She was the one I had heard singing in a low voice. In order to get a better look at her, I took the cover off my telescopic sight and took a look through it. It was Zina Stroyeva. She was sewing or knitting something, softly singing. Not far from her, a sub-machine-gun was resting on a gas mask bag.

This encounter with Zina was unexpected for me. A week before the battalion commander had summoned her and I hadn't seen her since. Rumours had gone around that Zina had caught the eye of battalion command, and they had decided to keep her at headquarters. What had caused Zina to come here? I continued to watch her. She was inexhaustible! I had often seen, once she put down her weapon, how she then started doing laundry, mending, and knitting . . . Zina laid her sewing down to one side, pulled a letter from the pocket of her combat blouse, and started reading it. Then she buried her face into her hands, and her narrow shoulders began to heave convulsively. Zina was crying! I knew the cause of maidens' tears: she was mourning the death of a loved one.

I quickly stood up and started back to the administrative platoon, so as not to disturb her in her grief. But I hadn't managed to go 100 metres, when I heard quick footsteps behind me.

'Hey you, wanderer!' Zina hailed me. 'Where are you going? Are you angry?'

'At you? Are you off your rocker? I'm just going to have a bite to eat with the guys. I'm very glad to see you again!'

Zina, looking into my eyes, reproachfully shook her head: 'Why are you lying? I can see everything. You think that it is far better for a young woman at the front to trade in her sniper's rifle for a submachine-gun and become the bodyguard of her field husband . . . To live in a safe shelter, to clatter around in a vehicle; after all it's much more peaceful than to fire a rifle at German infantry.'

Stroyeva grabbed me by the hand; tears were glistening in her eyes: 'Really can you, the only man I trust and believe, think that way about me?'

'Calm down, Zinochka, I've not for a minute thought badly about you. You're a soldier, and you're carrying out the commander's order . . . but you must make sense of your own feelings.'

'To hell with philosophy! Once I had listened to my own heart, but now it is reason's turn. I beg you, give me your rifle.'

'Why?'

'What, don't you know anything? You see since morning, German snipers have blocked the approach to Lieutenant Morozov's company outposts. They've killed three of our guys. These snipers must be located and finished off, or else they'll shoot an entire platoon. And you're just strolling off somewhere! I'm coming to you for cover, but your tracks have become cold . . .'

'No, Zina, don't beg for my rifle . . . I won't give it to you. I'll find them myself.'

I turned and quickly headed towards the trench. Stroyeva followed me, quickly stuffing kerchiefs, her sewing kit, and whatever else into her pockets.

'Step more lightly, you're hurrying. All the same, I'm not going to leave you.'

'Zina, I'm not giving you the rifle.'

'I'm not going to leave you alone,' the young woman said, grabbing me by the sleeve. 'Wait for me here, while I run back to our bunker, or we'll no longer be friends.' Stroyeva quickly ran off to the headquarters bunker, and before I had even managed to roll a cigarette for myself, she had returned with a sniper's rifle in her hands.

'Let's go,' Zina said resolutely, drawing even with me.

I saw in a flash how Major Ogurtsov glanced out of the bunker, and then dived back into it again. He was a strange man: he even slept in his helmet. The soldiers didn't like him; they thought he was a coward. The battalion commander plainly didn't want to be seen with me. By order of the regiment commander, I had been categorically prohibited from entering the front-line trenches because of my wound. But in the given case, when death from German snipers was threatening a platoon of soldiers, the Major gave the appearance that he hadn't noticed me.

When we entered the trench, a runner from the battalion commander caught up with us and relayed an order to Zina: 'Stroyeva, immediately return to the battalion commander!'

'Wait a bit, Yosif, I'll be right back.'

I took a seat on a stump. I thought back to Kruglov's rifle company, which we had left so unwillingly. I recalled Major Chistyakov with his fine, but sparing smile. I became depressed . . .

Almost out of breath, Stroyeva ran back to me. Her pretty face, flushed from her quick run, expressed a certain firm and fierce resolve.

'Why did the battalion commander call for you?'

'He told me he was going to send me to a penal company for insubordination. That's why.'

I advised Zina to go back.

'Never! What, you don't understand? I'm a sniper and I'll stay as one. That's why I headed to the front in the first place . . .'

I recognized Zina's character, which I had been able to study in the past. She was moody, and her moods could change rapidly. Sometimes she would go around preoccupied and pensive, or else she would begin to laugh, joke, sing and dance. Often, she would sit for hours without raising her eyes or twitching a brow. But this taciturn mood would be replaced by some sort of devil-may-care attitude. I loved to see her then, when a genuine Russian boldness would wake up in her. It sometimes happened that she would walk right up to you, narrow her eyes, and give you such a smile that your blood would begin to boil. But as soon as you tried to hug her, she would slip away, like a swallow from a hawk, and even shake her finger at you.

Now, however, the young woman was next to me again, the Russian sniper, stern, brave, and ready to enter into a dangerous duel with the enemy. Over the past month, our spirits had somehow grown close to each other.

I recalled how one morning, when we were putting our quarters in order, Zina came to visit our bunker. She had taken me by the hand: 'Osip, I was in Leningrad and dropped by to see your son. He's a fine little boy, and how he delighted me!' She was standing next to me, then without looking at me, she had added: 'He took me for his own mother. He climbed on my lap, wrapped his arms around my neck and began to kiss me. He said, "Mama, you'll now be coming to see me?" I just couldn't disappoint him. But when I got ready to leave, Volodya said, "Mommy, bring me some sugar." So I promised him.'

From that day, Stroyeva tried to be alone as much as possible. Whenever she encountered me, she would lower her head and stand there quietly. One morning, when I headed to the sniper's emplacement, Zina was already there. Sitting at the periscope, she was unravelling a large, woollen mitten and knitting little children's booties. She spent every free minute making something for Volodya.

Now before reaching our sniper's nest, we had to move unnoticed across an exposed area of about 150 metres. Our sniper's nest had been set up among some metal beams, which had been twisted by a bomb blast and were sticking up in the air on the western side of the damaged brick building. We knew that the enemy kept this objective under constant observation. If the Germans managed to spot our movement in the ruins of the building or in the area around it, they would immediately begin lobbing mortar shells, and sometimes call in artillery on us.

I crawled into the nest first, covered the embrasure with a shelter half, and opened the gun port halfway. Then I gave a hand signal to Stroyeva. Zina quickly set up the periscope.

We carefully examined each wrinkle of the terrain: each little gully, each little mound, even a branch, tossed up by the Germans onto the trench's breastworks.

'Where are they? I don't see anything. Where are the shots coming from?' Zina said, turning the periscope from side to side.

'Don't rush, we won't find them quickly; after all, you yourself know how meticulous they are, and they do everything without taking excessive risk. We'll keep searching.'

'But in the given case, they can't avoid risk,' Zina chuckled. 'They know splendidly well that they can't keep shooting Russians in the back as they are crawling along the bottom of the trench for a long time without going unpunished; a meeting with our snipers is unavoidable.'

No-man's-land seemed as exposed to us as a ribbon of road through the steppe. Sultry heat haze hindered long-range vision.

Stroyeva, turning onto her back, raised first her left, then her right hand, wiggled her numb fingers, and wrinkling her face from the pain, said: 'We won't find them from here.'

'Just take another look for a place, from where the Germans can see the entire bottom of our trench at the turn. Without being able to see the bottom of the trench, they wouldn't be able to kill our guys.'

Zina shot a quick glance at me and shifted closer to the eyepiece of the periscope. Then she neatly gathered her legs beneath her and fell silent.

'Yosif, take a look at that birch tree close to their trench. Are there not Germans lying on its shaded side?'

Many times I had looked at this birch, which a shell blast had uprooted. Its dried-out roots now stirred in the wind like the legs of an enormous, overturned beetle, looking to right itself.

This time I hadn't given the birch my customary attention, when several shells passed overhead with a shriek, one after the other; columns of black smoke and earth shot into the sky, concealing the enemy's positions from our eyes. It was our artillery, giving support to our infantrymen.

'Eh, that's no help,' Zina said, frowning in annoyance. 'To flush a beast is no big deal, but to spot one . . . They're not where they should be, but they're here somewhere.'

I examined every piece of the toppled birch tree, from its top to its roots, and each clump of scorched grass, searching for the concealed enemy.

'There they are!' Stroyeva joyfully and suddenly exclaimed. 'Look over there: young guys, concealed in the shadow of the trunk. Our artillerymen are pounding their trenches, but they're lying out in front. Look at the pattern on those uniforms! See the camouflage they're throwing at us? Dandy, huh?' Zina reached for her rifle: 'Yosif, don't be upset with me; after all, I found them.'

I restrained her arm: 'We have a score to settle with them. But we can't shoot from here, and you know that. Let's go to the back-up position.'

'You go, and I'll keep an eye on them. If they try to slither away, I won't let them leave no-man's-land alive.'

'I'll go, but you don't fire. You're risking your life . . .'

I went downstairs. A runner from the battalion commander pounced on me: 'Well? Have you started firing? Where's Zina?'

Paying him no attention, I quickly dashed down the trench line. Heavily panting and swearing, the messenger ran after me.

I hurried to the reserve sniper emplacement. I heard two shots in quick succession. On the run, I couldn't make out their origin, but for some reason, my heart clenched.

Running into the emplacement, I quickly opened the embrasure and looked over no-man's-land to where the German snipers had been located. Two grey-green figures lay motionless, nestled into the ground. Stroyeva had shot the fascists while I was changing position.

I quickly closed the embrasure and hurried out of the emplacement, where the battalion commander's runner again met me: 'What, have the Germans shot more of our guys?'

'Get away from here. Why the hell are you hanging around here?' I shouted at him.

'I've been ordered to find out, whether you shot the Germans or not.'

'Tell the Major that Stroyeva shot two Germans in no-man's-land, and how many more there might be, and where they're hiding, I don't know.'

'You're lying!'

I threw myself to the bottom of the trench face-first as I heard incoming artillery rounds. There was first one, then a second and third explosion. Sheltering behind the turns in the trench from the shell fragments and flying clumps of dirt, I crawled back into the sniper emplacement. The battalion commander's messenger was already there, sitting in the corner, covered in grey dust. His lower jaw was trembling. His eyes were wide like those of an eagle owl as he silently looked around.

As soon as the artillery barrage ended, I rushed to the ruins of the brick building, to find out what had happened to Zina. The traces of ammonium nitrate were still smoking in the craters. Dust and smoke stung the eyes. With difficulty I clambered through the rubble. I found Stroyeva lying on her side, curled up like a little child, her right arm clamped over a wound on her left arm. Blood was streaming through her fingers.

'Yosif, don't scold me, I didn't manage to get away, and now I've been hit . . .' was all Zina said.

Chapter Eighteen

The Staro-Panovo Operation

July 1942 . . . With the fall of darkness, at the order of the regiment's chief of staff, the students of the sniper school were issued dry rations for three days, and we headed for the front lines. The white night was ebbing. An enormous moon emerged in the middle of the night sky, as if the glow of the evening sunset was passing it from hand to hand to the morning dawn. The air was filled with the light scent of flowers. In the shrubs, some sort of little bird was flitting about. Eh, what a fine night you are tonight! In your calm, everything seems near and dear, as if my little son Volodya is whispering something to me.

The sun hadn't yet managed to peek over the horizon when the earth gave a muffled gasp and began to shake. Fiery arrows penetrated the mist of the morning fog over our heads. It was our *Katiusha* multiple rocket-launchers launching their payloads towards the Germans. The Staro-Panovo operation was under way on our sector of the front. Literally within the first several hours of the offensive, all the enemy's fortified lines were broken. Although we did not manage to exploit the initial successes, this offensive was a serious warning to the enemy.

Our artillery worked over the enemy lines for more than an hour. For the first time since the war began, I was witnessing the enormous fire-power of massed Soviet artillery. While the preparation was proceeding, I was standing with a group of schooled snipers in a trench on the right flank of a rifle battalion to which we had been assigned.

It is difficult to express the condition of waiting troops before an attack. The majority of the soldiers were just trying to keep themselves busy in some way. Some were idly picking at the trench wall with a bayonet, while others, squatting, were thoroughly cleaning grime from the breech of their gun and the bayonet, as if they had only just spotted it. Soldiers a little younger tried to huddle together, while the 'old guys', who had already participated in more than one attack, were smoking hand-rolled cigarettes, spitting them out, and then lighting another one, never taking their eyes off the enemy's positions.

Anxious moments: we were waiting for the order to go . . .

A short, barrel-chested major walked up to us – the battalion commander. He was cleanly-shaven and even freshly scented.

'Who's the senior sniper here?'

'I am, Comrade Major.'

'Once we reach the first German trench line, change your position only at my command; the signal will be a yellow flare. Keep watch over the flank. If you don't have enough strength to withstand enemy pressure, report it; I will be with the 1st Rifle Company.'

At once everything fell silent. The troops stood quietly, holding their weapons at the ready, waiting for the signal. Suddenly, a single rifle shot rang out. No one paid it any attention, as if it was just someone's cough. Everyone knew, however, that this was the shot of a German sniper, who had just taken the life of a comrade, but at this minute no one thought about it.

Ten minutes passed. We looked at each other in bewilderment: had the attack gone wrong? Then suddenly our artillery again rained shells on the enemy. The last echo of the artillery fire hadn't yet died away, when signal flares soared into the sky. Attack! Men clambered over the parapet and hopped out into no-man's-land, but sensing their exposure and seized by momentary consternation, they froze in place. This lasted only for an instant, perhaps a second, and then we all rushed towards the enemy line. Our Ilyushin Il-2 'Shturmoviki' roared overhead.

No matter how many times I went into an attack, I was seized by such rage that I almost didn't know what I was doing. To the left and right, I could hear the explosions of grenades, bursts of automatic weapons fire, and rifle shots, mingling with the shouts of men and the peremptory voices of commanders. Once you reach the enemy's trench, though, you immediately come to your senses.

On the enemy breastwork, two of the young snipers had taken a prone position, covering with their fire the attack on the enemy's next line of defence. It was the giant, hulking Sergey Naydenov and the puny, but devilishly nimble Nikolay Smirnov.

Once, the guys had asked Naydenov to climb up onto some scales: he weighed 116 kilograms [almost 256 pounds]. But he had astonishing agility. The sniper's rifle in his hands looked like a toy gun. He reloaded it cautiously, gripping the bolt lever with two fingers, as if fearing to break it. He was a fine fellow – calm, accommodating and brave.

'Sergey! Everything's turned out splendidly, huh? Just yesterday evening, the Nazis were shouting: "Rus! Give up, we're going to

Leningrad!"' Smirnov said. 'But now we're punching their snouts. Seryozha, take a look how they're running!'

'Don't just admire them, shoot them!'

The bantam strongman sniper Puzanov was lying beside me. They said that he could play with a 33-kilogram [about 72 pounds] weight like a child with a ball.

'Comrade Commander, take a look over there. Germans are in the station ruins behind our guys. Do you see them?'

'I see them.'

I began to observe closely a German officer, who with a small group of soldiers was picking his way towards the ruins of Ligovo Station's terminal. Before opening fire on them, we had to establish the number of Germans and their intentions.

As I watched, more and more groups of Germans were making their way towards the brick ruins of the station, crawling from shell hole to shell hole. It was clear that the enemy was massing for a sudden counter-attack on the flank of our attacking units. In order to foil this plan, I gave the snipers the order to open fire.

Smirnov even clicked his tongue in satisfaction, firing off cartridge clip after cartridge clip. Naydenov, in contrast, slowly and deliberately fired bullet after bullet; his eyes were shining, and a drop of sweat was hanging on the end of his nose.

The Nazis, caught under the destructive sniper fire, halted their advance and became pinned down. Suddenly, the sniper Puzanov lying next to me quietly drew his elbows into his abdomen and slowly slithered to the bottom of the trench. I could hear his quiet voice, pleading for something to drink. Soon a medic came running up to the wounded man. Hearing his pleas, the medic replied: 'You can't drink anything, brother, you've been shot in the gut.'

The Germans, taking cover in the ruins, opened a furious automatic fire. We engaged the enemy infantry for not more than five minutes, although they had several times the number of men of us snipers. However, they couldn't sustain this gun duel with us for very long, as our precise fire picked them off one by one. Soon the fire from their side diminished, before it quickly went silent altogether.

We had liquidated the danger of a flank attack, and our rifle battalion continued to push on to the ruins of Ligovo Station. This was the first piece of our land, ripped from the bloody paws of the fascist executioners in front of the walls of Leningrad. Fighting for this strip of ground had been going on for nine months, but now at last it was again ours. Inspired by this initial success, we occupied new lines, and continued to press the enemy.

Next to a shattered enemy timber pillbox, Sergey Naydenov and Nikolay Smirnov were digging in with spades, hastily fashioning a new sniper emplacement. The remaining men took up staggered positions to either side. Our deployment now suggested a flock of cranes in flight.

'Sergey, did you see their trench?' someone asked.

'What can I say? It was a real piece of work, even the walls were lined with wattling. But they couldn't hold it . . . Fie, you rascals!'

'Our artillery did some excellent work!'

Someone in the bunker replied, 'Yes, you can't say anything else but that it worked in the Russian style!'

'It was the only way to smoke them out; look at how deeply they were dug-in.'

'A costly start, but we'll find the path from here even to Berlin.'

Lightly-wounded comrades were walking past us, heading for the rear. One of them took a seat on a log next to Naydenov's embrasure.

'Well, how are things going for you here, guys? Are the Fritzes pressing you hard?'

'They're pressing us, yes, but look – we've managed to take the steam out of them.'

The wounded man handed Naydenov a tobacco pouch and paper: 'Roll a cigarette for me, brother. The vermin have badly wounded my hand, and I can't put one together myself.'

'What, have they struck a bone?' Naydenov asked.

'Apparently so; my fingers won't move.'

'Hold on,' Naydenov said as he handed the cigarette to the soldier, 'I'll get a light for you.' Sergey pulled a piece of flint from his pocket and struck it forcefully with a narrow strip of iron. Sparks flew, and the wick began to smoke.

'Here you go, hold on, but smoke it quickly. See over there? The Germans have started to move again.'

The wounded man smoked the entire cigarette without haste, and then stood up: 'Eh, there's not enough strength to advance . . . Don't yield to the Germans what you've already regained. Well, so long, and thanks for the light.'

. . . That evening the group of snipers was ordered to escort prisoners. Passing between the Russians, the prisoners bowed and smiled timidly, glancing to both sides. Once in the city, the fascists walked slowly, their heads lowered and with their hands in their pockets. There were a lot of old men, women and children standing in the streets. The Germans shot quick side glances at the green vegetable patches, which had been planted on the grass plots where flowers had once been.

I remember how on the corner of Mayorov Street and Sadovaya Street, there was a boy about 7 years old holding the hand of a young woman, asking: 'Mama, why are the fascists hiding their hands in their pockets? Why, are their hands dirty?'

The woman, not answering her son's questions, shot a hostile glance at the Nazi soldiers and kept walking. The boy several times looked back at the prisoners, who were walking lazily like hard labourers, their hobnailed boots clattering on the cobblestone paving, and shook his fist at them.

We returned to the front lines early the next morning, and after several minutes, Vasiliy Yershov appeared. He was holding the barrel of a heavy machine gun under his arm.

'Uncle Vasya, where's Romanov?' I asked.

'He's here. Alive.'

Yershov rejoiced at seeing me, and then immediately frowned. His thick wide brows furrowed, and without looking at me, he said, 'We thought . . .' Then he sternly asked: 'Just how did you wind up here?'

'With my pupils, Vasiliy Dmitriyevich. As they say, we're conducting field training.'

'Not a business for you, brother! You shouldn't wade into this game with one eye. Here, in addition to the two eyes in your forehead, it wouldn't be a hindrance to have two more eyes in the back of your head. But it . . .'

'Where are you dragging your machine gun?'

'Back from repairs, a shell fragment ruined the sight. I learned that you were here with your students and came by to chew you out.'

I was silent.

Vasiliy Dmitriyevich was out of sorts. The reason for this became clear to me a little later. Disapprovingly shaking his head, he laid the machine gun on a plank bed and began to wipe and clean it diligently, loudly sniffing his nose.

Naydenov slowly pulled a tobacco pouch and paper from his pocket, and having picked up his enormous hooves, so as not to trip anyone passing by, said: 'You, brother, anyhow, have known our teacher for a long time, so why have you lashed out at the man for no rhyme or reason?'

'Can I ask if you've been fighting beside him for a long time?'

'This is my first time.'

'That's obvious.'

'Have a smoke! Why are you so angry?'

'I wasn't grousing at all, I was just speaking the truth.'

I stepped out into the trench. It was a peaceful summer morning. There wasn't a cloud in the sky. From somewhere, clipped words carried to me: 'Come on, come on! All together now! A plank! Place the plank under the left wheel . . . Ah, damn it! Careful with the foot! Watch out for your feet . . . Now then, fellows, once more! Heave-ho!'

It was anti-tank artillery changing their positions, preparing for the battle to resume.

Our offensive at Staro-Panovo brought us our first victories. In the first hours of our offensive, the German armour, artillery and air force weren't operating, since they had been paralyzed by the sudden strike of our forces. Only in the afternoon did the German artillery begin to conduct counter-fire, but fortunately it was inaccurate. The struggle against the furiously resisting enemy infantry continued. Only mine-fields and still-intact machine-gun nests, from which the Germans continued to put up stubborn opposition, held up our advance into the depth of the enemy's defences.

I dropped by a neighbouring bunker. The door of the soldiers' quarters had been torn off by a bomb blast together with the jamb. From a jagged hole in the shelter, a plume of tobacco smoke rose.

'Mitya!' a voice came out of the darkness. 'You're simply our hero! It is simply splendid! Just how did you reach him through that storm of fire, huh?' A deep voice responded, 'What's there to be amazed about? A soldier here knows his own business.'

'Here, my brother, it's not enough to be simply a soldier . . .'

'Ho-ho-ho!' the deep voice again rumbled. 'In war, brother, you'll find out everything there is to know about a man: whether he's dense or has an agile mind, and what sort of heart he has. In combat . . . how should I say this . . . people are exposed for who they really are. There's no masking it.'

'What do you know about it, guys?' a strong voice hastily began to say. 'There's no sort of heroism here. I managed to make my way close to this bunker before anyone else, and then I just stuck a bundle of grenades into it, that's all.'

'What's right is right,' answered the deep voice.

In the bunker, everything lapsed into silence. Soon you could hear the sound of snoring.

Somewhere quite nearby on the enemy side, a conversation carried to my ears, a chatter of a weapon, curt commands, and then it became silent there, too.

I returned to my bunker. I found Uncle Vasya leisurely telling a story there: 'Once, in the first days of the war I was cleaning this very machine gun with my young friend Grisha Strel'tsov. At first he was timid in battle, but then he got used to it, and that's not all, he became reckless. Another time he was lying there beside me; then he nestled up next to me and talked to me about something or other, and then he cuddled up like a little kid and fell asleep! Oh! How passionately he hated the occupiers!' Yershov sighed deeply: 'Once, where it was very dangerous, I was protecting him, but it happened I couldn't save him, and they killed Grisha. He was like a son to me.' With that, Yershov clapped his palm on the jacket of his machine gun: 'No matter how many fascists I shoot from this here Maxim, they're not enough for the life of one Grisha.'

Vasiliy Dmitriyevich gave a cough, and turning away, he quickly wiped his eyes. He attempted several times to roll a cigarette, but couldn't do it: his hands were shaking, tearing the paper and the tobacco spilled onto his lap.

'Uncle Vasya, allow me,' Naydenov said, 'I'll do it.'

'Thanks, friend, for some reason I'm not myself today.' Yershov eagerly stretched and shook his head. 'My hands are tired from this machine gun, and as you can see, I couldn't fall asleep. The Germans, no doubt, are anxious to get back what we took from them, although indeed it is our own hard-won land.'

Vasiliy Dmitriyevich hastily rose to leave, and said, 'Well, fellows, thanks, it's time for me to get back, or else who knows? I might lose my way on my own soil and wind up in the wrong trench!'

Parting, Uncle Vasya gripped Naydenov's hand most firmly of all: 'If you have a need for fire support – my little friend and I can help you out, just let us know.'

'Thank you. We can also give you help, whenever you have the need for it,' the snipers answered in a chorus of voices.

I escorted my old friend out of the bunker. In the trench, Yershov told me: 'A couple of evenings ago I received a letter. My woman writes that the Secretary of the district committee supplied them with some bread and firewood. My thanks to him. But there was also such grief in the letter that I don't even want to talk about it: my younger son has died.' Uncle Vasya lingered for a moment with me, as if trying to recall where he needed to go, but then gave a bitter wave of his hand and added: 'We also called the lad Grisha . . .'

The machine-gunner abruptly spun around, and without saying goodbye, started off in the direction of Gorelovo Station. Soon his tall, slightly stooped figure disappeared in the trench. Watching Yershov as he walked away, I was thinking about my own son.

Sometimes at the front, everything would be quiet for a few hours. But experienced front-line soldiers know the danger lurking behind this desired calm: the sentries' senses of sight and hearing become heightened, lest they instantly fall into enemy hands or get a knife in the heart.

I walked over to some sappers as they quickly worked to reverse the enemy's former positions and emplacements, turning their embrasures from east to west. The sun rose. A lark, flapping its wings, circled in the air and started singing its simple song. A signalman, bent over from the load on his back, was running in the direction of Ligovo Station. In a ravine, a soldier approached the little stream in the bottom of it, washed out his mess kit and spoon, and after taking a look around, washed himself.

Suddenly the ground shook from a powerful artillery salvo. A messenger from the battalion commander came running up to me: 'I've been ordered to direct you to a new firing line.' Lowering his voice, the messenger added: 'We're expecting a German tank counter-attack. You must hurry, Comrade Commander.'

We had taken up a new line south-east of Ligovo Station, close to the highway. The artillery fire from both sides intensified with every minute. At the foot of a low mound, anti-tank riflemen had already taken their positions. Behind a nearby ravine, artillerymen were bustling around their anti-tank guns. Despite frequent shell bursts, they took no cover.

We were prone, literally hugging the earth. The strip of no-man's-land was about 300 metres in front of us. To our right and left, despite the heavy enemy artillery fire, the anti-tank rifles began to bang away with muffled reports, while nearby the anti-tank guns discharged their rounds. Suddenly an enemy tank emerged from a cloud of dust and smoke. It was firing from its main gun and machine guns. Anti-tank shells passed over our heads with a terrifying shriek. The grey armoured vehicle came to a stop with a shudder.

Nazis, running in a dense line from one piece of cover to the next, were moving on the attack. At the start of the attack, our rifle volleys rang out in concert. As the enemy infantry approached, the fire intensified and merged together into a crackling roar, like a lit string of fire-crackers. The machine-gun fire became more furious.

Someone's sonorous voice from the anti-tank guns' position rose above the din: 'Tanks on the left!' The snipers fired at the German infantry running across the field.

For a certain time, the artillery barrage lifted, allowing their infantry to finish the battle that had begun. The hammering of the machine guns became clearer. Here and there, mortar rounds exploded. One minute more, another – and we lunged forward into hand-to-hand combat.

Naydenov knocked the weapon from one Nazi's hand with a blow from his rifle-butt, then reached and grabbed the German by the collar with one hand and threw him to the ground. Shouting 'Off our land, toad!' Naydenov re-gripped his rifle and delivered a powerful back-handed strike with the butt of it to the German's head.

The hand-to-hand struggle ended as suddenly as it had begun: the foe, unable to withstand the violent impact of our soldiers' counter-attack, buckled and ran. The ranks of the field grey-clad soldiers melted away. It became tougher and tougher to catch one of the fleeing enemy troops in our telescopic sights.

Sergey Naydenov ran up to me: 'Comrade Commander, for some reason Vasiliy Yershov's machine gun has fallen silent; permit me to go find out what has happened with him.'

'Where do you see Yershov's machine gun?' I asked the sniper.

'It's over there on that knoll to the left of the road.'

'Had Uncle Vasya really been killed?' Chasing away this awful thought, I watched Naydenov's every movement as he moved towards Yershov's position. Sergey crawled into a shell crater and stopped, wiped his face with the sleeve of his blouse, and started crawling again. A shell suddenly exploded almost next to Naydenov. For a moment I lost him from view. When the smoke dispersed, Sergey was lying motionlessly on his side.

'Guys!' Smirnov shouted. 'Naydenov has been killed!'

But Naydenov was still alive. I watched as he carefully detached his canteen from his belt with his left hand and raised it to his mouth.

Everybody exclaimed at once: 'He's alive!'

About 100–150 metres remained to reach Yershov's machine gun. Naydenov, having rested for a minute in his spot, quickly started crawling forward again, unnaturally dragging his right leg and arm. He passed near an immobilized German tank.

'He's wounded. Does he have enough strength?'

Completely unexpectedly, a hatch on the immobilized German tank opened. First the arms, then the head and shoulders of a tanker emerged. The Nazi was intending to shoot the crawling Russian soldier. I fired first. The enemy tanker collapsed back into the tank and the hatch banged closed.

'There's still somebody else in the tank; I've got to keep watch,' I thought to myself. Naydenov, plainly, noticed none of this, or else he would have stopped by the tank. He kept crawling towards his destination. He disappeared from view, and after a minute I saw him again at a trench entrance: he was standing, propped against the trench wall with his left hand and speaking with someone. Then he glanced back in our direction and disappeared again.

The day was gloomy and humid; the clouds were floating low above the ground. By noon, the fighting sputtered to a close. The snipers took a seat to have lunch in the open trench. Just then someone loudly shouted: 'Air attack!'

I looked around. Behind us the artillerymen were frantically covering their guns and ammunition cases with canvas, shelter halves and greatcoats. The enemy bombers were flying stealthily just above the scattered cloud tops, like thieves approaching a home. The first three bombers released their loads, and the din of falling bombs and their explosions drowned out all other sounds. We were rocked from side to side as if we were in a hammock. A blanket of smoke and dust covered the ground.

The bombers, freed from their deadly loads, flew away, but a terrible ringing remained in our ears. Wiping my eyes, I was breathing heavily through my mouth, when suddenly someone gave a tug on my leg. It was Sergey Naydenov: 'Comrade Commander, are you alive? I've brought a message from Yershov. Both his legs are fractured. An artillery doctor is checking him out.'

'Seryozha, are you also wounded?'

'I just have a nick, but you see Uncle Vasya is badly injured, he's delirious. He didn't recognize me when I reached him, and all the way he was either cursing out the Germans or talking as if in conversation with his wife.'

I followed Sergey at a run over to the place where Uncle Vasya was lying. Yershov was feeling about with his hands all around him.

'He's searching for his machine gun,' Sergey said, and turning away, he began to blow his nose and furtively wipe his eyes.

'Guys, where's our machine gun?' Yershov whispered in delirium. 'Artem, a fresh belt quickly! Mitya, where's the iodine? Sanyusha . . .

drop by . . . the district Secretary, thank him . . . for the help, and give him . . . a soldier's thanks. Look after the kids, send them to school, don't worry about me, I'm OK . . .'

For five days, we struggled with the adversary for the ground we had won from them in front of Leningrad. Over the next six days, the Germans introduced fresh forces into the fighting and pushed us back to Ligovo Station, where we managed to halt them and dig in. That's how the Staro-Panovo operation ended.

Chapter Nineteen

Encounters

The Gor'ky House of Culture was jammed with military men. Soldiers and officers were crowded around the massive double doors inside. From time to time the doors swung open and a dapper major wearing horn-rimmed glasses pushed down on the end of his nose appeared. Bringing a sheet of paper up close to his glasses, he unintelligibly called out a few last names, and then like a cuckoo in a cuckoo clock, he disappeared again behind the doors.

More and more fresh crowds of military men entered the hallway. I was standing by a window. Suddenly a pair of hands grabbed me from behind and gave me a tight squeeze, and someone stuck a cigarette into my mouth.

It was Akimov. He looked at me, smiling widely. Sergeant Andreyev was standing beside him, waggishly saluting me.

'Fancy meeting you both here!' I said. 'For what should I congratulate you, friends?'

'It's a military secret,' Akimov replied, pressing a finger to his lips. 'It wouldn't be bad to wind up on the list of Heroes [of the Soviet Union, the highest Soviet combat honour].' He was still the same tireless joker. Two military Orders already decorated Akimov's breast – the Red Banner and the Red Star.

Andreyev said, 'He deserves to be a Hero. After all, he blew a German tank onto its back, just like it was a dung beetle.'

'An ordinary matter. All sorts of things happen in a scrap. You just hope for the best and try to stay out of trouble. And you, Yosif, what's the occasion for congratulating you?'

'For the medal "For courage".'

The door flew open, and again the bespectacled major appeared. No one responded to the announcement of many of the names.

They called for Akimov. He straightened his shoulders, raised his head, gave us a wink, and with a precise step marched up to the oak door, opened it in a businesslike fashion, and disappeared into the shadows inside. A few minutes later, he re-emerged and rejoined us.

'Look! Look! Our Akimych sauntered back like a dandy, but just see why! Attaboy, Hero!' the sniper Nikolay Smirnov cried out.

As he was leaving after receiving his own decoration, Andreyev told me: 'Comrade Senior Sergeant, don't leave, wait for us at the gates.'

A new group of front-line soldiers arrived. Orlov was among them, who had managed to leave the hospital in time to take part in the latest operation. From one glance at Orlov, I understood that something had happened. But what, and to whom?

'Have you seen Romanov?' I asked Orlov.

'No, he's been away on some assignment.'

'And where's Sabinov?'

Orlov took a hard drag on his cigarette, coughed fitfully and dryly, and rapidly drummed his fingers on the windowsill.

'Where's Sabinov?' I repeated.

Orlov glumly looked at me: 'Leonid's in the hospital with wounds to his eyes. Whether he'll be able to see or not is unknown.'

At last the major called for me. In the spacious office, high-backed chairs were standing along the walls. Sitting behind a desk covered with a fringed brocade tablecloth, was our division commander Major-General Trushkin, wearing a new general's tunic. He was grey-haired, and had the tired face of an old man. Next to the Major-General, a small, but solidly-built man with a weathered face wearing a worn-out civilian suit was seated; his dark hair bristled like a hedgehog. He smiled courteously, looking at us. The General sat with both elbows heavily leaning on the table. His eyelids were heavy and yellowish, and when he glanced at me, his lids slowly rose. The wrinkles on his face now and then smoothed out, as if yielding their place to an aged smile. The General was holding a large red pencil and tapping it on the desk as he conversed with his neighbour.

Behind a small, round table covered with red cloth, sat the division's chief of combat troops, a swarthy young man with a luxurious black moustache, Lieutenant Colonel Lyubavin. He was quickly ticking off the names of the honourees on a list lying in front of him on the table, reading the documents and handing oblong boxes together with the papers to the General. The rhythmic ticking of a metronome emitting from a loud-speaker gave this minute a stern solemnity.

Suddenly the ticking stopped. A voice replaced it: 'Attention! Attention! Citizens, the district is being subjected to an artillery barrage. Stop the movement of all transport vehicles, and the populace is to take cover.'

Sirens were wailing outside. Their sounds filled the air and gripped the heart.

The man in civilian dress glanced at the General. Trushkin, paying no attention to the warning or the ruckus outside, continued to hand out the decorations. It seemed as if he was thinking, 'Don't be surprised, esteemed guest. You earned your honour to just such music, and you'll receive this honour to the same.'

Exiting out into the yard, I couldn't find my comrades. Crossing the wasteland that had become the House of Culture's grounds, I emerged on Novosikovsky Street; the air was filled with smoke and red dust. Women and children ran past me, crying something on the run and waving their arms, but their voices were drowned out in the thunder of explosions.

I stood in a building's arched entrance, tightly pressed against a wall, so that a blast wave wouldn't hurl me onto the bridge. Suddenly someone behind me touched my arm. Looking back, I saw a woman covered in brick-dust from her head to her feet. There was no fear in her calm eyes. She unhurriedly told me, 'Get into a shelter, Comrade, right this way.'

Climbing down several stairs, I opened a door sheathed with iron and entered a quite spacious cellar, already furnished by people. A lamp was burning. Along the right wall, there were beds, both large and small, desks, and numerous suitcases and bundles. To the left, there were two jerry-built stoves and little kitchen tables. Next to the door was a plank couch, covered with white oilcloth, and a makeshift medicine cabinet – apparently, this corner was a little medical station.

An old woman walked up to me. She was wearing an armband that read 'Attendant'.

'Lo, God has brought you to us,' she said soothingly. Suddenly the entry door flew open with a bang, and a peremptory voice shouted from the entrance: 'Aunt Pasha! Call the doctor!'

Two women carried in an 11 or 12-year-old blood-soaked girl on a stretcher. She was constantly moaning and calling for her mother: 'Mama, where are you? Give me your hand, I'm in pain.' The girl turned her head from one side to the other, casting an anxious gaze on each of us. The doctor, gaunt and all in white, entered the cellar through a spare entry. He gave the girl an injection and asked me to lift the girl from the stretcher and lay her on the plank couch. I carefully took her into my arms. The girl gave a subtle wince and requested water.

The doctor began to apply a needless bandage . . . Within several minutes, the girl passed away. Aunt Pasha folded the dead girl's thin arms on her breast, tied them together with a strip of gauze, and gave the sign of the cross three times over the girl's body.

It became stuffy in the cellar: there was not enough air. I exited the cellar and climbed the stairs into the yard. The artillery barrage had ceased. The silence now was startling. From the Narva Gates, a solitary trolley car departed in the direction of the front. It moved slowly, its wheels clattering on the rail joints.

I stood there for some time at the House of Culture, waiting for my comrades, but neither Akimov nor Andreyev appeared. My eyes were still seeing the image of the dead child. Her death strikingly reminded me of the death of my older son Vitya. I was almost wild to go and see my motherless son Volodya, to be with him together if only for a minute, but I had no separate pass card for this, and I was forced with bitterness in my heart to reject this idea. I stood for several minutes on the corner of Narva Prospekt, and then set off for the front on foot.

Chapter Twenty

The Brown Rat

Just before sunrise, the blond-haired joker and merry-maker Ivan Dobrik, a renowned Leningrad Front sniper, came running into my dugout. As usual, mixing together Ukrainian and Russian, he gushed out the purpose of his visit: 'You know, old boy, snipers have appeared on our sector. Give us some help, brother, or else life is impossible. Yesterday evening they killed two of our riflemen, Ivanin and Smirnov. The snakes, they're nestled in some spot from where they can see our trenches and lines of communications, and we can't detect them!'

The sniper's face with its high cheekbones was flushed with agitation and from his rapid walk to see me. His large blue eyes flashed with alarm.

Dobrik was an outstanding sniper and as slippery as a fish. When 'on the hunt', he typically liked to creep out into no-man's-land, set up on the edge of a shell crater, and from there he would hunt down enemy observers, and sometimes kill the sentries at machine guns as well. But Ivan knew that a particularly dangerous struggle was now in front of us.

Enemy snipers were cold-blooded and superb shots. A large group of specially trained soldiers supported the snipers by offering various ruses to smoke out the positions of our own snipers: they set up dummies, opened fire from different locations, raised helmets above the trench line, and created commotions in their own trenches. I had witnessed this masquerade many times in my own experience.

I couldn't leave together with Dobrik right away. In parting, Dobrik told me: 'So, tomorrow you'll come and help me duel with them.'

'But don't go out yourself; I'll look in on you with my guys in the morning.'

'Fine! I'll be waiting. But I'll keep an eye on them, in case they start acting up over there.'

Ivan Dobrik departed. Later that evening, however, I learned that he had been badly wounded in the back of the head by a mortar fragment.

As soon as twilight had gathered, I went to Stroyeva to discuss with her how best to prepare for the duel with the Nazi snipers. I also had to alert the other comrades.

When I stepped into the communications dugout at regiment head-quarters, Zina, curled up into a ball, was fast asleep on a plank couch. Two soldiers were sitting in front of the telephone apparatus, smoking hand-rolled cigarettes and conversing in a low voice. I walked up to the sleeping woman and cautiously laid a hand on her shoulder. Zina woke up in a flash, rolled over onto her back, grabbed my head and firmly pressed it to her breast. The soldiers exchanged glances.

'Yosif! You're alive? Oh, I had just dreamed . . .'

The signalmen laughed: 'It was just a dream. In reality, may he live to 100!'

We stepped out of the stuffy, smoke-filled dugout. A prime mover was passing nearby. With a howling engine, its clattering tracks were chewing up the earth. I told Zina about the appearance of the German snipers and laid out my plan of action.

'I make only one request of you,' Zina said. 'Don't go out with your pupils. I'll have a chat with Tolya Bodrov, and we'll decide together what we should do.'

With the sun still below the horizon, Zina, Bodrov and I arrived in the 1st Rifle Battalion's sector. We took up our positions before the sun rose and began to observe the Germans' trench line. What wasn't over there! Rags of different colours, tin cans, buckets, bottles, bricks, pieces of plywood, bones, helmets, pieces of scrap metal, rolls of barbed wire, gas masks . . .

Bodrov had already been on this sector. He looked at me and gave a shrug: 'Just try to find anyone among all this junk.'

Zina handed Bodrov a notepad: 'Tolya, take a good look, it's a sketch I made of their defences with all its ornamentations. Perhaps with a fresh eye you'll notice something new.'

I peered at the enemy's positions. Soon I spotted a prone fascist next to a rusty bucket on the breastwork. He was nestled in on the shady side of a scorched tree, his shoulder up against the trunk: the sunlight couldn't reach his face and arms. His head was wrapped with a dark rag; only his chin, mouth and half his nose were exposed. I pointed out my finding to my comrades.

'Well, I'll be!' Bodrov drawled. 'What a rascal, look how he's settled himself in!'

Stroyeva, fitting a spare armoured plate to her embrasure, couldn't resist razzing Bodrov a bit: 'You, Tolya, look sharp, or you'll overlook things.'

'My foot, I'm not overlooking anything. It's not my first time to see that creature.'

'Don't rush to conclusions, Tolya. What if that's only a dummy?'

'What the hell do you mean "dummy", take a closer look: you're shaking in your shoes from fear.'

I didn't take my cross hairs off the fascist's head, waiting for him to turn in our direction. Just then, a large brown rat came running up to the prone German. Without any concern, it approached his face, sniffed first his chin and then his mouth, and then rose on its hind paws. Startled by someone or something, the rat darted down the front of the German's shirt.

'Screw you, devil! Where the hell did that just come from!' Tolya was gaping in surprise.

'Tolya, shut your trap, or even better, bite your tongue!'

The chagrined Bodrov gave a dismissive wave: 'Fie, devil, just how did I fail to make it out? Stop your chuckling, it's the first time I've seen such a prop.' Then he added, 'And I, by God, was just about to fire, but I felt sorry for the rat.'

'You would have planted a bullet in his skull. Look for a real one; he's got to be around here somewhere.'

This incident reminded me of a meeting with an old acquaintance, Petr Andreyevich Timonin. I ran into him on Lenin Square, when I was going to visit my son Volodya in the second half of February 1942. At the time, I could hardly recognize this former top-class gymnast. Emaciated, Petr Andreyevich's skeletal face was ashen, and his eyes were sunken. His mouth appeared unnaturally large, and his lips trembled.

In a word, he was at the end of his rope. His athletic, lithesome body had become hunched over, and his arms were hanging like dead sticks. Petr struggled to recognize me, but then immediately began to talk about his family: 'You know, Yosif, Zoya Nikolayevna managed to slip through aboard the last train on 28 August, via Mga Station. Yes, yes, don't be surprised – she literally slipped through, because at that time fighting was going on with German tanks just 2 kilometres away from the Station.'

'And you, Petya, where are you living now?'

'Me?' With the tip of his tongue, he slowly moistened his trembling lips, and looking in the direction of the Neva, he shivered from the cold. 'I live like a prisoner. At first I got meals at a dining hall, but when they stopped feeding people there, that's when it all started.' Petr Andreyevich extended his arms, and then continued: 'Just look at my arms, not a bit of meat on them, just tendons. But my work requires a lot of strength, because you see I now work as a railroad's deputy chief of freight. You yourself know the situation at the front; but the people are weak.

You instruct someone to check the serviceability of the boxcars, and he never reaches the place. I must go myself, though I don't know where to find the strength, and we can't let down the front. So you run yourself dizzy.'

We started to cross the Liteynyi Bridge. A cold wind was howling in our face. Petr Andreyevich tugged his fur cap down a little lower, raised the collar of his greatcoat, and laboured to keep pace with me, his boots shuffling in the snow. Reaching Tchaikovsky Street, he suddenly stopped beneath a loudspeaker and began to listen to the music coming from it. As if excusing himself for his weakness, he said: 'You understand, Yosif, no matter how hard things are for me, I love to listen to music. I recall on 20 January, I returned to my room. It was cold. I had one thought – to find something to eat. For the hundredth time, I began to rummage through the shelves in the cupboard and search the kitchen table; I looked in the stove and behind the stove in search of a morsel of bread or a handful of groats. Nothing. So then I took the frying pan and began to scrape it with a knife. The crumbs of crust freed by the scraping lay on my tongue and fell onto the bed. There was absolutely nothing else available . . .'

Petr Andreyevich fell silent. He started to search for something in his pockets.

'In the city, you understand, they often stop you and demand to see a pass. Now, where was I?'

'You were on a bed.'

'Yes, yes, there I was, lying on my bed, and suddenly the radio began to play "The Dance of the Swans".' Petr Andreyevich paused to lick his lips, and leaning on my arm, he continued: 'I always love to listen to music with my eyes closed. So there I am, lying on the bed and picturing not the dancing swans, but train after train coming, loaded with bread, sugar and cases of butter. What didn't my hungry brain imagine!'

We stopped to rest a bit. Petr Andreyevich leaned against the wall of a building. I took the arm of my acquaintance, and we trudged along further.

'Petr, you haven't finished telling me about the music,' I reminded him.

'Oh, yes, I totally forgot. Well, when the music stopped, I opened my eyes and saw a large brown rat directly in front of me on the windowsill; yes, yes, it was brown. It didn't take its tiny, voracious eyes off of me. You understand, I couldn't lie there, so I gathered my last strength, stood up – and caught sight of some spilled grains of kasha under the nightstand.

I began to sweep them into a little pile, and then spotted a briefcase in the corner behind the nightstand. I noticed that a hole had been chewed through its side. Next to it on the floor was a little pile of kasha. I opened the briefcase and gave such a loud cry that the brown rat scurried from the windowsill and disappeared. I found a kilogram package of kasha in the briefcase. You understand, the rat helped me find it. My wife had not remembered to take the kasha out of the briefcase, or I had not thought of it myself; I don't know, but we had forgotten about it . . . This kasha saved my life.'

'Is he really alive?' I wondered to myself, never taking my eyes off the enemy's trench line.

A shot rang out, but from which side, I couldn't determine.

Zina laid her rifle flat.'Osya, come here,' she called. 'Look, what the heck are the Nazis doing?'

I took a look through the periscope. Two Germans were engaged in something unbelievable: taking turns, they were bending over, and then straightening back up; one stood back up and rested a wooden mallet on his shoulder.

'Guys, they're playing croquet,' Bodrov said. 'They're looking for fools in our trench, the tricksters.'

After long searching, I nevertheless spotted the German sniper. He was lying about 30 metres away from the dummy, in among some stone rubble. I indicated his position to my comrades, and then suggested that they take a look to see whether or not another enemy marksman might be lying in wait near the croquet players.

A couple of minutes later, someone started to cough in our trench, and I saw how the sleeves of a German wearing a camouflage cloak, who we had believed to be dead, slowly straightened out. The fingers of the fascist's hand, wrapped around the rifle stock, raised the barrel above the ground and then held it steady. The muzzle of the rifle was pointed in the direction of my embrasure. The foe was aiming at one of a small group of our men, who were moving out of their outposts. I was compelled to fire at the hand, to try to avert a shot that would have been fatal to one of our comrades.

The enemy rifle jerked upward, collided with the edge of a piece of rubble, and dropped to the ground. I closed the gun port.

Zina asked, 'Well, did you finish off that one behind the pile of rubble?'

'No, Zinochka, he was ready to shoot at one of ours, and I had to fire at his hand.'

'Pity; he got off easily, the scumbag.'

'Where did the croquet players go?'

'They disappeared after the shot.'

Bodrov and I took a seat on the floor of the emplacement and had a smoke. Stroyeva continued to observe the German line while chatting with us.

. . . The slanting rays of the afternoon sun fell on the edge of the sniper emplacement. The first yellow leaves were slowly circling in the air and falling on the floor of the trench and on the still green blades of grass, decorating it with a yellow pattern. A gossamer thread extended through the air – all of this spoke of the coming autumn. My cigarette died out. I had forgotten that I was sitting in a front-line emplacement.

'Guys!' Zina called to us in a half-whisper. 'Osya, take a look; someone else has appeared by that clump of sage.'

I slowly turned the periscope in the direction Zina had indicated and spotted a head. The arms and weapon weren't visible. The fascist's eyes were looking in the direction from where my shot had come.

'Comrades, let me go out into the trench, and I'll at least make this sharp-eyed snake move!' Bodrov said. 'Tolya, stop joking and keep your eyes peeled!' Zina replied.

'My eyes are tired, and I have a crick in my neck – it won't turn.'

I didn't intervene in the discussion. Bodrov himself knew what could and could not be done.

I knew that Tolya wouldn't make it across the exposed area of the old trench unnoticed, before he reached the main lines. I held the cross hairs of my rifle scope on the eyes of the prone enemy. He immediately spotted the crawling Bodrov. His blond eyebrows started and rose; his eyes were looking slightly to the side. I could see flecks of dirt on his face. The Nazi, twisting his mouth, said something, his thin lips moving, but he himself didn't pick up his weapon. I waited for the other German, whom we hadn't yet managed to spot, to show himself. My temples were pounding. In the expectation of a shot, I started to count the seconds, but I immediately lost track and had to start over. Stroyeva was lying as if she had become stone. Only the eyes of the fascist were moving. From this beast's tactics, it wasn't hard to guess that we were dealing with an experienced sniper: he didn't rush to fire at the crawling Russian, but was waiting instead for a more important target.

Suddenly the German dropped and began to squirm backwards towards the corner of a shed.

'Look, Yosif, the viper is slithering away. He plainly noticed something. I'll move off just a bit to the side at once, to get a better angle.'

'Don't worry, Zinochka; he's not getting away from me.'

There was the sound of a single shot. The fascist's arms flopped and he died on the spot.

The brown rat, which had been scurrying among the rusty tin cans, was startled by the shot. It scurried quickly away along the enemy breast-work.

Chapter Twenty-one

Joyful News

Another autumn had arrived – the second autumn of the blockade . . . A year of toil and struggle had hardened Leningrad's defenders. A turning point in the war was in the air.

Frosts had dried up the puddles and firmed up the mire. The trees were dressed in fanciful garb, decorated by a multitude of glittering silver icicles, and powdered with a white dusting of snow. Feathery snowflakes more and more frequently whirled through the air. Winter was approaching. The earth had become resonant – we could even hear the footsteps of moving men in the German trench line.

One night a fresh unit arrived to replace us. Andreyev asked, 'What, fellows, are we going on the attack together in the nippy weather?' An unfamiliar lieutenant replied, 'No, Comrades, go rest, before the Germans see you moving out.'

Leaving the trenches, we strode quickly, still stooped over – a habit we had developed after spending an entire year in the trenches without rest. The troopers were now and then looking around, as if fearing that the enemy was following, stepping on the heels of the men marching in front of them, swearing and celebrating.

After a three-week rest, our former 14th Rifle Regiment, now the 602nd Rifle Regiment, re-entered the front lines, occupying a sector on some heights overlooking a valley that separated Pulkovo [located about 17 kilometres south of Leningrad, Pulkovo is today the location of St. Petersburg's international and domestic airports] from the railroad. The ruins of the Pulkovo Observatory were plainly visible from our vantage point, as was a wide flatland dotted with low scrub.

As we took over this sector of defence, we were informed that we faced Romanian troops here and that it was possible to live rather peacefully with the Romanians [Pilyushin and his comrades are misidentifying Spanish troops of the Spanish Blue Division as Romanians, here and in the following few pages. There were no Romanian units with Army Group North, and the Spanish Blue Division indeed occupied this area south of Leningrad between August 1942 and October 1943]. The departing soldiers told us, 'We used the same well for water. But SS units are positioned behind the Romanians.'

Sergeant Andreyev critically examined the trenches and checked the condition of the firing positions and dugouts: 'Your bunkers are low and cramped and you have shallow communication trenches. What is this, brothers? You neglected everything around here. Today there are Romanians, but tomorrow the SS, and then what?'

'We weren't planning to be here for a century. But it will do for fighting.'

'Stop being clever; it's obvious to everyone how you've been fighting here. You scrubbed your mugs in the same stream with the Romanian fascists . . . you've been fighting . . .' Andreyev concluded dismissively.

'To each his own,' a scrawny sergeant snapped back with a sneering smile, before disappearing in a flash around a corner of the trench.

At sunrise, I stepped out into the trench and began to observe the enemy line. I couldn't believe my own eyes: in no-man's-land, an unarmed Romanian soldier wearing a ragged, homespun coat was walking upright, fearing nothing, as if back in his own country. He was swinging a bucket, and upon reaching the stream, he stopped and stared in our direction.

I could make out his every feature through my telescopic sight: a swarthy face, large eyes, a black moustache, and a prominent, hawk nose. His imperturbability, to be honest, disarmed me. He dipped the bucket in the water, glanced once more in our direction, then set off back to his own lines, whistling.

I fired at the bucket. The Romanian calmly clapped his hand over the hole, through which water was streaming out, and smiling, wagged his finger at me. Immediately, several Romanians stuck their heads above the parapet and started to shout, 'Bravo! Bravo!'

No matter how peacefully the Romanians were behaving on our land, war remains war. The time to drink water from the same goblet had passed. The Romanians seemed to understand this, and despite the frigid weather and frequent snowstorms, laboured to deepen their trenches. Our riflemen probed their defences for a weakness.

The Romanians often forgot to close the doors to their bunkers, and since the gun slit and door were in alignment, we could see right into their trench. Once in a while we managed to kill one of their officers by firing through the embrasure and doorway. It was not a particularly difficult shot. The Romanians figured out what was going on and started to screen the doors of their rifle bunkers.

On one quiet night, our ears caught the sound of Russian speech. It was so surprising, that word of the appearance of some Russians instantly flew around all the regiment's units. Soldiers and officers spilled out into the trench.

A young woman's voice carried to us: 'Look! Look! Trolleys are running!' Another voice, also a woman's, replied: 'It must be Leningrad!' Then everything got quiet. Only the muffled sounds of axes and picks working.

The sniper Smirnov shouted into the darkness, 'Comrades! From where have they brought you?' Complete silence reigned for several minutes. Then we heard: 'We're from Vi-teee-bsk [Vitebsk]!'

Smirnov started to pace up and down the trench, clenching his fists. Then he stopped and grumbled: 'Oooh, the vermin; they've brought our women to the front.'

'Perhaps they're Vlasovites?' someone asked.

'Damn it, what do you mean "Vlasovites"? They're our dames from Vitebsk. They've been brought here to dig fortifications.'

For the rest of the night, Smirnov didn't fire a single shot. Indeed this was understandable. I knew that the girl he loved was in fascist captivity.

I recall that it was during these days on the defence at Pulkovo that we learned the wonderful news about the hole punched through the German blockade. Petr Romanov, who came running up to our trench, informed us of it. Taking a seat on a cartridge case, he pulled a map out of a folder: 'Take a look, fellows, how our guys have smashed the Germans on the Volga! They've surrounded von Paulus's grouping like this' – Petr traced a red line on the map with his finger – 'and now they're battering it. Soon we'll learn the details of this battle.'

Everyone's throat went dry from the exciting news. 'That's the way!' was all I could say.

'That's still not all,' Petr continued triumphantly. 'Celebrate! Today the forces of the Leningrad Front and Volkhov Front have started an offensive to break through the blockade of Leningrad!'

'Well! At last! How do you know this?' the soldiers encircling Romanov vied with each other to respond. Petr replied, 'I heard it over the radio.'

Romanov continued excitedly: 'The operation's concept consists of eliminating the enemy's Shlissel'burg-Sinyavino corridor through a decisive meeting blow of the forces of both *fronts*, in order to link up the *fronts* and lift the blockade.'

'But you know, couldn't the Germans be hiding major reserves in the forests?' I observed.

'It's possible. But you take a look here' – Romanov drew his finger from Shlissel'burg to Nevskaya Dubrovka. 'Here's the shortest distance between the Leningrad and Volkhov Fronts. Here the depth of the German defences is only 12 to 14 kilometres. If both sides simultaneously bombard this area from the east and west, then the Germans won't be able to deploy their reserves.'

'Only if we can do it,' I countered. 'The Germans have a strong belt of fortifications there, and we'll also have to force a crossing of the Neva. It is difficult; oh, how difficult!'

I didn't manage to express all of my happiness and doubts, because at that moment enemy artillery rained down on us with particular fury. Romanov shot an inquiring glance at me. I covered the embrasure and began to prepare hand grenades. Stroyeva was glued to the periscope.

'The Germans have blown a fuse, and are brewing up something serious,' Romanov said, checking his pistol. 'It's apparent that they feel the end is coming. Their heavy artillery is pummelling our lines: listen, the earth is moaning. Keep watch, after such a barrage an infantry assault will surely come.'

'Do you really think the Romanians will attack?' I asked.

'What else can they do? They have SS behind them; there is nowhere else for them to run.'

The last thunderous shell explosions died away. Romanov shook our hands and quickly left the emplacement. I opened the embrasure and immediately spotted Germans running towards our trench. I thought, 'Aha, they don't trust the Romanians!'

The enemy's attempt to crack our main line of defence had no success. Prisoners reported that the Romanian units had been withdrawn from the front line on 6 January 1943, and had been replaced by the German 23rd Infantry Division.

That evening, returning to my bunker, I bumped into Naydenov in the trench. I asked him, 'You've recovered? Come on along with me. Tell me, how is Uncle Vasya doing?'

'I rode to the hospital with him in the same ambulance. The entire way, Vasiliy Dmitriyevich was delirious, either talking to his wife or saying something to his kids. Then he got quiet – he had fallen asleep, I thought, but when we arrived at the hospital and they grabbed our stretchers . . . you understand, Osip . . . he was dead.'

Naydenov turned away. I couldn't ask Sergey any more questions – my heart was breaking. I didn't want to believe that our brave Russian soldier Vasiliy Yershov would no longer be with us.

* * *

Enemy artillery kept our lines under constant bombardment, but the infantry didn't try to attack again. Desultory exchanges of rifle fire went on day after day. We were all waiting for the order to attack. I asked Romanov more than once about any news arriving from the breakthrough sector of the blockade. He always replied, 'No information, but nothing is coming in over the radio – the Germans are jamming the transmissions.'

The day 18 January 1943 arrived. Sergey Naydenov and I were keeping watch over the enemy's line. Suddenly there was a wild stirring in our trenches, shouts, and chaotic gunfire. Soldiers and officers were embracing each other, and fur caps were flying into the air.

Naydenov told me, 'I'll go and find out what's going on.' A few minutes later, Sergey came running into the emplacement, shouting 'Victory! Victory! Uraa!' With that, this Goliath began to dance in the cramped emplacement, tapping his boots on the floor. Then he grabbed me by the shoulders and hoisted me into the air like I was a child.

'Put me down, quit horsing around,' I howled. 'You're going to break a bone!'

'Victory, Osip, victory!'

'Yes, I know, but tell me what's happened!'

Beside himself with joy and still tapping his feet, Naydenov told me: 'Our forces have linked up with the Volkhov Front. The blockade has been broken. Uraa! You understand? It's broken!'

For the rest of this day, the soldiers and commanders walked around intoxicated with joy.

Two days later, I was granted leave to go visit my son in Leningrad. There was so much jubilation on the streets of Leningrad! At literally every step, I was being stopped and embraced, congratulated on the victory, and being given tobacco and vodka. One old woman stopped me, and shaking my hand, she told me: 'Thank you, sonny, for sweeping the road clear to the rest of the country. It has become easier to breathe, dear ones.'

Not finding the words to respond to the Leningrad woman, I wrapped my arms around her frail shoulders and in the Russian custom, kissed her gaunt, wrinkled face.

Chapter Twenty-two

Soviet Army Day

The adversary was still threatening to take Leningrad. But the defenders of the heroic city were steadfast. Their strength consisted in not only how many guns and tanks had been repaired and put back into service; how many pillboxes had been built and how many kilometres of anti-tank ditches and interlaced trenches had been dug. The strength of Leningrad's defenders was in the ring of anvils and in the chatter of sewing machines, in the new patches on the façades and roofs of buildings and in that which is called courage on the battlefield.

For the winter period, the sniper school suspended operations. We all left for units in the front line, where in fact we did perfect our skill in firing at living targets.

Cautiously stepping along the narrow, icy path at the bottom of the trench, I walked up to a machine-gun emplacement and stopped, in order to try to locate the position of an enemy heavy machine gun by listening for it. Previously, for night-time firing the Germans had placed tracer cartridges in their ammunition belts in order to control the accuracy of their aim. This made it easier for us to locate them, and without any particular risk to send bullet after bullet into the embrasure of the enemy pillbox. The Nazis had learned from the tactics of the Soviet marksmen and had stopped using tracer bullets. This made our nightly hunt for German machine-gunners extremely difficult. Now they could only be detected by the muzzle flashes when they fired, and the first reaction of a man who sees such flashes in front of him is to dive face first to the ground. Here, our worker-friends in Leningrad helped us out. They fabricated special armoured shields with a very narrow gun slit for us . . . The nightly struggle with the enemy machine-gunners resumed.

However, the Germans responded to this approach as well, and started using only light machine guns at night, while also frequently changing their positions. Then hand grenades began to play a decisive role in our struggle against them. Many of my comrades employed them masterfully against the Nazis in their trenches.

A new day was approaching . . . the pre-dawn air was frigid, and the temperature was dropping. I was still standing at my armoured shield, never taking my eyes off the enemy line. Suddenly I caught the sound of a quiet song; someone not far away was singing, repeating the same couplet of the song: '*A dark night, my love, I know you are not sleeping . . . By the child's bed, you're quietly shedding a tear.*' This song, which was widely popular at the time, touched the soul of every front-line soldier.

Suddenly the singing broke off. A short time later, I heard rapid footsteps approaching down the trench. It was Naydenov. Seeing me, he told me with a smile: 'Osip, Zina has come back from the city, saying that she paid a visit to your son. Go, I'll keep watch for a while on your behalf.'

The edge of a blue envelope was protruding from the pocket of Naydenov's jacket.

'A letter from home?'

'No, from Svetlana.'

'Where is she?'

'At the front. Even though she didn't reveal the hospital where she is working, from her words it is plain that it is a field hospital.'

Naydenov, shifting from foot to foot, looked at me, peevishly gave a wave with his hand, and turned around. At this moment, a breathless messenger from regiment headquarters came running up to us. He was heavily sweating. He asked, 'Fellows, which one of you knows where to find the sniper Pilyushin?'

'I'm Pilyushin, what of it?'

The messenger wiped his steaming face with the sleeve of his quilted coat and said, 'I've been searching for you all over the trenches of the 1st Battalion; we must go immediately to the regiment commander.'

'What has happened?'

'How should I know? I've been ordered to find you, and that's all.'

The messenger and I ran the 3 kilometres back to regiment headquarters without a rest. The sentry, standing by the headquarters dugout, spotted us even at a distance and shouted, 'You're late! That goose flew off; it couldn't wait for you.'

'What goose?' I asked, dumbfounded.

'A real goose, like any other one, only wild. It hurt its wing in the summer, so it spent the winter with us. It would fly around 20 to 30 metres, land on the snow, take a rest, and then fly a bit further.'

The sentry lowered his voice, then added: 'Understand, it flew right under the nose of the Colonel, who immediately wanted to dine on goose. "Who's the well-known sniper here?" he asks. "Pilyushin," they say. So he sent for you. But that goose didn't begin to wait around for you, and it flew off on the sly. That way – towards the highway.'

'What colonel? What goose? What are you talking about?'

'How should I know? You'll see for yourself.'

I stepped into the dugout of regiment commander Putyatin. A colonel unfamiliar to me greeted me, who, by the way, I had seen somewhere before.

'Are you the sniper?' he asked me.

'Precisely so.'

'How many killed Germans do you have to your credit?'

'On the defence, sixty-two. On the retreat I wasn't counting.'

'That means you don't know how many Germans you've killed?'

'No, I know, Comrade Colonel.'

'I've summoned you to check whether you're really as accurate as has been reported to me – that you can hit a German in the eye.' The Colonel removed his watch from his wrist and twirled it under my nose: 'Here's your target, do you understand?'

'Understood, Comrade Commander.'

'I'm going to set up this target at 200 metres. If you hit it – good for you, but if you miss – I'm going to take away your sniper rifle. Understand?'

'Clearly, Comrade Colonel.'

Just then did I notice that the Colonel was swaying a bit. The Colonel drew a white sheepskin coat around his shoulders and grabbed a fur cap with ear flaps. Leaving the dugout, he stepped off 250 paces along the railroad embankment and laid his cap on the snow. He propped his watch up on it.

Returning to me, he said: 'I'll allow you to fire from any position. Understood?'

'Understood, Comrade Colonel.'

'Well then, fire!'

Submachine-gunners, scouts, and staff members started to stick their heads out of the nearby bunker, and curious people began to gather. Muffled laughter and voices could be heard: 'Will Pilyushin really shoot at a watch?'

'He'll do it. For him, a watch is a large target.'

'I'm sorry about the watch. Take a look, no way: it's golden, with an illuminated face.'

Any other time, I wouldn't have stooped to shoot at a watch. But the Colonel, looking at me with a frown, kept repeating: 'Shoot, shoot, do what you're told.'

I fired. A messenger ran to the fur cap. He picked it up, like a platter containing soup, and gingerly carried it back with outstretched arms to the Colonel.

'Where's the watch?' the Colonel asked.

'It's all here, Comrade Commander; here's the strap, the buckle and glass fragments . . .'

'Son of a gun!' The Colonel slapped his thighs. 'No goose meat to taste, and now no watch either! Well, thank you, sniper!'

In the forward trench line, my altogether tireless and reliable friend Naydenov was waiting for me. I knew that Sergey didn't like it when people pitied him. Once it had happened that one of the comrades had told him, 'Seryozha, you should lie down for a minute; your eyes have become like a mouse's.' Sergey had answered, 'Bah! Go on with your nagging! When a fascist raps on a window for a soldier's mother, should the soldier be sleeping?'

He was tireless and courageous. In the daytime, hiding behind an ice chunk, he would lie in wait for a German officer or observer, while at night he skilfully pelted the German trench line with hand grenades. During the war years, I studied a lot of human behaviour and firmly came to see that a brave man doesn't talk or yell about danger – he silently seeks encounters with the enemy and kills him. That's just the way Sergey behaved.

The morning dawn was peaceful, and so silent that it seemed to have stopped breathing. The front was still sleeping. The sun's rays penetrated all the nooks and crannies in the trench, chasing away the darkness and dissolving the shadows, and a bright haze hung above no-man's-land. Spring was moving with a measured, but confident pace, like a landowner walking around his fields.

Entering a bunker, I stopped at the threshold for a moment in order to let my eyes adjust to the dark interior. Zina rushed to me. I don't recall what had happened to me, but before I could even greet her, I had to gulp some air and lean myself against the frame of a bunk bed. For some reason, my meeting with Zina had particularly agitated me.

'Yosif, what's wrong?' Zina asked with alarm. 'Are you wounded? You don't look yourself.'

'No, no, Zinochka, I'm completely fine . . . How is Volodya?'

'Don't worry for your son; he's a marvellously strong little fellow.'

Stroyeva wanted to say something more, but she didn't have time. Naydenov came running into the dugout at that moment and started to shout: 'Comrades! The Germans are plotting something.' Catching his breath, he explained: 'They put up a piece of plywood on their breast-work, which has something written on it in black letters. I didn't have time to try to read it, when one of the Germans shoved it over and it slid down the front of the parapet. A hubbub and shouting arose in their trench. Suddeny one of the Fritzes climbed up on the breastwork and started waving his arms. He was shouting something loudly. I called over: "Hey! Come on over, I won't shoot." The German wagged his hand – "I can't", it meant – and disappeared.'

The three of us ran to the sniper emplacement.

'Did the German see you?' Zina asked.

'No, I shouted through the embrasure.'

'All the same, Seryozha, you must shoot at such targets.'

'But what did the company *politruk* say recently? That there are different sorts of people among the Germans, so try to pick them out . . .'

Naydenov's story strongly interested us. What could be going on over there on the German side? What was on that board out in front of the Germans' line? Stroyeva cracked open the firing slit and took a look through the periscope at the spot where the plywood was lying.

We never took our eyes off the enemy trench until the onset of darkness. Despite our intense scrutiny, we didn't detect anything serious: the enemy trench was still the same picture, while the plywood sheet continued to lie on the snow in front of the German parapet. The riddle of the sign became clear only several days later, when we captured a prisoner. But that story will be told a bit later.

On this particular day, when the Germans tossed out the board – it was Soviet Army Day – they fed us a fine holiday meal. An unfamiliar sergeant, wearing an artilleryman's shoulder straps, came by our bunker to see us. He was so blond that it didn't seem he had eyebrows or eyelashes. His large blue eyes cockily looked us over.

Having taken a look at everyone in the gloomy dugout, he declared, 'He-he! Brothers, it's just like a resort here!' Stroyeva replied in a quiet voice, 'And you, buddy, what route did you take to visit our resort?'

'Up the Volga, Miss, up the Volga. There we gave the fascists some real hell. Now we've come to help you out, of course.'

'For your help, I thank you, but you're unlucky with the "resort": you're a bit late, you see, we've closed it for repairs.'

'The road's a long one, you yourselves know it: on foot and on vehi-cles, so we're laying over for a bit.'

'What a prickly one you are, Sergeant!' Naydenov intervened, taking a seat next to the artilleryman. 'Don't stick a finger in your mouth. Come on, have a smoke, and explain to us how you distinguished yourselves there. Perhaps you'll have a bite of lunch with us?'

'Thanks for the offer. But I'd prefer a drop of vodka . . . Don't get upset over that "resort" remark; we know how you've lived and are living here. But why don't I hear any front-line gabbing here? Even the sentries over the last *verst* [a Russian unit of distance equivalent to 1.067 kilometres] have been standing there like telephone poles.'

Stroyeva, narrowing her eyes, replied, 'No two poles are alike; you can put up rotten ones by the hundreds, and they won't last and will fail, but just one good one will remain standing.'

Zina, gathering the dishes from the little table, watched the artilleryman closely, as if weighing him. I also observed his every move with great interest and measured his every word, because there was the scent of gunpowder around this man. The sergeant rose to his feet, and like a master in his own home, began to step off the size of the bunker, holding a strap of his knapsack with his large hand.

'What, you've come alone to our aid?' Naydenov asked.

'No, not alone; together with my battery. I'm a spotter, Semyon Korchnov, but the guys all just call me "Siberian".' Korchnov removed his cap, and a lock of blond hair fell down over his tall forehead: 'It's hot here, guys.'

'Just take off some things,' Stroyeva offered.

'There's no time. I ran by to see you for a minute to ask you the location and type of firing positions the Germans have. Soon we're going to start knocking them out. Oh, and one more thing. I've brought you a little gift from the men of our battery.'

The Siberian shrugged off the heavy knapsack and placed a hand on Naydenov's shoulder: 'We've saved all of this for you on our way up.'

Korchnov began to pull packs of cigarettes, biscuits, sugar, cakes of dehydrated peas and buckwheat, and rations of salt pork from his knapsack and pockets of his fur coat, saying: 'We know, we all know, how you have atrophied here.'

'Thanks for the gifts, but we're no longer starving here,' Naydenov said, as he vigorously wiped the breech mechanism of his rifle.

'I see your plumpness: skin and bones . . . So you need to regain some weight now.'

'We don't need fat; we'd rather have strong muscles,' Zina replied. 'Oh! You are a prickly one, Miss!' the artilleryman said between his teeth. 'We'll see how you are in battle.'

'There are no ladies in the army, Comrade Sergeant, there are brave soldiers. Unfortunately, we also come across cowards.'

Korchnov didn't reply. He, like a war horse, became alert to the sound of distant artillery fire. I had already grown to like this artilleryman. I was drawn by his warm, straightforward ways, his unfeigned pluck, and his salty, soldierly humour.

'What's that firing?' the Siberian quickly asked.

'The Fritzes are bombarding Leningrad with long-range guns. Have you really not been in the city?' Naydenov asked in return.

'No, I haven't managed to do it; we passed through the suburbs at night.'

The artilleryman thoughtfully gazed at Sergey, who was still cleaning his rifle. Then without saying another word, the Siberian began to hurry out into the trench.

Stroyeva stopped him: 'There's no rush, Sergeant! You won't see the Germans' positions from here; they're firing from Krasnoye Selo. Better you tell us what you saw on the Volga.'

'We'll chat about that another time, but now show me the enemy pill-boxes on the front line.'

Naydenov, Korchnov and I took some armoured plates and headed out into the trench. Stroyeva remained behind in the bunker.

Walking down our line of defence, we familiarized the artillery spotter with the position of the Germans' weapon emplacements and bunkers. 'It's difficult to remember everything; it would be nice to have a diagram to see,' Korchnov said, stepping into our sniper's nest.

Naydenov struck a match, and I showed the Siberian a sheet of paper attached to the wall of the emplacement: 'Take a look, does a diagram like this one suit you?'

'That's nifty. Which one of you thought it up?'

'Our Zina.'

'A fine woman, though a real sharp one.'

'Senya, you're nobody's fool: she's the best sniper in our division,' Sergey said, raking the embers in the little stove.

The artilleryman let these words pass unnoticed, never taking his eyes off the diagram.

'And what's this?' Korchnov pointed at a fresh sketch.

'Earlier today the Germans tossed a sheet of plywood into no-man's-land.' Naydenov relayed the story of the board in detail to the Siberian.

'Aha!' the spotter excitedly replied. 'A familiar trick! Guys, I saw this subterfuge back on the Volga! It is nothing but camouflage. They used the sheet to conceal an embrasure they had cut into the trench wall. Behind this plywood sheet was the concealed muzzle of a machine gun or what have you. Be careful, comrades.'

The words of the Sergeant caused us to prick up our ears. We decided to inform the platoon commander about it and to increase our observation of the enemy.

Soon Zina showed up at our nest. She stopped at the entrance and said with a smile: 'Hey, fellows, I have everything ready, so I'm inviting you to the table.' None of us knew what she had brewed up. We quietly waited for an explanation, but Zina didn't say anything more. However, seeing her diagram in the artilleryman's hands, she asked: 'Is the diagram suitable?'

'And how! Permit me to use it! I'll bring it back within several days,' Korchnov requested.

'Take it, but you must return it.'

'You can be sure of it.'

The spotter, who had obtained such a vital plan of the German sector of defences, started to hurry back to his battery, but Zina blocked his way: 'No, dear comrade, on such a day not a single good host would let a guest leave, without treating him to whatever God has provided. Please celebrate Soviet Army Day together with us.'

'Damn it! I forgot completely!' Korchnov gave the woman a sly wink, patting the canteen hanging on his belt with his broad hand. 'On such an occasion, a cup each wouldn't be a sin.'

When we returned to our bunker, we saw a festively decorated table. A steaming aluminium teapot was resting on it. There were slices of sausage in the lid of a soldier's mess kit, fried salt pork in an enormous cast-iron skillet, and pieces of bread in a helmet. Next to each of the six mugs sitting on the table, there were two cubes of sugar and a chunk of chocolate.

Zina invited us to the table with a sweeping gesture.

'No one touch anything just yet,' Zina said with a smile. 'Two more comrades will be here shortly, and then Korchnov will tell us how they gave the fascists hell on the Volga.'

'Zinochka, permit us just one swallow of vodka each. It will moisten the tongue!' the Siberian requested.

'No! Intoxicated men flatter more than they tell the truth.'

Soon Romanov and Andreyev showed up. We noisily took our seats around the holiday table. Zina sat down next to me. Waiting for a moment when no one was looking, she tightly squeezed my hand.

'Volodya asked me to do it . . .' She lowered her head.

Chapter Twenty-three
The Ruhr Mine Worker

The next morning we saw that the plywood had disappeared from in front of the German parapet. The Germans had removed it overnight. Nothing else seemed to have changed in the vicinity where it had been lying. Korchnov's conjectures hadn't proved correct this time. The same rusty cans, buckets, and rolls of barbed wire were scattered on the German breastwork, just as they had been before . . . But what had been written on this piece of plywood? Who was the German who had stood up, leaving his cover and risking his life?

The front-line days and weeks passed in turn. We started to forget about the plywood, and would have forgotten it entirely, if one unexpected episode at the front hadn't reminded us of it.

One night in the first half of March 1943, we learned that our former company commander Viktor Vladimirovich Kruglov had returned after a lengthy absence. As soon as Zina learned that he was at the command post, she forcibly dragged Andreyev and me to Kruglov's bunker. We hadn't even had time to exchange greetings with our combat-friend, however, when the door of the bunker flew open, and in flew a cringing German in a tattered camouflage cloak; right behind him, a fuming Sergey Naydenov appeared in the doorway. Where and when he had managed to capture this prisoner, no one knew. The German, catching sight of a Soviet officer, hastily started to sputter a stream of unintelligible words.

'Petya, tell him to be quiet,' Kruglov appealed to Romanov. 'If we need something, we'll ask him.'

Naydenov growled, 'That's just how he gave me no peace along the entire way here, chattering like a machine gun.' The German fell silent, pulled his head into his shoulders, but his cold blue eyes followed us with interest.

'Where did you capture him?' Kruglov asked Naydenov.

'There were two of them, Comrade Major. They were creeping into no-man's-land. We kept our eyes on them, and when they approached our trench, we nabbed them. The sergeant in charge kept one with him, and ordered us to bring this one to the company command post.'

'Tell the sergeant to bring the other one here too.'

Naydenov quickly disappeared into the darkness of the trench.

'Petya, ask him what he was doing in no-man's-land.'

'He says that they were coming to warn us that they had received fresh forces. They're allegedly preparing to storm the city.'

'Tell him that's an old story, and now tell him to lay out everything frankly. Give him a sheet of paper – let him write down what he knows.'

Romanov gave the prisoner a sheet of paper and a pencil. The German brightened considerably and quickly began to scribble lines.

Soon the other prisoner was led into the bunker. This one was a husky German with red hair and a bullish head, seemingly around 35 to 40 years of age. His thick, short neck strained the collar of his filthy, worn uniform. The German's large eyes looked directly at us, without any timidity. He quietly took a seat on the edge of a bunk, and spreading his legs widely, placed one enormous hand on his knee, and with the other wiped the back of his neck, while shooting side glances at Naydenov.

Seeing his comrade leaning over a sheet of paper, the red-headed giant in a stentorian deep voice said: 'Streich, what are you writing? A last will and testament to your son, or a complaint to von Leeb? Toss it aside, Streich. We're in a pickle. If you don't have enough of your own sense, then you'd better know that the Russians won't loan you any. You and I have finished fighting, and thank God.'

Romanov walked up to the red-haired German: 'What's your name?'

The prisoner, finding a Russian officer in front of him, leaped to his feet, but answered simply and proudly: 'Artur Goldrein, a Ruhr mine worker, fighting since 1939.' Then giving a wave of his hand to his comrade, cheerfully laughed: 'What did I just tell you, Streich? We're up the creek! But God grant that each get out of the game in this way!'

'What were you doing in no-man's-land?'

'Probing for mines, clearing a passage for our scouts. But once we put our foot in it, our guys didn't come.' Goldrein wonderingly spread his arms and continued: 'It had to happen, for four years I've been crawling around between the lines, and nothing ever went wrong – until now. Well, what of it! Let someone else take over my job, because I'm through with this dance with death.'

For some time we'd been paying no attention to the other German; he was still writing something, at the same time listening to the conversation between his comrade and the Russian officer. Romanov, walking up to him, said: 'Can you recall which one of your soldiers back in February put up a plywood sheet on the breastwork, which had something written on it?'

'Ha, ha, ha!' the red-haired German burst out laughing. 'The plywood! It was one of our oddballs, who had thought to joke a bit over the Russians. He took a sheet of plywood and wrote on it with a black paint: "I congratulate the Ivans on Soviet Army Day." Joker!'

'Well, what of it?'

'Our side doesn't like such jokes. This soldier, I heard, received a bullet in the back of the head for his bit of fun. Too bad for the good man.'

'Is it true that fresh troops have moved into your positions?'

'What the hell kind of fresh troops? They've all gone mouldy long ago. They've all been patched up, like me and my hand, and Streich and his butt. Ha, ha!'

'Have a lot like them arrived?'

'Everything we have needs to be reduced ten times. Reckon for yourselves: if a division has come up, how many men would it really have?'

They began to take away the prisoners to regiment headquarters. Goldrein noisily parted with Romanov, but turned around at the door and jokingly waved his large paw to everyone: 'If you're ever in Germany, my greetings to the *Führer*.'

When the Germans left, we gathered around Kruglov, vying with each other to offer our congratulations on his promotion to major. We asked him to tell us where he'd been fighting all this time and how he'd wound up back with us again.

'Before my wound I was on the Karelian Isthmus, and from the hospital I asked for my old place. I'd become bored,' Kruglov replied with his typical miserly smile.

'Comrade Major, how are the Finns behaving?'

'Finnish fascists and German fascists are all alike, seeds from the same apple. But the Finnish soldiers, just like the German ones, have stopped believing in the promises of their commanders. They also have their own Artur Goldreins.'

Kruglov walked up to me and asked: 'Tell me, old man, how is your son?'

'I haven't seen him for three months. Zina spent a few days with Volodya, and says that the little guy is getting along well.'

Kruglov looked over at Stroyeva attentively.

'And how is your own family doing, Viktor Vladimirovich?' Zina asked, a little embarrassed.

'They're all alive; back in the summer they were evacuated out of the city.'

Kruglov lapsed into silence. Then he spoke up again: 'Well then, fellows, now I've taken over your battalion. We'll be fighting together.' The soldiers who had known Kruglov previously, received the news of his return joyfully.

Chapter Twenty-four
A Soldier Hurries

A morning in early April . . . deep silence. An overnight freeze had hard-ened the walls and bottom of the trench, making it so resonant that any rustle or the footsteps of a person walking along it were audible at a hundred metres through the frosty air. A chilly breeze constantly stirred the dried blades of last year's grass.

At such a time back in 1942, in the evening the Germans usually left their shelters and went into the trench, talking loudly, laughing, singing songs, and playing harmonicas. But by the spring of 1943, laughter and songs in the enemy's trench became rare. A certain restraint was percep-tible in the Germans' behaviour. They even stopped firing during our propaganda broadcasts over their lines.

I found Naydenov in the trench next to a machine-gun emplacement. He was busy with his favourite activity. An open case of hand grenades stood at Sergey's feet. On the edge of the parapet lay several empty cartridge cases. Sergey removed a cartridge from a clip and carefully extracted the bullet from the cartridge. Next he sprinkled some of the gunpowder onto the palm of his hand, pulled a piece of cotton wadding from his pocket, tightly packed it in the cartridge with a ramrod, and reloaded the rifle. Then he took a grenade, stuck a fuse in it, put it on the muzzle of his rifle, and carefully adjusted the launch angle. After this, he took a specially carved stick, placed one end of it on the trigger and cautiously pressed the stick with the toe of his boot. The gun fired . . . After each shot, Sergey saw off the launched grenade with a happy wave, saying: 'Wait, there will be another one right away,' or 'There's another one coming.'

He liked to play this game both night and day. Naydenov's grenade-launching often enraged the Germans, and they would retaliate with a furious mortar barrage. Then Sergey would calmly hoist the case of grenades and head into a bunker.

The disturbed soldiers inside would scold, 'Where are you going with that case?' Sergey would answer imperturbably, 'Why the fuss? I can't leave them in the trench; for all I know, a random shell will land on it, and there could be a disaster that wouldn't do any of us any good. Once the Fritzes calm down, I'll go and give them some more entertainment.'

On this particular morning, though, the Nazis responded with not only a mortar, but also an artillery barrage. The alarmed shouts of the men on watch duty rang out: 'Germans!'

The stacked pyramid of rifles was quickly taken apart. I only now noticed that Stroyeva's rifle, which was usually next to mine, was missing. I didn't have time to ask where she went. The comrades hastily took up their firing positions. Naydenov and I ran into a secondary sniper's emplacement. Sergey quickly opened the embrasure and looked out across no-man's-land: 'The louses didn't manage to sneak up on us, so now they're coming at us with all kinds of racket.'

I had noticed many times that even when under reliable cover, nearby shell explosions and the hum of flying fragments will cause a soldier to hug the earth. The body tenses, hearing becomes acute, and a sniper's vision becomes particularly sharp. Nothing at this minute can divert your attention from your combat duty, or from the face or helmet of an approaching adversary.

'Did our guys have time to leave their forward outposts?' I thought aloud. 'They got away, I saw them,' Sergey tossed out, not taking his eye away from the eyepiece of his telescopic sight.

Suddenly the artillery fire from both sides ceased. For a moment, there was such silence that it was painful to the ears. Then all at once, heavy and light machine guns began to bark, and rifle fire began to crackle.

In the middle of no-man's-land, a German officer emerged from the smoke. Crouched low, he was shouting something, waving a pistol over his head. But his shout was drowned out by the roar of battle.

'Osip, fire at the submachine-gunners, and leave the officer to me,' Sergey requested in a pleading voice. 'Just look how that son of a bitch is agilely leaping across the craters, better than a gun dog!'

Naydenov fired, and reloading his rifle, shot me a quick glance, as if he wanted to say: 'Got him, that Nazi adjutant! He's been feeding the lice in the trench; now let him feed the maggots. That's what lies ahead for him!'

The Germans, spraying their fire, reached the middle of no-man's-land, where they became pinned down by our machine-gun and rifle fire. Their attack had plainly failed . . .

Suddenly Naydenov tugged at my sleeve: 'Take a look where the Germans have appeared. They're being clever . . .'

The Germans were trying to outflank us on the left, but their manoeuvre was detected in time. A company of submachine-gunners under the command of Vladimir Kuleshov came to our aid. He was a fear-less man, but also swore incorrigibly and was fond of the bottle. One time, one of his men let loose a string of curses, and Kuleshov approvingly clapped him on the shoulder: 'Good man, you know the Russian language well.' He didn't like lackadaisical, sluggish soldiers. He'd tell them: 'Brother, you left your rage at home, but here it would have been most useful.'

To the left and right of our section of the trench, submachine-guns fired without interruption. When my rifle became fouled, I ran out into the trench, in order to grab a wounded comrade's weapon. Taking a look around, I spotted a killed submachine-gunner. He was laying face-up; a quite young man, he had his submachine-gun pinned to his chest with one arm, while the other was loosely slung over his head. He seemed alive: his wide, unblinking blue eyes were staring up into the sky. Even in the heat of battle, I was reluctant to take the weapon from his hand; it seemed that he might jump up and start shooting.

In the middle of the hectic firing, shouts of 'Ura!' could be heard. Naydenov suddenly covered his embrasure and told me, 'Yosif, look! The guys have left the trench to drive the Fritzes out of no-man's-land. We need to help them!'

We crawled out of the emplacement and without even thinking, hopped over the breastwork. In short rushes, we approached a scene of hand-to-hand struggle. We leaped into a shell crater to catch our breath and get our bearings, and tried to figure out where the enemy was and where our guys were. I rose slightly from the crater to get a better view, when suddenly I felt a stabbing pain in my stomach. I slid down to the bottom of the crater and curled up tightly.

Sergey quickly asked me, 'Are you wounded?'

'In the gut . . .'

'Shit! Can you crawl off to a medical tent?'

'I don't know . . .'

'I can't carry you there – we'll get killed for sure.'

I detached my canteen from my belt, to take just one gulp of water to try to extinguish the fire burning inside me, but Sergey grabbed it from my hands and tossed it aside: 'Forbidden! You know that.'

Naydenov hastily bandaged my wound, rolled me onto my back, and grabbing the collar of my coat, dragged me back to our line. For the first time in my life, the fear of death gripped my heart, when a short time later I was laying on an operating table and the surgeon was probing around in my gut with forceps. From time to time, he would lean over and take a close look at something. He then applied an adhesive patch to the wound, whispered something to a nurse and left the operating room. They laid me on a stretcher and carried me into a ward. Then a doctor dressed all in white and with a neatly-trimmed beard came to my bed. With fingers as long and bony as stalks of bamboo, he cautiously pressed my abdomen in various places, always asking: 'Does this hurt? Does this hurt?'

I didn't feel pain in any one particular place, my entire belly was hurting. Day after day passed . . . Sometimes, my pain would disappear for a few minutes; these were minutes of indescribable bliss. Sometimes I dreamed that I was home again with my wife and children, and we were strolling along the Neva embankments. I would wake up with extreme pain in the groin. The pain immobilized my entire body, making it impossible to move. At those times, I thought: 'Is this really the end?'

Once someone grabbed hold of my arm. I opened my eyes. The surgeon Ivanov was standing slightly stooped over my bed. He was taking my pulse, looking at his watch. Straightening, the surgeon commanded two elderly attendants, 'To the operating room!'

Then once again the operating table, an anaesthetic mask, and blessed sleep without pain or terrors. I woke up when the operation was finished. A nurse was delicately applying a dressing. The surgeon, a stocky man with a bald head on a short, muscular neck, was washing his hands over an enamelled blue bowl and loudly whistling Lensky's aria [from Tchaikovsky's opera *Eugene Onegin*]: 'Will you come, fair maiden, to shed a tear over a premature urn . . .'

Involuntarily, I thought 'Is he really whistling my requiem?', as I looked at a glass jar standing on a table next to me, which contained a blunt-nosed bullet in a clear liquid. A surgical instrument was boiling in a nickel-plated tray on an electric hotplate. In a basin next to the table, bloody bandages and two human fingers were lying.

A nurse, seeing that I had woken up from the anaesthesia, took a piece of gauze, tenderly wiped my face and chest, and gave me a little water to sip: 'Dance, soldier! Everything went well: they extracted the bullet. There it is, in that jar. You'll soon be back on your feet.'

The surgeon wiped dry his hands, tossed the towel over his shoulder, and walking up to me, roughly pressed the end of my nose with his fingers: 'You're a lucky man! The bullet took a stroll through your stomach, just like a mademoiselle through a birch grove . . .'

'But doctor, I thought you were whistling Lensky's aria for me.'

'No. You're going to live 100 years and longer.'

Our conversation ended. Two attendants wheeled an operating table into the operating room. A man in bloody clothing was lying on it. He was moaning and repeatedly shouting two words of command: 'Canister! Load!! Canister!!!' They carried me out into the ward.

The days passed. The pain in my abdomen faded, but I was still running a temperature, and they forbade me to get up.

During one morning doctor's visit to the ward, one of the wounded asked the doctor to discharge him and return him to his unit. The doctor said nothing in reply, but as soon as he left, a ward nurse approached the wounded man.

'Look how untiring these front-line men are!' she told him. 'You haven't even had time to come to your senses from that blow to the head, and you're already spoiling for another fight.'

My neighbour, an older soldier with a bandaged head, wistfully replied: 'Don't castigate us, dear nurse; we're in a hurry to end this war as soon as possible. We're homesick for our native region, for the aroma of freshly-turned earth, for fine singing. Oh! If you only knew how well our Novgorod gals sing in the fields. Yet you're saying "Lie down, listen to the radio, and put on some fat." No, dear nurse, the soldier's heart will calm down, only when the rifles are stacked for the last time.'

My neighbour lay on his back with his left arm tucked under his head. The right sleeve of his shirt was empty. He stared pensively somewhere into the distance.

*   *   *

After twenty days I was discharged from the hospital. Before leaving for the front, I dropped by to visit my son. Volodya had grown and seemed mature beyond his years. He knew who was bombarding the city and where he should take cover during a barrage, and that somewhere there was a 'Road of Life', over which they trucked in bread and sugar for the adults and children. He kept asking, 'Will the Germans go home soon, Papa, and will we be living with Mama at home again?' I replied, 'The Germans, son, won't choose to go home; they have to be shown the road.'

I noticed with surprise that my son was pressing three fingers to the palm of his left hand. I asked him, 'Volodya, why are you holding your fingers like that? Is your hand hurting?'

'No, they aren't hurting. That's how I count when Granny Katya will come to see me. I want Mama to come, but she doesn't.'

'But doesn't Mama Zina come to see you?'

'She has, but rarely, and I want her to stay with me all the time.'

Volodya showed me his toys, and I got acquainted with the good nanny Lyudmila Yakovlevna. Volodya and I skipped lunch and took a walk together. When we returned, the other children took turns coming up to me, and laying a little hand on my shoulder or resting their head on my arm, listened hungrily to my every word, while gazing into my eyes. Then, dropping their heads, they would walk away, pick up their toys, and keep an eye on Volodya and me from a distance.

Volodya lay down to sleep, but he didn't let go of my hand. I kissed my sleeping son and went to visit Aunt Katya, but she wasn't home. Leaving a note and some money behind for her, I walked back to the front lines.

The reunion with my front-line friends was boisterous. Naydenov kept sticking a tobacco pouch filled with fragrant tobacco into my hands until I just didn't want any more: 'Smoke up; it's fine tobacco.' Zina impatiently asked me about Volodya.

That evening, Naydenov and I went out into the trenches. We had to lay in wait for a German, who was carrying dinner to one of his officers in a bunker in a shattered brick building on the outskirts of Pushkino.

A June day was fading . . . calm fell over the lines. A crimson sunset stretched across the western sky. Looking at Leningrad from the Pulkovo heights, we saw something unusual: the city with all its domes and smoke-stacks now and then became submerged in a fog bank, but then it would reappear on the surface, like an enormous ship sailing in some direction . . .

Naydenov grabbed my elbow: 'Do you hear? Somewhere in these bushes a nightingale is singing . . . a little bird, but it isn't afraid of the gunshots. It has flown back to its dear home . . .' The nightingale's warble indeed in peaceful times caresses the hearing, but here, in the front-line trench, it was pitilessly touching the heart.

The night passed normally with an uninterrupted fire-fight and tussle with the Germans. The sun rose. Suddenly somewhere not far away, a single artillery piece discharged. The wind grabbed the cannon's roar and carried it away, as if trying to prevent a violation of the start of a wonderful summer day. We hadn't even been able yet to determine who had fired, when the artilleryman Korchnov walked up to us.

'Semyon, was that you who fired?' Naydenov asked.

'It was me, why?'

'Oh, you and your restless skull! The guys have only just laid down to rest, and there you are with your clapperboard.'

'That, brother, isn't a clapperboard,' the sergeant protested. 'That's nothing other than a genuine 45mm gun!'

'It's a noise-maker, but what's the use of it?'

'What?' the artilleryman erupted. 'Just what do you know about our business? A 120mm gun can't do from long-range what I can do with this baby over open sights. You need to understand.' With that, Korchnov took Naydenov by the arm: 'Come on, blockhead, I'll show you.'

After passing several turns in the trench, the artilleryman stopped and pointed to a deep crater in the breastworks of the German trench, right where the Nazis had established a firing position.

'Do you see? I took notice of it last night, and early this morning I scratched it off the ledger. And you say that I'm making a din for nothing, disturbing the soldiers' sleep. Now you see what that action accomplished; there are only fragments of the target scattered about,' Korchnov declared not without pride.

From our combat experience, Naydenov and I both knew that Korchnov's shot was no help to us. That enemy emplacement, which had already been detected, presented no dangers: we constantly kept our sights on it. It made no sense to destroy it, since the enemy would replace it with a new one somewhere else, which would be much more difficult to destroy than one that was already known. But I held my tongue, knowing that any initiative can be positive for the front-line situation, and it must not be discouraged.

'It was a splendid shot, what else can one say?' Naydenov praised the artilleryman through his teeth. 'But some other time they'll fire and fire, and every shot misses, which makes me so furious that I'm ready to pummel the gunner. But this shot, as they say, was as good as a sniper's!'

'That's true, all sorts of things happen with us as well,' the spotter agreed, scratching the back of his head. Enemy mortar rounds flew over our heads one after the other.

'They're angry, and probing for our gun, but we have it concealed in a safe little location.' Just as a precaution, we stepped into a machine-gun bunker.

'Senya, where have you been? We haven't seen you in a while,' the machine-gunner Maksim asked.

'They nicked me, and I disappeared into a hospital for a couple of weeks.'

'Where were you when you were hit?'

'With the 1st Rifle Battalion. The guys and I were working over this one little German bunker; they noticed us, the devils, fired a barrage, and my leg got a scratch.'

'And here I thought you'd skipped over to a different "resort",' Naydenov cautiously intervened in the discussion.

'I was just teasing you, Seryozha, with that "resort" comment. I said it in jest, but you're taking it too seriously. It will be better if you tell me how you distinguish one German from another, when you say: "I killed an observer, a messenger, or an officer."'

Sergey responded: 'You can immediately recognize an officer from a soldier by his face: a well-groomed mug, but glowering eyes; when one appears in the trench, the soldiers on duty raise a cry, well, just look at where a helmet pops up. Now, you look for an observer somewhere around a roll of barbed wire or among the rusty cans on the breastwork. It's very difficult to find him. The messenger is a moving figure; it's easy to pick him out.'

'And who is this one-eyed sniper among you, do you know? They say he's training soldiers; I'd also like to learn from him.'

Naydenov with a sideways glance at me put a finger to his lips and then turned in my direction. I acted as if I hadn't noticed anything.

Sergey replied to Korchnov's question with this: 'As soon as you begin your instruction, I'll tell you.'

Naydenov and Korchnov went out into the trench, while I remained in the bunker to observe the enemy's defences.

Chapter Twenty-five

A Competition

For several days, we had been detecting an unusual amount of movement and noise in the enemy's trenches. In the evenings, the Germans had been whistling loudly, shouting, and singing to the accompaniment of harmonicas. I didn't know what had made them so happy. I knew only one thing: that nothing at the front has the capability to make a man so angry, as happiness in the enemy camp. Even the most level-headed fighters were scowling, chewing their lips, and hurling the choicest invectives at the Nazis. Now from the other side they were shouting: 'Hey! Ivan! Soon your Moscow will be German.'

One night I encountered Petr Romanov in the trench. He was moving slowly, paying close attention to the Germans' hubbub. I asked him, 'Petya, do you know why they've started acting so high and mighty?' He replied: 'We've received a report that on 5 July German forces launched an offensive on the Orel-Kursk axis with the aim of swinging around Moscow and taking it from the rear. That's why the Nazis are animated: they say that if they take the Soviet capital, the war will be over. In addition to this, there are other reports that the Germans are concentrating forces on the Mga and Sinyavino sectors, in order to close a ring around Leningrad again. That's why they're so merry; they still believe in their *führer*, the morons . . .'

'Petya, how can we spoil their mood, huh?'

'If our guys in the Orel-Kursk bulge can smash them in the nose, they'll quiet down on their own, but it wouldn't hurt to give them a rap at the same time somewhere else.'

The days passed. The nervous tension among the men at the front grew with every passing day. Often heated arguments erupted, always on the same question: when would we finally throttle the Germans? The mood of the soldiers in the front lines during these days was reminiscent of a volcano ready to erupt. Only strict military discipline could curb the soldier's combat impulses. We were waiting impatiently for the order to attack.

Of course, at this time the situation around Leningrad didn't permit a major offensive against the Germans. But the high command, considering the soldiers' fervour to attack, launched isolated heavy attacks on the Germans. Such was the case even now.

On 12 July, the units on our sector of the defence suddenly attacked the Germans. In a single impulse, we threw ourselves at the enemy line. We were all ready to die, if only to crush the enemy. Who was running to the left of me, to my right, or in front of me – I don't recall. But this moment of attack, when every soldier seemed to be gripped by the same fire, remained forever in my mind.

Leaping across the smoking shell holes, I ran into a thick cloud of smoke and immediately collided face to face with a husky SS trooper. We stopped momentarily. I had an enormous advantage: the barrel of his machine pistol was directed away from me, while my bayonet was pointed squarely at his chest. The Nazi tried to alter his unfavourable situation, but didn't have time . . . I leaped into the German trench and saw a wounded Naydenov. Sergey was leaning against the trench wall, gulping air through his open mouth. I hastily applied a bandage to the wound, and he crawled away to get medical assistance, holding his left arm.

In the twilight of the white Leningrad night, around every trench turn, savage close-range combat was going on: there were short bursts of submachine-gun fire and solitary pistol shots, the explosions of grenades, the dull thuds of rifle-butt blows and the piercing screams of men being stabbed . . .

On the first night of the battle, we only managed at dawn to get a bit of rest and a bite to eat. Exhausted by the constant fighting, the soldiers ate quietly, their eyes focused on their mess tins. Each of us felt a sense of satisfaction with the results of the night's fighting, but the death and wounding of our comrade-friends took the lustre from our successes. This night had been particularly difficult for me: Zina and Naydenov were not around me. At the very start of the battle, Zina had been wounded in the leg, and Naydenov, in the shoulder and head.

For three days, the Germans couldn't reconcile themselves with the fact that they had been driven back from Leningrad another 500 metres. They literally rained shells down on us, counter-attacked repeatedly, but we refused to yield any of the ground we had gained.

On 16 July the company's Party organizer came to me at dawn and announced the happy news: our forces in the Orel-Kursk bulge had stopped the Germans and then gone over on the offensive themselves. The threat to the Soviet capital was passing. We breathed more freely. On this morning, even a shovel seemed like a feather in our hands, and the sun seemed to rise in a different way – it quickly sprang above the horizon, and bathed the earth with its bright, warm rays.

For several days in a row, I had to keep watch on the German trenches alone, without a partner. Only now did I really understand which of my friends had made my life bearable after the loss of my right eye.

I became friends with Maksim Maksimovich Maksimov, who was the gunner on a heavy machine-gun team. The soldiers all called him 'Kettle', and the 45-year-old man responded good-naturedly to this jesting nickname. But in combat, his comrades called him only by his last name. Maksimov was simple and kindly when addressing his comrades. His pleasant, open face and large blue eyes were always smiling during a conversation. It seemed that nothing at all could make this man angry. He threw himself into any task. When cleaning his machine gun or filling an ammunition belt, or digging a well, he liked to hum some tune to himself. But Maksimov was a different man in combat: his smile vanished, his eyes narrowed, and he became prickly and bad-tempered.

'Boris, another belt!' Maksimov would curtly order. 'Listen, buddy! Keep your trap shut! You'll swallow a bullet!' he would shout at the ammunition carriers. The machine gun in his strong hands fired without jamming, and he fired without fatigue.

At times, Maksim Maksimovich's behaviour reminded me a lot of Uncle Vasya. In his habits and manners, there was a certain fatherly affection, which drew everyone to him, but especially the young soldiers. But Maksim's life had been entirely different from Uncle Vasya's. Maksim came from a small Russian town, and he had long worked as a carpenter. That's why the machine-gunners' bunker always looked particularly fine and solid. Maksimov lugged around a carpenter's tool of sorts in his backpack. He was especially fond of telling young soldiers how to behave in battle.

Once, when he was squatting in the trench, his back against the trench wall, smiling and puffing his beloved pipe, which he never took from his mouth except when eating and sleeping, he leisurely started a discussion: 'For example, a battle is going on. Now, my brother, the soldier's eye must be sharper than a needle. You must remember that your eyes are backing up the commander's eyes. Don't just look around without any purpose; bullets have a real fondness for rubberneckers: one of their snipers will drill you in the forehead. You must figure out for yourself where the commander is located and what your comrades are doing!'

Seeing that he had an attentive audience, Maksim Maksimovich lay a pinch of tobacco into the bowl of his pipe, lit it up, settled in more comfortably, and continued: 'Each little mound, every little wrinkle in the ground is cover for a soldier in combat. Remember this! Take me for example . . . I earned my first wound out of stupidity. Although I'm not a young man, I wanted to demonstrate my agility, and I neglected to seek cover. But a bullet isn't a fool, and it found me . . .'

One of the young soldiers interrupted Maksimov: 'That's just what it said about using terrain in the Manual.'

'What a choirboy! When they were reading the Manual to you, dear brother, a bullet wasn't humming in your ear, and now when one ploughs into the ground right in front of your nose, you'll have a lot to think about. Where in the Manual does it tell you where you'll be when you meet the enemy, huh? What kind of treat does he have in store for you? On which side of your body should you lie, when shells are exploding all around you? Here again, you have to figure it out yourself. I didn't have a chance to read the Manual; I'm not educated, fellows . . . That, of course, is a bad thing. But this is now my third year of experiencing what the Manual only talks about. I've had a lot of opportunities to bury my nose in our native soil, to take cover from bullets and shell fragments. There's nothing shameful about it. That's indeed how I fight, and I don't consider myself under any obligation to the Germans.'

Maksimov had a large family. For some reason, however, he didn't like to talk about it, though he thought about it constantly. I learned about this completely unexpectedly. Maksimov and I were somehow standing sentinel together, and it was -33° C. We stepped into a damaged dugout, in order to find shelter against the biting wind. Maksim Maksimovich pressed up against my side with his back and fell silent. Suddenly he bellowed: 'Frosya, give me a piece of bread!'

I nudged my comrade in the ribs: 'Who are you asking for bread? Who's this Frosya?'

Maksimov, smiling with embarrassment, looked at me: 'Fie, it was just some sort of attack! I was having a dream that I was at home, and I'm looking as the wife pulls loaves of bread from the oven and sprinkles them with water. I love the aroma of fresh bread! There's nothing better. That's why I shouted in my sleep . . . I went completely bonkers. Frosya is my wife.'

One morning Petr Romanov came to see the machine-gunners. He was now the company commander. Maksimov, seeing him coming, quickly smoothed his combat blouse, removed the pipe from his mouth, took several precise steps towards Romanov, and clearly enunciating each word, formally reported: 'Comrade Lieutenant! The machine-gun crew is ready for combat!'

Romanov exchanged greetings with the soldiers, took Maksimov by the elbow, and said: 'Get ready, Comrades, for a shooting competition. But you, Yosif, have been ordered to appear at regiment headquarters today. If you're in the city, pay a call on the wounded.'

The machine-gun crew under the command of Sergeant Maksimov began to prepare diligently for the competition. Over and over again the machine-gunners checked the firing mechanism and adjusted the tension of the recoil spring. Each component of the machine gun was cleaned and polished to a mirrored shine. Several times in the course of the day, Maksim Maksimovich asked me about the rules of the upcoming competition.

Comrades joked, 'What, Maksimych, are you planning a wedding with your namesake?'

Puffing his pipe, the machine-gunner replied, 'At a wedding, you yourself know that they pop the bottle, but here, my brother, it is a different matter – to defend the company's honour in a shooting competition. That's a bit more difficult . . .'

It wasn't difficult to understand the mood of the machine-gunner, whom I already knew fairly well: he very much wanted to check his accuracy by shooting at targets, before entering into a decisive clash with the enemy. Maksimov had not managed to fire a machine gun at targets even once on a shooting range. He understood how necessary this was, in order to convince himself of his ability to fire at living targets. That's why Maksim Maksimovich could not forget about the upcoming competition even on this joyful day that marked the victory of our forces at Orel and Belgorod.

The defeat of the German fascist forces at the battle of Kursk sharply changed the behaviour of the Germans around Leningrad. Under the given circumstances, there could no longer be any talk about any sort of superiority of the Nazi forces over the defenders. The Nazis became subdued: they were sitting in their bunkers like ground squirrels in a burrow before an oncoming storm. But the enemy's long-range artillery fell with even greater fury upon the city's living quarters. Now the artillery duels continued around the clock.

In the morning Maksimov met me in the trench. His eyes were burning with a special light. 'Osip, the company commander has ordered you and me with my crew to go to division headquarters.'

'Fine, Maksimych, go on ahead and I'll catch up with you.'

In the dugout of the officer on duty at division headquarters, I was greeted by a youngish lieutenant. He was ruddy like a ripe apple, his face still untouched by the blade of a razor. It was hard to take my eyes off his rosy lips and bright blue eyes, which even in a front-line dugout were reminiscent of a bright blue sky. Voluminous curls of brown hair decorated the youth's uplifted head, while little ringlets covered his small ears. He tried his hardest to give the impression of an experienced front-line soldier, but with little success – his cracking voice gave him away.

An enamelled *Komsomol* pin gleamed on the lieutenant's chest and below it shone two military Orders and the medals 'For courage' and 'For the defence of Leningrad'. He greeted me deferentially as his senior in age, handed me an order from division commander Major-General Trushkin, and added: 'You'll be boarding with the commandant's platoon. The time and location of the field exercise has been indicated in the order.'

The rules of the competition had been affixed to the order. Each division would select a fully-staffed rifle platoon. The platoon would be augmented with one heavy machine-gun and one light machine-gun crew each, two company mortars, two anti-tank guns and eight snipers. The platoon would have to advance 5 kilometres over difficult terrain, reach a start line and attack the 'enemy'. It would have one hour to carry out the mission; cannons and machine guns would move together with the riflemen in combat readiness; those who dropped out of formation along the route could not be replaced. There was a note written on the corner of this page of rules in red pencil:

> I designate master target-shooter Y. Pilyushin as responsible for the marksmanship training, and Lieutenant Yu. Grudinin as platoon commander. Major V.V. Abramovich will inspect the readiness of the platoon for the competition and report to me.
> Trushkin
> 23 August 1943

I asked, 'Where am I to find Lieutenant Grudinin?' The young lieutenant replied, 'Let's get acquainted, I'm Grudinin.' We warmly shook hands.

'How many days do we have for training, Comrade Lieutenant?'

'Five.'

It was necessary not only to sight in the weapons, but also to work out every minute and to think over how to conserve the strength of the soldiers for the concluding attack on the 'enemy'. After all, the men had spent a long time on defence, and had become unaccustomed to rapid and lengthy marches, especially while wearing a pack. For a front-line soldier, who had spent two years in a trench, it wasn't so simple to march 5 kilometres in one hour with full combat gear across difficult terrain.

The snipers spent one day from sunrise to sunset sighting in their rifles. Sergeant Maksimov also fired his heavy machine gun. I saw the precision with which he aimed his gun and the care with which he pressed the trigger. But what's this? The bullets were tracking far to one side. Confounded by this, Maksimych checked the setting of his sights, rubbed his eyes with his fists, once again checked the sights, and then gave me a look. I saw fear in his eyes. In order to calm the comrade, I dropped down beside him and checked the sights.

'Everything's correct . . . Just let the master armourer adjust the foresight a tad, and everything will be fine.'

Maksimov went white: 'Do you understand, my brother, what you're saying? For two years I've been firing this machine gun! Two years! It turns out, I was just wasting cartridges?'

I was truly sorry for Maksimov, but I couldn't help him now. I just said, 'Do you see now how important it is to sight in your weapon at a firing range in a timely fashion?'

On 28 August precisely at six o'clock in the morning, our fully-staffed team was already at the infantry training area. An enormous, boggy field stretched before our eyes, overgrown with low brush and dotted with the mock-ups of tanks, guns, mortars, heavy and light machine guns, and targets depicting moving infantry.

'Osip, where should I set up my machine gun?' Maksimov asked.

'On either flank. Your task is to cover the attack of the riflemen with your fire. If you don't manage to do this, we'll lose the competition. You know yourself that the enemy won't attack under machine-gun fire.'

'I know that, but what about here?'

'Forget that you have targets in front of you; just remember one thing: a fascist is peering out from behind each target, and you know what to do with him.'

'You bet . . .'

The comrades sitting on the side of the road were looking hungrily at each target and every fold in the ground: they were already picturing that they were on the attack. From experience I knew that people participating in their first competition are perceptibly nervous, even though everything necessary has been taken into account during training. The closer to the start of the competition, the more a soldier's heart will pound.

Even Major Abramovich, an old, experienced participant in many competitions, was plainly nervous. Screwing up his brown, slightly almond-shaped eyes, he was pacing back and forth on the road, kicking along a little stone with the toe of his boot. I knew Abramovich from back in 1941, when he had been a platoon commander and had often visited us in the front-line trench at night together with his riflemen. Then he took command of a company, at one time worked on the staff at regiment head-quarters, and now he was Division's deputy chief of operations. We had been friends through all this time, despite the difference in ranks, main-taining amicable relations as fellow sportsmen.

By eight o'clock, all the competition's participants had gathered. By a drawing of lots, our team went second. We climbed into a truck and rode to the assigned starting location. As we were driving under a railroad bridge, one of the guys jokingly shouted: 'Hey, Maksimych! Leave your namesake behind the embankment, and we'll pick it up on the way back.' Maksimov replied, 'You're quite a joker, brother; no doubt your own knees are shaking.'

The platoon commander Yuriy Grudinin was standing on the cab's running board. He playfully gave his curls a shake and started singing:

We'll remember those who commanded the companies
Those who died in the snow,
Those who waded through the swamps to Leningrad
While wringing the necks of the foe . . .

A chorus of voices took up the song. The truck was heading down a country road, rocking from side to side. To the right and left of the road stretched rows of vegetable gardens planted and tended by the citizens of Leningrad. Women and children were picking crops. Catching sight of us, they straightened their tired backs, and leaning on their shovels, gave us friendly waves. One young woman adroitly tossed a large bunch of carrots into the back of the truck. She shouted something, but the noise of the engine drowned out her words.

When we arrived, we were given our orders on the spot, and the team from the 109th Rifle Division deployed on the course start line. Two hours later, a motorcyclist rolled up to us. He briefly reported, 'The 109th Division is to proceed with the execution of its mission!' Then he drove away.

. . . In the distance ahead, I could see men, women and young adoles-cents run out onto the field in front of us with shovels. They started to dig potholes in our path. One gaunt little old woman brought us a bucket of water, offering to each of us a full cup while she encouraged us to take one: 'Sonny, drink up a little cold water, it will make it easier for you to lug that damned weapon.'

Maksimov was running in front of me, lugging the Sokolov wheeled mount of his machine gun. Coming up to the old woman, he wiped the sweat from his brow with his sleeve, took a cup from the woman's caring hands, and emptied it in a gulp. Then he carefully embraced the old woman around her thin shoulders and kissed her: 'Thanks for your help, dear.'

Our team took first place in the competition. Leningrad women indeed helped us in this, as they did in all our combat successes on the lines of defence.

Chapter Twenty-six

The Unknown Visitor

At sunset our team left the infantry training grounds. The trucks rolled along the streets of the city in no hurry, and only after reaching the Krasnokabatsk highway did they speed up. All the while we gazed at our beloved city, which slowly submerged into the evening twilight. At this hour of the day, Leningrad was somehow particularly beautiful. The trees, exhausted by the daytime's sweltering heat, spread out their leaves to meet the cool of the evening, the beautiful Neva is covered by a light mist, and along its banks plumes of smoke and steam lazily rise from the factories into the clear evening sky, undisturbed by any wind. Along the streets, trolley cars run, clattering and throwing out showers of sparks.

At this hour, Leningraders were returning home from their garden plots. They were stopping on the streets and along the sides of the road, escorting us with a silent gaze towards where flares were regularly appearing and disappearing in the sky. Wherever we had occasion to bump into Leningrad's residents, the months of the terrible famine that they had experienced would immediately spring to our minds. Even now, when those fatal days were passing, upon meeting these courageous people, your hand subconsciously reached for your cap – you felt like removing it, deeply bowing, and saying, 'Thank you, Leningraders, for saving the city from destruction and fire for future generations.'

Our truck took a sharp turn to the left, and reducing its speed, headed towards the front lines. The first person I met in the trench when arriving was Sergey Naydenov. He was smiling as he walked up to greet me, well-groomed and freshened up. His clean-shaven face exuded health, and from under the stiff collar of his new combat blouse there peeked a narrow white strip that fringed the sniper's deeply tanned neck. Sergey was holding a brand new carbine with a lightweight telescopic sight. Walking up to me, he quietly placed his hands on my shoulders and hoisted himself up, just like a 3-year-old tot, then clownishly requested, 'Well now, teacher, assess this student's suitability for a rifle unit!'

'Let go, you devil, you're going to break a bone!'

'Give me a letter – then I'll let go!'

'I don't have your letter, let me go.'

'Don't be clever, the fellows told me that you have the letter, Osip. Don't torment me, my soul is suffering!'

I gave Sergey his letter, which had been handed to me at division headquarters to deliver to him. He examined it from every angle and cautiously opened the envelope. His eyes hungrily ran over the lines on the page, which had been written in pencil. The sheet of paper slightly trembled in his strong hand. Sergey re-read the letter several times, then dropped his arms, deeply sighed, and stared off into the distance. He had forgotten my presence.

'What are they writing from home?'

'Just read it . . .'

I took the letter and read:

Greetings, our dear. Yesterday we received the letter from you. I read it, laughing and crying with joy that you are still alive. Father went off to fight, sent us two letters, and hasn't written again. Kostya and I are working at a collective farm, while Nadyushka is home. She will start school this year. That will be a joy! She often takes your photograph, places it among her toys, and has a conversation with you. When she goes to bed, she places your picture under her pillow. She herself blows out the lamp, hugs me around the neck, and says: 'Mamochka, sleep; Seryozha and I are already sleeping.' She doesn't remember Father. My son, each night and day we are living with you in our thoughts and hearts.

This distant, but living voice from someone else's family strongly shook me up. I once again experienced the full depth of my grief. At this moment I desperately wanted to see my son, if only to spend a minute together with him.

'Osip, I was in the same hospital with Andreyev.'

'How is he feeling? Will he return soon?'

'Poorly. Sometimes he recognized me and spoke normally, but at other times he'll hardly even look at you and speaks all sorts of rubbish. The bastards gave him a strong blow to the head, and he hasn't been the same since.'

'How's Zina?'

'I bumped into her at the office, when I was being discharged.' Sergey handed me a little metal token from Stroyeva. 'She was requesting a discharge, but the doctor refused: her leg is still bad.'

Naydenov gave me a peevish wave of the hand, hoisted a case of grenades under his arm, and walked off down the trench line. I headed back to my bunker, stretched out on a bunk, and laid there with open eyes until the morning dawn.

On 1 September, a holiday for all school teachers, we all headed to company commander Romanov's bunker to congratulate the former school teacher, after shaving, putting on fresh undercollar strips, and gathering some flowers for him. When we arrived, we were informed by the radio operator that Romanov was on a visit to the 1st Platoon, but should return shortly.

We took our seats in the bunker wherever we could find one: on the bunks, on crates, in a niche to store grenades. We set the flowers in a tin can on the table, lit two candles, placed our packs on our knees, and assumed solemn poses. Bazanov was instructed to present the flowers to Romanov and to congratulate him on the start of the school year.

Romanov entered the bunker and stopped in disbelief when he caught sight of us. We rose to our feet. Bazanov handed our commander a bouquet of dried wild chamomile and festively pronounced, 'Comrade Company commander! We congratulate you on the start of the school year!'

At first, Romanov didn't understand what was going on. Then I saw how joyously his eyes began to sparkle. Broadly smiling, he pressed the bouquet of faded blossoms to his breast with his left hand, while the fingers of his right hand fidgeted with the buttons on his shirt or smoothed his hair with embarrassment. Finally he spoke up: 'Thank you, my combat-friends and comrades, for not forgetting this joyful day for all Soviet school teachers. How fine you all are for remembering this day!'

The Lieutenant, waiting while everyone took their seats again, stood by the bunker entrance, still happily flustered. Recomposing himself, he carefully laid the flowers on the table and opened a folder. Then he spoke, drawing out his words very much like a teacher would: 'Today, comrades, your school lesson will begin a bit unusually – with political information. I have good news for you: our forces have completed the destruction of the Nazis at Orel and Belgorod. Our counter-offensive began in two locations: from the area north of Orel to the south, and from the area east of Orel to the west. After a month of fighting, the foe has lost 4,605 tanks and assault guns, 1,623 artillery pieces, 2,492 aircraft, and more than 132,000 officers and men killed or taken prisoner. Our forces are driving the shattered remnants of the Nazis to the west. I think that even we won't be letting the fascists spend another winter around Leningrad. The Germans will remember this lesson!'

The telephone began to buzz. The Lieutenant picked up the phone. After a minute he set it back down and said: 'We've just been informed that an important guest has arrived in our battalion. He may even visit our company. Therefore I ask all of you to return to your squads and take up combat positions . . . Thanks again for your attention and for the flowers.'

Bazanov gave us the code words: 'Get lost!' We quickly left the commander's bunker. When I arrived at the sniper's nest, Naydenov was already sitting at the periscope.

'Have you noticed any changes in the enemy positions while I was gone?' I asked.

'No, just the same camouflage: cans, rags and all sorts of rubbish.'

Naydenov covered the gun port and took a seat directly on the emplacement's floor.

'It's rather hot today.' Sergey angrily pulled his forage cap off his head and wiped his sweating face. 'As if just in spite, not a single Fritz is showing himself.'

I took a seat at the periscope to check a few familiar places, where sometimes a German periscope made an appearance. Seeing nothing suspicious, I lingered by the gun port, searching for enemy observers or officers, who usually checked their posts around this time. They would often sneak a peek over their breastwork, in order to take a look in our direction.

At times, when sitting at a periscope, you would become queasy from the nauseating scent of decaying corpses, but nothing could avert it. No matter where you looked, there was one and the same thing: scorched earth, shattered trees, craters and rolls of barbed wire.

Suddenly the sounds of music carried from the German side. I tried to pin down where it was coming from, but I couldn't find the source of it.

Then suddenly I saw the camouflaged shield on the embrasure of an enemy sniper emplacement slowly move to the side. With just the same caution the sharpshooter positioned his rifle and became still. I couldn't delay, for at any moment the German might kill one of our soldiers. Not seeing the enemy's face, I fired at the dark opening of the gun slit. The rifle in the German's hands jerked upward against the top of the gun slit, and then fell back into the emplacement. I pulled back my rifle, covered the firing slot, and glanced at Naydenov. Propped against the wall of the emplacement, he was sleeping tranquilly. I couldn't move to a different location and continue my observations – I couldn't leave behind a slumbering comrade. Having woken up, he would undoubtedly open the gun port, which German marksmen could be keeping under observation. After all, not a single sniper's shot, no matter from which side it came, went unnoticed.

I touched the sleeping Naydenov lightly on the shoulder. Sergey in a flash leaped to his feet, grabbed his rifle, and fixed his frightened eyes on me: 'Huh? What? Germans?'

'Wake up! The Germans haven't moved; I woke you up to warn you that I had fired.'

'Aah! How did I fall asleep? Forgive me. I spent all last night at the same firing position.' Sergey, with a fitful yawn, settled back down into his previous place.

'I'm going for breakfast, Sergey. It will be your turn when I come back. Just make sure everything is in order. If the guest comes, let me know.'

On my way, I dropped by the machine-gunners' dugout to visit Maksimych. The soldiers were eating breakfast and attentively listening to a comrade, who was reading a copy of *Leningrad Pravda*.

'On the 13th of August, Soviet forces of the Southern Front . . .' the reader shot a glance at me before continuing: 'with a decisive assault took the city and port of Taganrog. Rostov Oblast has been fully cleansed of fascist occupiers.'

'Great news, huh, guys?'

'Over there things are going fine, but we're still hunkered down in front of Leningrad,' Maksimov said as he filled his pipe. Then he turned to me: 'Osip, I'm just thinking of doing a little night-time firing on the German rear with my machine gun.'

'An excellent idea, only you'll need to mount the quadrant sight.'

'But, obviously, that's no simple doodad; none of the machine-gunners have seen one.'

'Yet you've seen the monocular sight for the machine gun, Maksimych? It allows you to fire at longer ranges.'

'I saw it once at a firing range, where I had a chance to examine one! They have all sorts of dials and screws there.'

'It's just the same as a telescopic sight on a sniper's rifle, only larger and arranged a bit differently. It is also mounted on an azimuth table. With its assistance it is possible to determine the range setting to one mil. Do you understand how important this is?'

'Osip, be a friend, help me get hold of one.'

Maksimych picked up his forage cap and donned it, trying to cover his right ear. I could see a deep slash in it.

'When did you get maimed?' I asked.

'You mean this nick?' Maksimych asked in return, drawing deeply on his pipe and carefully patting his right ear. 'It's a memory of my schoolboy years; I fell from a horse . . .'

'Don't believe him, Comrade, it was someone giving him a lesson: he was stealing carrots from somebody's garden. But he didn't learn his lesson,' the machine-gunner Gavrila, who didn't like Maksimov, said sneeringly.

I glanced at Maksimych to see how he would react to this scathing retort. But the machine-gunner acted as if he didn't even hear the jibe. He calmly kept cleaning his namesake, and grabbed a spare gun barrel, greased it, and inserted it into its jacket. Sensing my questioning gaze, he said: 'I'm not angry with him: the man has a bad character. He's badly put together. Incidentally, he's a dandy soldier. In peacetime he was even afraid to cut the head off a chicken, but at the front he's got used to everything. He recently shot a Fritz and smiled afterwards, just as if he'd bitten into a tasty apple.'

Gavrila shot a sly glance at Maksimych, and quietly continued to fill an ammunition belt. Escorting me out of the dugout, Maksimov once again reminded me, 'Osip, don't put it off for long; track down a quadrant sight.'

One day soon after, all the preparations for firing on targets in the enemy rear had been completed just before the arrival of darkness. According to our calculations, a supply road leading to the German front line from the direction of an urban park in Pushkino should come under Maksimov's machine-gun fire.

Once it became dark, Maksimov came to our bunker and took a seat next to me on a bunk. He proposed, 'Osip, I have everything ready; let's go fire the machine gun.'

Maksimov walked slowly up to the machine gun, which had been set up out in the open, wiped his eyes with his palms, carefully checked the sights, and then spat on his hands and rubbed them together so vigorously that it seemed sparks would fly from them. Staring in the direction of the enemy, he gripped the handles, freed the safety, and pressed the trigger with both thumbs. The feed mechanism instantly went into motion; jerking, the cartridge belt hastily climbed into the open slot of the feed block, and the bolt hammered out a series of shots.

Maksimov gave a long burst at the unseen target and froze, without releasing his grip on the machine gun. Then he strained to hear any results of his firing. Everything was silent in the enemy's position: not a sound or a stirring. So how could we determine the results of the firing? We had seen this winding supply road only on a map. It skirted a low hill, and then intersected a light patch of woods before running across a field to the German front line.

The next evening, the chief of the division's reconnaissance came to our bunker and asked: 'Which one of you conducted the night-time machine-gun fire on the enemy rear?' Maksimov rose to his feet and said, 'I did, Comrade Captain.'

'Attaboy! You have forced the Germans to search for a new route to the front.' The captain pulled out a map: 'Now fire on this little lane; the Hanses are using it as well.'

Maksimov returned to his machine gun that night and fired belt after belt of ammunition, constantly adjusting the sights. Inspired by the results, he spent the entire night periodically placing fire on the roads and paths in the enemy rear.

The next morning, Naydenov sought us out. He was agitated by something: 'Guys, I just now had some guests – battalion commander Kruglov and some bigwig. He was bearded and loved to crack jokes . . . the visitor was interested in how I lob hand grenades onto the German trenches, then he himself went through all the procedures and fired a shot. Then they walked off from me to one side and started conversing about something between themselves. I only managed to catch the visitor saying that two divisions of the most notorious 'black cormorants' have been brought from France to the Germans' assistance: one division to the area of Strel'na, and the other somewhere around the settlement of Gorelovo. They apparently want to attack us on the ground, and simultaneously break into the city with a naval assault landing from the Gulf. Just look what the bastards are planning!'

'What about the battalion commander?' Maksimych asked.

'He said only crazy men can dream up something like that.'

'And the visitor?'

'I didn't hear anything more; they walked away from me.'

'What rank was the guest?' I asked Sergey.

'He didn't have any bars on his shoulders, but you couldn't count all the Orders on his chest.'

The desire to catch a glimpse of this visitor made me restless, but neither Kruglov nor Romanov made an appearance in our trench. Everyone was curious about the mysterious visitor: 'top brass' but with no signs of rank and a chest covered with Orders. Who might this be? Soon everything became clear.

The next morning during a political talk, Major Kruglov visited us in the bomb shelter together with a comrade in a camouflage jacket with no signs of rank. Kruglov greeted us, then took a seat on a bench next to the entrance and asked the deputy political commander Perov to continue the discussion. The visitor also sat on the bench, took off his forage cap and placed it on his knees, and then looked around the faces of the officers and soldiers with small, piercing brown eyes. Naydenov nudged me in the side with his elbow and whispered: 'That's him.'

'Quiet, let me listen.'

When the discussion ended, Kruglov introduced us to the guest. He was the commander of a partisan detachment, operating in the enemy rear in Leningrad Oblast.

'Stepan Afanasyevich,' Kruglov turned to the partisan, 'tell us please about the combat operations of your detachment, and about how the Soviet people are living on occupied territory.'

Such a silence fell over the shelter that we could hear the rustling of mice on the floor; as if by command, everyone was looking at the visitor.

The partisan, holding his forage cap in his hands, slowly moved forward into the centre of the shelter. A well-built man with a balding head, he looked around us with his dark, deeply-set eyes, as if assessing each one of us. A kindly but still crafty smile appeared on his long face. The partisan held his left hand in the pocket of his faded jacket. When he began to speak, his pleasant and resonant voice filled the shelter:

When I flew off to Leningrad our male and female partisans asked me to give the defenders of Leningrad a brotherly greeting and a wish for combat successes. So that's why I'm here . . . We partisans, dear comrades, are helping you fight. Our foes are not only the fascists, but also traitors. Sometimes we happen to live in the same village with these dogs, or even sleep under the same roof with them. For example, recently our partisans captured an officer from the German 18th Army headquarters by the name of Reiche. He didn't want to talk with us. In his words, partisans were 'bandits'; he demanded that we turn him over to 'Russians' and that was all. What would you want to be done with such a 'creature'? We knew of him already earlier, and knew that he was a terrible beast: he had executed hundreds of Soviet citizens. But there is something even more terrible than him. He was an open foe, but when a man carries a Russian name, and secretly passes the location of a partisan camp to the Gestapo, or the identities of our messengers, then you have something genuinely awful. At some time, the fascist and the traitor will have to hang from the same branch. Yet the most agonizing thing, dear comrades, is when you must be present at the execution of Soviet citizens. Your heart is wildly pounding in your chest, because you cannot save the life of one of your own people. It is hard, very hard, to maintain your composure, and not hurl yourself on the fascist executioner . . . and you must smile, when the SS officer looks at you. The Germans take partisans prisoner only very rarely, even if we are wounded or sleeping. They torture us . . . Well, who's going to tell them where his family is: the wife, the kids, the father, the mother, or an armed comrade? So they torture you more . . . they string you up and beat you half to death. Sometimes they shoot you, but this they do only with old women and adolescents; they hang the partisan women and men. But we pay them back; we always have some rope and a solid branch handy for the fascists and their allies.

So-called 'special purpose' forces [German *Einsantzgruppe*] under the command of the Nazi Stahlecker are operating to liquidate the partisans and the Jewish population in the Baltic region.[3] This Nazi Stahlecker is a terrible and cunning fellow. He operates entirely through other people's hands. His criminal associates, local Nazis and police, shoot, hang and burn Soviet citizens. Our traitors – Ukrainians, Russians and Belorussians, Estonians, Latvians, Lithuanians – also help them. The Nazis instruct these miscreants to fill the common graves with the bodies of Soviet people.

'What sort of people are these *polizei*?' one of the listening comrades asked.

'*Polizei*?' the visitor asked back. 'These aren't simply people that the Nazis force to serve them. Many of them voluntarily joined the Nazis, in order to carry out a fully conscious crime against their fellow countrymen.

'The *polizei* operate in a place known to them, where they know every person and each forest path. With their assistance, the Gestapo learns where communists, *Komsomol* members and the families of partisans live. It is true that some of our own comrades are among the *polizei*; they help us fish out the traitors, but our justice is swift over these miscreants – a hanging, and that's the end of it.'

Each word spoken by the partisan fell on the hearts of the Soviet

---

3. Dr. Franz Walter Stahlecker was the commander of the German *Eisantzgruppe* A until he was killed in a clash with partisans near Krasnogvardeysk on 23 March 1942, some time prior to this partisan leader's report.

soldiers like droplets of molten metal. Stepan Afanasyevich went on to list the names of executed people, and recounted the villages and settlements that had been put to the torch by the enemy. He was calling us not to commit cruelties, but to retribution. He spoke calmly and confidently, without haste, like the way a prosecutor lays out a case.

The soldiers listened to the partisan commander with lowered heads. No one offered him any more questions, but from this day on each of us sought to meet the enemy in open combat with a particularly unquenchable thirst.

When the partisan commander departed, Maksimov offered him his silent mate – his pipe: 'Give this trifle from me to your best machine-gunner.' The 'unknown visitor' embraced Maksimov.

Chapter Twenty-seven

The Final Meeting with My Son

In September and October 1943, Major Kruglov's battalion was located in the second echelon. We rehearsed encircling and assaulting enemy fortifications, pillboxes and bunkers; crossing water obstacles and mine-fields; and techniques of street fighting.

I was a constant presence at tactical and firing exercises, and the re-equipping of the rifle units took place before my eyes: old weapons were exchanged for new, more improved weapons. By November 1943, Kruglov's battalion was fully equipped and staffed, and prepared for offensive battles.

Before our return to the front, I was granted leave of absence to see my son. It was one of the happiest days of my life. To spend a few hours with Volodya, to hear his voice, to reassure my little boy that he wasn't alone, to express my gratitude to those who protect the lives of orphaned children – this can be nothing other than a joy!

Passing along the streets of the city, I saw with what care the urban dwellers were preparing for the third winter of the war: they covered up shattered windows and doors with boards and plywood sheets, and patched roofs and the façades of buildings. On the outskirts of the city, where there were still wooden homes, the Leningraders were disman-tling them to prepare fuel for the winter. The iron sleeves of chimney pipes jutted out towards the street from each window of a residence, like arms bent at the elbow, and next to the pipes one could see pieces of glass arranged like small windows set into plywood sheets for daytime illumi-nation of the interior of the home. There was not a speck of dirt on the streets or in the courtyards. Keeping to the northern side of the streets, city residents cautiously strolled along the walls of the buildings.

In the Children's Home, where Volodya was living, an electric light was burning, and children dressed in warm little outfits were running around a clean, warm room set below street level. I set my son on my lap and saw that the little fingers on his left hand were unclenched. That meant Aunt Katya was still alive and unharmed.

'Papa, Nanny brought me this little bear. It squeaks when you press its tummy. Nanny also told me that soon we would all be living together: Mama, you, Nanny and me. Is that true, Papa?'

It was very difficult to answer such questions from the child; I lied, if only to soothe his little, but sensitive heart: 'That's right, son. And just who bought these fine little booties for you, huh?'

'Mama!' Volodya answered with delight. 'She can't come herself; her leg hurts, so she sent them with her sister.'

Volodya also showed me his new woollen anklets with childlike pride. 'Mama also sent these,' he added.

On my return to the front, I dropped by the hospital to visit Zina. Unfortunately, I was unable to see her: the hospital was under quarantine.

It was already getting light when I passed the Pulkovo Observatory. A field kitchen was set up in its heavily-damaged ruins. A soldier emerged from a cellar with an axe in his hands; giving a yawn, he started to chop firewood. Another one, a bit older, wearing a snow-white apron and dressed in an old combat blouse that was just as clean, brought up a hog carcass from the cellar on his shoulder, and began to cut it into pieces on a wooden block. The cook opened the lid of a kettle, dropped in some meat, tossed a few pieces of cordwood on the fire and, turning to one side, rubbed his eye with his fist like a little boy. Taking another look, I recognized him: 'Andrey Petrovich!' I shouted to the comrade. 'Is a hot cup of tea possible?'

'Only today without sugar! Drink up, sniper, to your health.'

We all sincerely loved our cook, a calm, easy-going elderly man, who was always ready with some hot soup and a good word. He somehow seemed to sense particularly deeply all the weight of the soldier's difficult work. He sometimes would sit on a case at the field kitchen, and his small, round head, seemingly jammed down between his broad shoulders, would begin to nod and drop onto his chest, but he'd still sit and wait. When a hungry soldier or officer would come around, he would always find a mess tin of soup or a mug of hot tea ready for him. It often happened that you'd return from the front at a late hour of night, and want to drop in on Andrey Petrovich not only to drink a mug of hot tea, but also simply to sit a bit with him and exchange a few warm words. The soldier in the cook's coat never asked where you had come from or whether or not you were hungry, but would simply place a mess kit with kasha in front of you and take a seat beside you, encouraging you: 'Eat up, eat up, likely you're worn out, crawling around over hillocks and through ditches. I know what the sniper's work is like.'

These warm words had a magical effect and would lift the fatigue from your shoulders. Sometimes, one of those present might fall asleep right at the table. Then Andrey Petrovich would cautiously step away from the sleeping soldier. 'Listen, my welcomed guest – he's become quiet,' the cook would say, shaking his round head, and removing his quilted jacket, he would wrap it around the sleeping soldier's shoulders. Then shuffling across the ground on his tired legs, he would head back into his kitchen, take a seat on a case, nuzzle up against the still warm bricks of his oven, and doze, waiting for a late-arriving soldier.

Moving down the trench, I glanced into the sniper's emplacement. There, Sergey Naydenov was already sitting at the gun port.

'How's your little one?' Sergey asked.

'He's growing.'

'Did you drop by to see Zina?'

'The hospital was under quarantine, they didn't let me in.'

Sergey gave a tug on my sleeve: 'Look at how that son of a bitch is running.'

I spotted the German, running across an open field towards the ruins of a brick building. Naydenov didn't have time to shoot. The German suddenly stopped, threw his arms forward, then his entire body rocked forward and he fell face-first to the ground without twisting. Only then did the sound of a single rifle shot carry to our ears.

'Damn it! You sit, sit and wait, and then one appears – and just like you, they snatch him right out from under your nose.'

Naydenov covered the gun slot and reached for his tobacco pouch: 'Did you meet the artilleryman Korchnov on the defence?'

'No, what of it?'

'They had an article about him in the newspaper: they say the Siberian fights well. There's even a photograph of him; Semyon is standing at full height next to his little pop gun.'

Naydenov dug into a bag for the paper, but hadn't had time to find it when Bodrov came by our emplacement and said cheerfully: 'What, my friends? You're sitting there with a closed gun port, and the Hanses are strolling around right under your nose, huh?'

'Anatoliy, don't squawk, we don't have Hanses, but a different breed called "SS". Here we're even setting aside a few just in case.'

'Just so, Seryozhka, let's have a smoke.'

'Go ahead, light up, but watch that you don't scorch your whiskers; look at what he's sprouted! What, are you driving at being a Guardsman?'

'Why not?'

Bodrov stroked his left whiskers with his index finger, then his right whiskers and gave Naydenov a wink. There was so much wiliness in the face of the sniper at this moment!

'What, are you envious? Or is there no room for such an ornament under your own nose? Without enough fertilizer, they won't grow, huh?' Bodrov joked.

'Akimov's schooling is immediately evident, you're flapping your jaws well,' Sergey answered, handing his pouch over to his acquaintance. 'But enough with the laughing, moustachioed man – tell us why you're here.'

'I came to you for help: one person alone can't find a German sniper. He's settled into some spot, where he can keep two trench turns in his telescopic sight. It's impossible to cross this trench section in the day; you can only walk it at night.'

'Did you listen to where the shots were coming from?'

'No, why?'

'Just how are we going to find him, if we don't even have a rough idea of where he might be?'

'Seryozha, you yourself know that the fascists are like wolves: they don't go out on a hunt alone, but in an entire pack.'

'Don't you have a partner?'

'No. Zakharov was wounded in the last battle and still hasn't returned from the hospital.'

The three of us headed to Akimov's company. We kept our eyes on the enemy's line until full nightfall, attentively examining each rusty can and every rag that lay scattered around on the parapet of the German trench, but nothing raised our suspicion that the enemy marksman might be lurking right there. Naydenov lifted his eye from the eyepiece of his sight, winced in pain, and began to rub his sunburned neck, while giving Bodrov a surly look.

'Seryozha, why are you mad at me? I don't have anything to do with this.'

'What do you mean, "nothing to do"?' Sergey shouted. 'Wherever we could do without you, you're always right there, yet you can't find a German viper that is right under your nose. So go spend entire days searching for it!'

Bodrov laid a friendly hand on the shoulder of his comrade: 'Hey, Seryozha, Seryozha! I understand you. If only our troops would take the offensive sooner, because it's shameful in front of our comrades on other fronts: they're driving the Nazis from our land, while we all just mark time here, scrutinizing these cans and trash, and cursing each other for killing an enemy before the other had time to do it. If only we could drive them out into the open, there it would be a lot more convenient.'

An icy rain fell all night long on the eve of the October Revolution anniversary. You just wanted to huddle up against something warm, to get some heat for your shivering body . . . But the enemy was nearby, and we had to stand on guard to protect the city of Lenin – the cradle of the proletarian revolution.

The rain stopped at dawn, and a cold north wind began to blow. The skies in the east became flushed, as if from the effort of trying to restrain the rising sun. But it couldn't stop the sunrise: the dawn split apart, releasing the fiery ball from its grip. The earth became bathed with a bright, but non-warming light. Wherever you looked around you, everything was dressed in glittering silver attire. The delicate branches of bushes were decorated with a multitude of icicles, and an enormous grey beard of water, gripped by the sudden freeze, hung from an old bird's nest. With the slightest breath of wind, all of this was rocking or trembling, radiating an iridescent brilliance. The icy fingers, striking against one another, gave out a slightly audible, extended melodic sound.

Tiny needles of hoar-frost, caught by the wind, slowly spun in the air and dusted the arms and backs of the soldiers standing in the trench. This first clear frosty morning had lavishly swept away autumn's colours. Even a piece of dried, totally scarred wood, sticking up in no-man's-land – even that was starting to play with its silver attire in the rays of the morning sun. I didn't want to believe that blood could flow, women could become widowed, and a child could be left fatherless on a day that was starting with such beauty.

'Osip, let's go have breakfast! I'm hungry, and my mittens have become like wet rawhide and need to dry out, or else I won't be able to hold my rifle,' Naydenov said, blowing on his reddened hands to warm them, having removed his mittens and stuck them under his belt. After breakfast, Naydenov climbed up onto an upper bunk to rest, while I headed out to see Romanov.

It was warm and cosy in the commander's bunker; the dirt floor was cleanly swept and a candle was burning on a table. Romanov was lying on a wooden trestle bed. Petr had an opened book face down on his chest.

Romanov gave me a long, anguished look. I had more than once seen the same expression on heavily-wounded comrades.

'Yosif, be strong. Hear me out. Yesterday Kruglov was at a ceremonial evening in the House of the Red Army, and along the way, he dropped by to see your son . . . Voloden'ka is no more, he was killed by a shell fragment on the 22nd of October.'

It became suffocating to me in the bunker. I ran out into the trench . . .

Chapter Twenty-eight

Waiting

In the first days of December, with snow already on the ground, several officers unknown to me spent several days in a row carefully examining our lines and the enemy's positions. In response to our question, 'When will we attack?' the commanders answered vaguely: 'We won't be spending the winter around Leningrad, fellows' – and not a word more.

Artillery spotters and artillery officers began to call on us in the trench more often than usual. They asked us to point out for them how and where the enemy had concealed his firing positions. Naydenov in turn started to visit the Guards' mortar [rocket artillery] men, who were finding a spot on the slopes of Pulkovo Heights to their liking.

We had everything ready by the long-awaited day – the day of launching the offensive. Our guns and mortars had sighted in or registered on each enemy firing position and every bunker.

On the night of 20 December 1943, fresh forces moved into our trenches; mostly they were young soldiers. They looked very sharp in their white sheepskin coats, spanking new grey felt boots, and with their factory-fresh weapons. Many of them were carrying submachine-guns. Fellow villagers and townsmen met, and friendly discussions sprang up. We learned that metallurgists from the Urals, weapons experts from Tula, vehicle builders from Gor'ky, and collective and state farm workers from the fields around Tver and Vologda had come to the assistance of Leningrad's defenders. Getting better acquainted, under the light of illumination flares we pointed out the position of the enemy's firing positions to our arriving comrades, and we even took some shots at them together.

However, at dawn, an unexpected order arrived: our 602nd Rifle Regiment was withdrawn from the front lines. By that evening, we were already in Leningrad.

As we marched along the city's avenues, I watched as soldiers or commanders sometimes suddenly dropped out of the formation to stop briefly in front of the burned ruins of a building, from which twisted metal beams jutted out, or simply in front of a heap of bricks. I also stopped at a large pile of bricks and scrap iron on Nizhegorodskaya Street.

231

'Why are you standing here?' Naydenov asked, drawing level with me.

'My wife and son were killed here.'

Sergey removed his fur cap and quietly stood next to me.

'Seryozha, you go on; I'll catch up. I have to visit one other place,' I said.

'Osip, let me go with you,' Naydenov requested, not wishing to leave me alone. He, of course, understood where I was planning to go. We quickly ran down Aptekarsky Lane and emerged on Karl Marx Prospekt.

'In which building was Volodya living?'

'Building Thirty-Four, across from the church.'

The entrance and windows of the building's façade had been tightly boarded up. Instead of a yard, there was a deep crater from a shell explosion . . . I couldn't take another step. I suddenly grew weak at the knees, and took a seat on a bench beside the door. At one time, Volodya and I had frequently entered the building through this door together . . . Minutes passed, and then I heard Sergey's voice: 'Osip, it's time to go, or else we won't catch up with our guys.'

'Yes, it's time. Let's go.'

We caught up with our company when it had reached Engels Prospekt. Towards morning we were already at the Lisiy Nos [Fox Nose] headland, where we halted for a short rest. On that quiet night of our rest, which we spent in the luxury of a heated building, I really wanted to be left alone. After the march out of the front lines, the comrades bathed and shaved, cleaning themselves of the dense layer of trench grime. Then they slept soundly and deeply. Struck by the sight of all these slumbering men, somehow – I don't recall – I fell asleep too.

I woke up from the light touch of someone's hands. Out of habit I quickly leaped to my feet. Sergey was standing in front of me with two mess kits in his hands: 'Let's eat, then you need to report to division head-quarters; some Cherepukha has summoned you.'

'Who said?'

'The company commander ordered me to pass this information to you.'

After a quick breakfast, I indeed set off for a distant cottage on the edge of the Lisiy Nos. This is where the headquarters of the 42nd Army's 109th Rifle Division was quartered.

The chief of staff Colonel Cherepukha immediately got down to business: 'There are 150 new sniper rifles that must be sighted in. The chief of artillery supply will be here momentarily, and together with him we'll decide where it would be best to do this.'

Someone knocked on the door. Major Razhnov, the chief of the division's artillery supply, entered the room.

'We've been waiting for you,' the Colonel said. 'I hope you're familiar with the sniper instructor Pilyushin?'

'Of course! They're ready to bite my head off over these sniper rifles.'

'It's good that you've been pressured. If they hadn't been pestering you, you would have overlooked these 150 rifles. Decide between the two of you where you will organize the test firing, but the rifles must be delivered to the regiments by 1 January.'

On this day I couldn't begin to pre-align the rifles' sights; I only had time to find a place to do the shooting and to prepare the targets. Then I headed back to my company to grab some rest and ask for some help in sighting-in the guns. Over the next five days, we completed our work and all the new sniper rifles were distributed to the regiments.

Among the soldiers and commanders at the tactical field exercises, around the campfire, in the building next to the makeshift stoves – everywhere, we heard conversations about when and how the offensive would begin. There was no longer any talk about defence. Some guys were insisting that as soon as the ice on the Gulf of Finland became a bit thicker, we would be going to the assistance of the Lomonosov [Oranienbaum] grouping. Others were reporting that the time had come for our division, which had been fighting in 1941 on the Finnish front, to take back the ground that we had yielded to the enemy then.

All of this soldiers' gossip was far from the truth, but could the average soldier even know anything about *front* command's strategic plans? But one thing was clear: the offensive impulse in the units had ripened.

There were no tactical exercises on the day of 11 January 1944. Battalion commander Major Kruglov with his deputy political commander and chief of staff went around all the battalion's companies, thoroughly inspecting our combat readiness – everything right down to our feet wrappings. Even without an order, it had become clear that we were going into battle, but where, on which sector of the front? The sergeant majors gave us dinner a bit earlier on this day, and distributed three days of rations to each soldier. With the fall of darkness, the battalion moved out and set off along the highway in the direction of Leningrad.

A sense of relief ran through all the ranks of the columns: we were returning to our previous sector of the front. We marched with singing. Snow crunched beneath our feet. The soldiers and officers marched quickly, as if wanting to leave behind the shattered and burned ruins as quickly as possible, and hurried through the empty, snow-covered streets of the city.

Looking at the faces of concentration on the comrades marching next to me, I thought: 'Soon, soon the sitting at Leningrad will come to an end. All signs make it clear: the days of the Germans are numbered.' A wave of joy washed over me.

'Osip, do you know what this street is called that we're taking?' Naydenov asked.

'Gaza Prospekt. Soon there will be the Narva Gates, and further on, Stachek Prospekt.'

'My father told me about the Narva Gates and Stachek Prospekt. In the Civil War he protected the city against the bourgeoisie, and now, as you see, I've had to do the same against the fascists.'

On Stachek Square [known today as Narva Square], Sergey, looking at the silhouette of a monument, asked: 'Who is that monument to?'

'Take a closer look, you'll find out who it is.'

'It's dark; I can't make it out.'

'To Sergey Mironovich Kirov.'

At daybreak we stopped for a rest in Avtovo and waited for further orders. At a given command, the battalion quickly turned off the road into the yard of an uninhabited home. The wind was playing with the torn sheets of roofing, now lifting them up like the flap of a soldier's greatcoat, then sending them back down against the eaves of the home with a bang. Soldiers, taking shelter from the wind, scattered into the different rooms. A few minutes later, voices came from the second and third floors: 'Guys! Come here! It's like a hotel up here!'

The yard emptied. Only the drivers remained outside, trying to warm themselves by jumping up and down next to the carts and slapping their shoulder blades with their hands. The horses, covered with hoar-frost, were crunching oats, snorting and shifting from feet to feet.

Romanov's company, in the expectation of receiving an order, dispersed through the rooms of the house, but no one took off their gear: they were waiting for the order. A half-hour passed, then an hour. Romanov didn't show up. The men, exhausted by the long and rapid march, immediately started to fall asleep as soon as their heads touched the floor. More and more companies approached from the road, and soon the entire house, filled with human voices, the stamping of boots, and the snoring of sleeping people, was humming like a beehive.

Turning over from one side to the other, I saw a narrow strip of light on the floor – it was moonlight passing through the boards that covered the window. The moonbeam, as if conducting a search of the sleeping men, slid across the floor and over their faces and backs and stopped abruptly. Tracking the path of the light, I huddled closer to Naydenov's back, trying to fall asleep, but sleep wouldn't come: the cold kept penetrating my body, causing me to shiver.

'What time is it?' Sergey asked, hunching his shoulders from the cold.

'It's too dark, I can't see. Sleep!'

'If you doze a bit here, you'll turn into an ice cube . . . I'm hungry.'

I sliced off a piece of bread for him.

'You don't need to do that. It's better if I go for some water; I'll boil some tea. We'll warm up.'

Naydenov grabbed a mess tin, and cautiously stepping over the sleeping men, began to pick his way towards the exit. I found a piece of roofing metal and lit an alcohol burner on it. Instead of water, Sergey returned with a couple of mess tins fully packed with snow. Other soldiers followed our example. Somewhere close nearby, artillery salvoes began to roar, and the floor beneath our feet began to shake.

'What, has it started?' The soldiers became alert, rubbing their eyes with their fists and taking seats around a boiling mess tin. 'Hurry!'

'Take a seat, brothers, and have a swallow of hot tea, there won't be sleep today.'

The cannonade intensified. Now the roar was coming from our right and left, and even behind us, as if our house was standing in the very midst of a forest of artillery tubes, which were belching salvo after salvo of shells with blinding flashes of fire and smoke.

'That's the way! Pour it on! They're hurling them somewhere far in the distance, because you can't hear the explosions,' noticed the machine-gunner Gavrila, cautiously extending his lips towards the burning edge of an aluminium cup. In the moonlight, Gavrila's eyes seemed bottomless.

No one was now sleeping; everyone was excited. Each man hurried to down a cup of hot tea, before setting off on the long-desired, but hard path to come.

One of the soldiers loudly shouted: 'Fellows, our Zina has returned!'

Naydenov leaped off the floor with the lightness of a ballerina. I watched as the tension drained from the faces of the comrades. They were now lit with smiles, and dozens of friendly hands were extended towards Zina as she approached. It was as if she was walking down a living corridor towards me. For me, this was the most difficult reunion in my life . . . The comrades knew that Zina had taken the place of Volodya's killed mother, and knew also that Volodya was no longer. Then as if to put off this unexpected encounter, in order to allow us to pull ourselves together, they surrounded Stroyeva, and showered her with questions. She ignored them, and reaching me, Zina quietly buried her face in my chest. Life inexorably follows its own course, and we didn't have time to give ourselves over to our own personal sufferings.

On that day, 13 January 1944, as soon as twilight gathered, Major Kruglov's battalion, observing all precautionary measures, moved into the front line and took up positions near Ligovo Station.

Chapter Twenty-nine

The Joyous Day

It was seven o'clock in the morning on 16 January 1944 . . . in the east, the sun was rising. The night-time fire-fight had subsided into scattered gunshots and machine-gun bursts. But none of the soldiers left their place in the trench in order to head into a bunker to drink a cup of hot tea or to warm their frozen hands. Everyone was waiting for something, never taking their eyes off the enemy's defences.

Naydenov and I crept into a sniper emplacement near the embankment of the Leningrad-Ligovo railroad. I opened the gun port, and Sergey began to burn some firewood in our little stove. At this early hour of a winter morning, a few fluffy snowflakes were whirling in the frosty air. Sometimes they descended to a point just above the ground, when suddenly, seized by a light, barely perceptible breath of wind, they would soar into the air again.

While on the defence, we had learned to value these minutes of calm. How precious they were to a man caught in protracted fighting!

Romanov and Stroyeva dropped by our emplacement: 'Greetings, snipers! What's the news?'

'Nothing to boast about. Not a single fascist is showing his ugly face,' Naydenov replied, rising so as to yield his spot on the bench to the guests.

Stroyeva lightly touched my arm, and I gave her my place at the periscope. Romanov pulled out an embroidered velvet pouch: 'Let's have a smoke, guys.'

'Who made such a stylish pouch for you, Comrade Commander? You, Zina?' Sergey asked. Stroyeva shook her head negatively.

'Guys, you'll never guess whose hands sewed and embroidered this gift.'

Romanov went silent. He attentively looked over the pouch, as if seeing it for the first time. At this moment, quite likely, his heart and thoughts were far from our emplacement.

'A Siberian woman sent this to me. Now when I take it into my hands, my mind sees this sweet woman; her hands, her concentrated face, and her dexterous fingers holding the needle and silk thread.'

Was she thinking, this distant unknown woman, that by sewing this pouch, it would stir some soldier's soul? Naydenov gingerly took the pouch, carefully put two fingers into it, and pulled out a generous pinch of tobacco. Returning the pouch to the commander, he carefully ran his fingers along the dark blue cord, on the ends of which were hanging two little rose-coloured tassels. It seemed as if he was caressing a tender young woman's hand. Speaking to no one in particular, he said, 'Russian women have a good heart. Thanks to them for everything.'

Suddenly Stroyeva raised her hand to alert us: 'Do you hear?' She tilted her head to one side and strained to hear something.

We all pricked up our ears. Our hearing caught the distant sound of artillery fire. I thought it was just a typical bombardment of Leningrad, but there were no shell explosions in our rear. Romanov glanced at his watch and said, 'It's 8.20 am. That's the forts of Kronshtadt's coastal defences conducting the next barrage on the enemy rear.' The company commander, hurrying to leave, excused himself: 'My conversation with you has wandered, fellows, but I still need to check on the machine-gunners, to see whether they have everything in order. Sergey, come with me.'

It was a bit of subterfuge by Romanov: he was taking Naydenov along with him in order to leave me alone with Zina. Stroyeva also understood this. When we were alone, she quietly said, 'Yosif, forgive me if you can; I didn't have enough strength, when I found out about Voloden'ka's death, to inform you of it right away.'

'What are you saying, Zina? How can I be upset with you?'

Quietly wiping away tears, Zina sat down on the bench next to the little stove and began to warm her hands. I took her place at the periscope and continued to observe the enemy trenches. Having searched for some time and not seeing anything suspicious, I glanced at Zina, who was being silent. The firewood was burning brightly in the stove, but Stroyeva was sweetly sleeping on the bench, her head resting on both hands.

I couldn't tear my eyes away from that dear face, from which sleep had wiped away the traces of grief. The two nostrils of her well-shaped nose smoothly expanded and contracted again as she breathed. The long black eyelashes of her closed eyelids occasionally twitched like a child's. In order not to disturb my dear friend's minutes of rest, I tiptoed away from the embrasure and began to warm my hands by the fire.

By now the sound of an artillery cannonade in the direction of Lomonosov [Oranienbaum] was clearly audible. It was the beginning of the destruction of the German-fascist forces in front of Leningrad. The

Lomonosov grouping was granted the privilege of firing the first shots that announced the initiation of the complete expulsion of the Nazis from their positions around the city. A few minutes later, the general artillery preparation for the offensive began.

At this triumphant and stern moment, I just had to wake up Zina. I wanted her to witness the awesome fire that the Soviet artillery was now unleashing on the enemy. Zina's eyes sparkled joyfully. 'The offensive!' she delightedly exclaimed. The two of us ran out into the trench together.

The entire area between the front lines and Leningrad was blanketed with the smoke from the artillery salvoes. Naydenov came running up to us: 'Guys! It's begun! When will it be our turn? I'm afraid we'll miss the tanks.'

Stroyeva took Naydenov by the elbow: 'We'll see them, Seryozha, they won't pass by us unnoticed.'

The Red Army men were emerging from their shelters one after the other. They all, as if on command, looked first in the direction of Leningrad, and then at the enemy trenches, above which smoke was billowing ever higher into the sky. The machine-gunner Gavrila was also here. The soldiers loved him for his good, courageous heart and sharp sense of humour. Although Gavrila was a very experienced soldier, he nevertheless wondered aloud: 'It's interesting; why aren't the Germans firing?'

Sergey looked at him with astonishment: 'What, have you lost your marbles? Don't you see that our artillery has stunned the devils? Just wait a bit; they'll come round and then they'll begin.'

'Then why the hell are we waiting? Why aren't we attacking?'

'Go ask the company commander.'

Shells were rushing by just over our heads. I had to grab my cap, so the shock wave didn't tear it from my head.

'What, a little breeze is blowing it, huh?' Naydenov laughingly asked Gavrila who was holding onto his cap with both hands.

The ground was shaking convulsively and rumbling. Zina proposed, 'Let's go to the machine-gunners' bunker. If we stay here, for all we know, we might get hit by a fragment.'

But just then, our ground attack planes flew quite low over the front lines. A little higher in the sky, there appeared a good hundred bombers or more, escorted by a large number of fighters. The sky was humming, lit up with the flashes of bursting shells. The bombers were flying slowly, as if admiring the terrible panorama of the combat below them, and searching for the necessary place, where they would deliver their needed loads.

Powerful explosions sounded somewhere nearby. Clumps of frozen earth tumbled from the trench walls and fell to the bottom. A continuous roar filled the ears, a foul smoke hindered breathing, and one had to grab something to keep from falling down. We made our way through the smoke to the bunker. The machine-gunners greeted us with exclamations: 'Aah! Sergey has brought his snipers to our aid.' They were playing cards. 'Our Sergey hasn't been lucky: he doesn't even have time to sit, before he's out of the game again.' Under the terms of the game, the losing pair of players didn't have the right to sit down, and had to wait their turn to challenge the winners again while standing.

'And you, Gavrila, win at first, but then you lose your cool,' Naydenov replied, taking a seat at the table.

The soldiers were trying any way possible to distract themselves from the roar of the artillery exchange, and trying to settle their nerves in a card game. They were laughing and needling each other, but their pale faces and trembling hands betrayed their agitation.

Gavrila held a fan of cards in his hand and parried Naydenov's attack: 'Come, come, give me another shot! What, you don't have one? Then sit down and play.'

'Draw another, braggart; you can't beat an ace with a jack.'

Suddenly a blast wave blew the door from its hinges. The cards flew through the air like jackdaws, stuck briefly to the ceiling as if they were wet, and then fell back to the floor.

'Gavrila, shut the door, or else we'll get a draught. You'll catch a cold; after all, you're the sickly one here,' Naydenov said, gathering up the cards on the floor.

'Seryozha, I have a well-tested remedy for colds: steam a bit in a *banya*, 150 grams of Russian bitters and then snuggle under a blanket with a woman. It will take a cold away as if by a hand.'

'Have you ever tried horseradish with black radish?'

'What of it?'

'It helps against chills.' [Even today, this is a common Russian folk remedy to boost the immune system and help ward off colds.]

The door was re-hung, the verbal crossfire ended, and the game resumed. The time was 11.10 am. A shell landed somewhere near the bunker and sand rained down from the ceiling.

'Fie, you devils; look how careless these artillerymen are: they just threw dust in my queen's eye,' Gavrila said, wiping the dust from his cards with his hand.

Zina, sitting on a case of machine-gun belts, was sewing a button onto a sheepskin coat. An older soldier was sitting next to her, enveloped in the smoke from his hand-rolled cigarette. A deeply pensive expression was frozen on his face. Zina attached the button, tied off the knot, and then quickly cut the thread with her teeth: 'Go ahead, put it on; you won't be walking around with open flaps in the rear.'

'Thank you, Zinochka. While watching as you were sewing, I was thinking of my own daughter.' The soldier donned the coat, buttoned it up, and picked up his submachine-gun.

Suddenly a sentry's head popped into the doorway of the bunker: 'Fellows! Our guys on Pulkovo Heights have gone on the attack!'

'He-he! Brothers, now the fun has started, and you, Seryozha, are bored!' Gavrila shouted, leaping to his feet. 'Machine gun to action!'

Jostling each other in the narrow entry of the door, the soldiers spilled out into the trench. Each of us wanted more quickly to witness the inspiring moments of the attack start, for which we had so longingly and seemingly interminably waited. But it was impossible to see anything even in our close proximity to Pulkovo Heights – there was too much smoke. We could hear the increasing roar of human voices and rifle and machine-gun fire. Fiery arrows streaked through the smoke in flocks, as if in pursuit of each other. It was the rockets from our Guards mortar units, firing on the enemy rear.

Someone's enthusiastic voice cried out: 'Maslennikov's Guardsmen [the 30th Guards Rifle Corps of Maslennikov's 42nd Army] have gone on the attack!'

'We can hear, we can hear, buddy; don't interfere,' Sergey said.

Each man wanted to sear this triumphant, long-awaited moment in his memory. None of the soldiers paid any attention to the near explosions of enemy shells and mortar rounds. Everyone gazed as if transfixed in the direction of Pulkovo, where apparently hand-to-hand fighting was already going on.

We stood in our trench until late evening, waiting for the order to attack. But it never came, and the disappointed soldiers and officers dispersed and went back to their shelters.

'Damn it, what's happening? We're sitting here snugly, while our neighbours are fighting!' Naydenov exclaimed in disbelief, reaching for the tobacco pouch in his pocket.

'They're Guardsmen, Seryozha, so they were ordered to start the attack first,' Zina replied, pouring tea into cups for everyone.

'The "Guardsmen", the "Guardsmen"! What, you think they're not people just like we are? They get the honour and glory, while we must wait . . .'

'Seryozha, the high command knows better, who should start the attack and where. Why argue?'

'It's insulting, Osip; you know we were also prepared.'

'It's still a long way to Berlin! Drink some tea and let's play cards,' Gavrila proposed.

Naydenov, not answering his comrade, gripped his cup and noisily gulped his tea. The sniper's eyes were shining with a malevolent light. He hastily finished the tea, stuck his cup into his knapsack, grabbed his rifle from the stack, stuck several grenades into his gas mask bag, and headed out into the trench.

Following after Naydenov, Gavrila said, 'Once again God has given me a troubled lad. Look at him; he's going out after the Fritzes alone.'

After midnight on 17 January, the enemy's heavy artillery stopped bombarding our lines. Only lighter guns and their five-barrelled rocket launchers continued to fire on us. Our artillery duelled with theirs throughout the night until dawn. On the Pulkovo Heights, the sound of fighting gradually receded ever more deeply into the enemy's positions. Even more persistently and loudly, you could hear the wondering shouts of our troops: 'Why aren't we attacking?'

On 17 January, a Party assembly took place in the battalion. Major Kruglov explained to us that according to our high command's plans, the Lomonosov [Oranienbaum] grouping with the support of Kronshtadt's sailors was to crack open the enemy's defences in the area of Staryi Petergof and Kotla Station and exploit in the direction of Russko-Vysotskoye, where it was to link up with the forces of Maslennikov's 42nd Army, which were attacking towards Krasnoye Selo and Ropsha. We would be informed when this link-up took place. Then it would be our job to destroy the encircled group of hostile forces thus trapped against the coastline of the Gulf of Finland. It only remained for us to wait for the order.

As we were leaving the commander's bunker, Zina grabbed Naydenov by the arm. Looking into his eyes, she asked: 'Well, is everything now clear to you?'

'I should think so!' Sergey answered with embarrassment, falling in step with Zina's shorter stride.

In the course of 18 January, the situation became extremely tense. Heated exchanges of rifle and machine-gun fire flared up here and there along our line. Enemy artillery now and then answered the fire of our guns and *Katiushas*. Our artillerymen worked over the lines of the enemy's defences with inexorable strength, because indeed there was much work to be done: we knew from the Staro-Panovo operation that the Germans had eighteen fully-fortified lines, with five or six rows of barbed wire in front of each line, and pillboxes and bunkers spaced every 100 to 150 metres along the trench line, tied together with communication trenches. The entire 10-kilometre depth of the enemy's defensive belt had been heavily sewn with anti-personnel and anti-tank mines. Yet a year and a half had passed since the Staro-Panovo operation – and the Germans had been busy ever since.

The artillerymen shifted their fire from one line of defence to the next. Just as women in a garden, having finished weeding one row move on to the next and a third, our artillery was working over this fortified belt of ground.

The day was winding down. Twilight imperceptibly changed into night. Naydenov, Stroyeva and I had dinner together with the machine-gunners in their bunker. Two loaded heavy machine guns were standing at the ready in the embrasure.

'Guys,' Gavrila asked us, setting aside his emptied mess kit, 'what if our artillery has just been wasting shells?'

'Wasting?' Zina asked.

'What if the Germans have pulled out?'

'Abandoned their lines?'

'They sensed that they were being surrounded, so they pulled out.'

Everyone was silent. Who can know the enemy's habits better than a soldier who has been face-to-face with him for years? Each of us knew the daily routines of the German soldiers. We immediately noticed the slightest change in their behaviour. Everyone also knew that the Germans were terribly frightened of becoming encircled during a battle. So now, when Soviet forces were fighting in their rear, could they hold their current lines? This question occupied our thoughts on those days, while we waited for the order to attack. Gavrila was especially vexed. He never stopped talking about this possibility in the bunker.

'Let's pay a visit to their trenches; everything will become clear,' Naydenov jokingly proposed to him.

'Ah, right, Seryozha, let's just run over and take a look at how they're living.'

'Fine, let's go look; I'm ready at this moment.'

Someone's voice rang out from an upper bunk: 'You're playing the fool, guys; who's going to let you take matters into your own hands?'

'You just sit there on that upper bunk and be quiet; we don't need your counsel,' Gavrila retorted.

The talk remained just that. None of us paid a visit to the German trenches.

On the morning of 20 January in the middle of breakfast, the door to the bunker suddenly flew wide open. The company commander's messenger Sergeant Bazanov flew in together with a swirl of snow.

'Guys! Guys!' He kept shouting one and the same word over and over, while twirling in a dance in the middle of the bunker with his hands above his head.

Gavrila asked, 'Hey, did you lose your mind running over here? Tell us *sensibly* what has happened.'

'Oh, you people of delayed action!' the Sergeant began to yell. 'You see our forces this morning linked up with the Lomonosov grouping in the village of Russko-Vysotskoye. Krasnoye Selo and Ropsha are ours!'

Bazanov's words struck us all like thunderbolts. The soldiers squeezed the poor red-headed fellow as if he had encircled the fascist forces on the coast of the Gulf of Finland by himself!

For the next hours, none of the soldiers even tried to get an hour of sleep. Everyone was waiting for daybreak, so at last we could begin the work of liquidating the encircled hostile troops in the towns and villages along the coastline. From the enemy side, heavy and light machine guns chattered all night, but there wasn't a single rifle shot or submachine-gun burst.

'They're firing from machine guns, but they're afraid to move out into their trenches,' Naydenov said, setting up an armoured shield on the parapet. 'Why do you need that shield, Seryozha?' Zina asked.

'I want to examine the terrain, to find a better way to reach their trenches.'

In the pale rays of the late January dawn, the outlines of objects began to emerge from the shadows. A cold east wind was stirring the bare branches of trees and blowing fine granules of snow in writhing waves across the frozen snow crust, sending them into the craters, the bottom of the trench and into the firing slits of the emplacements.

With the arrival of dawn, the blood began to pound in the temples all the more strongly. The heart was tormented by a thirst for vengeance. There was a desire to pay the enemy back for all the sufferings inflicted on the defenders of Leningrad. The ears caught every sound and rustle coming from the enemy line. We waited for the command to attack. Zina was standing next to me, leaning with her shoulder against the trench wall. Her vision was focused on Leningrad, illuminated by the rays of the morning sun. Then she energetically shook her head, straightened up, and turning towards Naydenov, asked, 'What are you thinking over, Sergey?'

'I was at home, Zinochka, talking with my Mama and sister. You know, when I left for the war, my sister was little. But now she can write herself, "Come home soon."'

Stroyeva gave a shudder, hastily covered her face with her hands and said flatly: 'I don't have Voloden'ka any longer . . .'

The loud shout of the company runner suddenly rang out: 'Snipers! Get to the company commander, pronto!'

Bazanov disappeared as quickly as he had appeared. Zina's momentary disarray instantly disappeared – just as if the wind had blown it away. She pushed away from the trench wall and glanced over at me, as if seeking forgiveness for her moment of weakness.

To the left of Ligovo Station, at the very foot of the Pulkovo Heights, units of the 189th Rifle Division were already engaged in fighting. There was a noticeable stirring in our trench line. The soldiers and commanders were checking for the last time whether everything was ready for the decisive charge forward.

We met Romanov next to the company command post. Despite the urgency of the meeting and even a certain abruptness in his motions before the start of battle, the commander's gaze was as soft as always, almost tender. Now the white scar, which lay across his left jaw, cut obliquely across his left brow and disappeared under his fur cap stood out even more clearly on his excited face, which been reddened by the cold.

'Not a step, not a shot without my command,' Romanov said succinctly and clearly, looking at his watch. 'We are through defending! Within several minutes we're going on the offensive. On the offensive, though, comrades, as you know well, sniper tactics change sharply. Keep watch for enemy machine-gunners and snipers, and we will deal with everything else. In general, you will be located with me.'

So here it was, the long-awaited minute! First one, after it another, and then a third green signal flare soared into the sky. Without a single shout, we rushed towards the German lines. We took the first and second trenches with unprecedented speed. We never stopped; we tore into the depth of the Nazi defences, destroying everything the least bit suspicious in our path.

Germans were crawling out of shelters with widely opened, twisted mouths; some of them were crying. There were also a few who threw down their weapons, gripped their head with their hands, and started running away. But where can one go to get away from the well-aimed bullet of an avenger?

At the fourth trench line Naydenov, stopping next to an enemy bunker, shouted: 'Guys! Look what the Nazis are doing with their soldiers!'

There was a very young-looking German soldier standing beside a heavy machine gun. His left wrist was chained to it; the ammunition belt was untouched. With his bayonet, Naydenov broke a link of the chain and freed the German from the machine gun. The condemned man looked at the Russian soldier with gratitude, saying something to him in his own tongue.

'Who is he?' Sergey asked Romanov.

'He's being punished.'

'What sort of crime did he commit to be chained to that machine gun?' Naydenov asked.

'He says that he's being punished for saying aloud, "We can't beat the communists."'

That evening, when the enemy's fortified lines lay behind us, we gathered in the settlement of Gorelovo to grab a bite to eat. One of the comrades dragged in a case of German rum. Gavrila poured a cup of the amber fluid and handed it to Naydenov: 'Sergey, go ahead, drink up. The guys are saying it's great stuff.'

'Thanks, chug it down yourself, as long as he's brought in this execrable stuff, but in any case I'll stick to Russian bitters. You drink a mug of bitters, and your insides begin to glow and you give a grunt of satisfaction, but you just can't get this stuff down your throat. Go ahead, Gavrila, have a slice of bread and butter. Eat a bit, so your breath doesn't reek of that filth.'

The divisions of the 42nd Army mopped the Nazi occupiers from the coastline of the Gulf of Finland. Once that was done, we moved out towards the highway.

Chapter Thirty

The Photograph

Marching shoulder to shoulder with my comrades, I saw that many of them, when reaching the side of the highway, stopped and looked in the direction of Leningrad. They were silently saying farewell to their native city and their Leningrader allies.

The first kilometres of liberated land . . . everything around was in ruins. Each of us had one desire: to see some peaceful Soviet citizens soon. However, no one came out to the road to greet their liberators. Marching through the streets of villages and passing the ruins and scorched chimneys rising from them, we quickened our step. Naydenov nudged my arm: 'Osip, did the Nazis really destroy all our people? If only just a dog would bark, it would be a bit easier on my heart.'

'During the fighting, the people hid. As things become quiet again, they'll return.'

'Where will they go?'

'Back to these scorched chimneys, Seryozha, and they'll build new homes. When we return home, you'll see.'

We marched through Krasnoye Selo at dawn. There were still several intact buildings here. On the outskirts of town next to the cemetery, there were German large-calibre field guns that had been bombarding Leningrad. Several of them lay toppled over or were out of their firing positions. Just beyond the cemetery, there were neatly laid out rows of German graves. An emaciated elderly woman was standing alone outside a cottage next to a pond. With one hand she was holding onto a fence pole, and with the other she was waving a greeting to the passing Soviet troops.

I thought back to the days of our retreats . . . I recalled that old woman with the fair-haired granddaughter, whom I had met among the refugees on my way to the front after my first wounding. Just where were they now?

We didn't encounter another single living resident on the road between Krasnoye Selo and Ropsha. The streets of Ropsha were piled with rubble. We had to pick our way through the ruins, clamber over knocked-out and burned-out tanks, self-propelled guns and transports, and dash through

247

the ashes of homes, some of which were still smoking. Once beyond the town, we sighed with relief.

Having passed the Glukhovo State Farm, we entered an area under enemy artillery fire. To our left we could hear the sound of fighting. Our regiments halted in some woods, close to the settlement of Dyatlitsy.

The first night in a log hut . . . Someone built a fire in the fireplace – the first soldiers' fire on liberated land. Each of the comrades wanted to toss at least a small dry twig or pine cone into this fire and to warm his frozen hands. Just how many memories of peacetime did this little fire conjure up in the soldiers! Sitting by the fire, I looked around at the faces of my comrades. They were thoughtful and sad. As I reflected on my own once-happy home and family, I sensed that my comrades' thoughts were flying away, just like the sparks from this fire, back to their own homes and villages. I thought of my own native Belorussia. Where now was my mother? Where was she, the dear old woman? I recalled my distant and yet simultaneously close childhood, when young men and women on the eve before Ivan Kupala Day would sing and dance in a ring around just such a night-time campfire.[4] So many tender words about love and friendship have been spoken on such a peaceful night! I remembered that grey-haired old man with his bucket of freshly-caught carp next to the pond, who had offered us his catch. Was he still alive?

On this front-line road around this first comforting fire on liberated land, we became lost in our thoughts and deaf to the sounds of nearby shell explosions. The soldiers, each immersed in their own thoughts, quietly cleaned their weapons, wrote letters home, brewed tea, or were stirring the kasha in their mess kits with spoons.

'Seryozha, do you hear? A dog is barking!' Gavrila was plainly happy.

'Just go to sleep, or else for all I know, even canaries will start singing in your rummy noggin.'

'First, I'll fry up a little fat, eat some kasha, and then I'll collapse until morning. Do you want a spoonful?'

Sergeant Bazanov, gazing with unblinking eyes at the fire, spoke up with a question: 'Guys, which of you happened to pass through these places during the days of your retreat?'

---

4. Ivan Kupala (John the Baptist) Day is a holiday celebrated in Russia, Belorussia and the Ukraine, marking the day on the calendar opposite the winter solstice holiday of Korochun. The night before the summer holiday is an occasion for mischief, but it also traditionally was a time for bonfires, around which young men and women would gather and flirt.

'Why?' Stroyeva took an interest in the question.

'My brother's grave is somewhere near Volosovo Station. A comrade wrote me about it.'

Bazanov's words brought a lot to mind: how many more graves of our combat comrades and dear ones would the boots of the Nazi occupiers trample!

Zina fell silent. Naydenov, hugging his knees, sighed deeply. One after the other, the comrades quietly lay down to sleep with their heads resting on their palms and arms, and soon the cabin was filled with the vigorous snoring of sleeping people.

The next morning, tanks and self-propelled guns were moving along the highway, followed by hurrying trucks with roaring engines. The cabin rocked and shook as the heavy tanks rolled past. The corner of the tent canvas that was covering the entry lifted and a head leaned into the cabin. I saw a face, reddened by the cold, and a pair of dark eyes, which were anxiously looking us over.

'Which of you are the snipers Pilyushin and Stroyeva?' a voice rang out.

'I'm Pilyushin, what of it?'

'The battalion commander wants to see you immediately.'

The battalion headquarters was located on the edge of the forest. Messengers from the company commanders, signalmen and submachine-gunners were bustling around the headquarters' tent, which had been set up on the snow. Two heavy machine guns were standing on sledges outside the tent. Nearby, the battalion quartermaster was distributing camouflage suits to scouts and snipers.

At sunrise on 24 January, it began to snow heavily; the falling snow reduced visibility to less than 20 metres. The order was given to fall in. Shivering from the cold, soldiers and officers stepped out of the cabins, formed up into companies, and twenty minutes later we were already marching along a country road towards Mestanovo. To our left, in the direction of Kas'kovo, artillery firing could be heard.

Major Kruglov's battalion was in the vanguard of the regiment. Stroyeva caught up with me and gave me a brand new camouflage uniform that had been taken from the Germans.

'I got it from the sergeant major, since ours are torn,' she said.

'Have you seen Sergey?'

'I saw him; he promised to come.'

A group of prisoners being escorted by two Soviet submachine-gunners was approaching in the opposite direction.

'Fellows, where did you catch these?' someone asked.

'In Kas'kovo. Only they're not Germans, they're Hungarians [again, this is likely a misidentification of members of the Spanish Legion, which was retreating through that area, trying to reach the Luga River]. We still haven't caught up with their main forces . . .'

The battalion approached a forest and halted. Scouts were sent forward to probe the woods. Bumping into an ambush is the most frightening thing in combat. The scouts moved into the woods with their weapons at the ready. On the edge of the forest, we saw a man in civilian dress appear among the trees like a shadow, who then disappeared into a patch of fir trees. Kruglov raised his arm. The battalion quickly deployed off the road into a line of battle in expectations of an enemy attack.

'Yosif, couldn't that have been a partisan?' Stroyeva asked.

'I don't know, Zina.'

'Partisans don't have any reason to hide from us,' an unfamiliar sub-machine-gunner interjected.

'There's no need to guess, the scouts will clear up everything,' his neighbour replied, holding his submachine-gun at the ready.

Suddenly we saw an old woman running and stumbling across a clearing, followed by a boy of around 12 to 14 years of age. They stopped on the side of the road and looked at the Soviet soldiers with joyful eyes. The woman, breathing heavily but smiling, placed a hand to her breast. Tears rolled down her pale, thin face. She didn't try to wipe them away. The adolescent was standing next to her, looking over all the soldiers with shining eyes.

Just then the woman, as if recalling something very important, franti-cally waved her hands and loudly started to shout: 'Sonnies! Dear ones! Don't go down this road, the Germans have recently thrown something across it!'

The adolescent walked up to Major Kruglov with a resolute expression on his face and said in a thin voice, 'The fascists have mined it. I saw it myself. At night I sprinkled a bucket of ashes to mark the place where they started to mine it.' Kruglov affably placed his hand on the boy's shoulder: 'What's your name, fearless one?'

'Shura.'

'Tell me, Shura, are there a lot of Germans in the village up ahead?'

'At least a hundred; they have two cannons and a lot of Hotchkiss machine guns.'

'Can you tell me, Shura, how we might approach the village unnoticed?'

'Let's go, I'll lead the way.'

'No, little friend, just tell me, and we'll find the path ourselves.'

The young adolescent, feeling that the commander was taking counsel from him just as he would from an adult, became more animated and cheerful. He sniffed his nose, and his little eyes sparkled with delight. Energetically pushing back his cap, he said, 'I'll show you, Pops. See that birch tree over there by the road? It is one and a half kilometres from it to the village.'

'I see it.'

'Now, to the left of it is a ravine – the Gestapo shot the Jews in it a while back – and if you take it you can reach the outskirts of the village; the Germans won't see you and there aren't any mines. I'll guide you there in a flash.'

'Thanks for the advice, Shurik. We'll make our way to the fascists without you, and you keep an eye on your grandmother.'

Stroyeva walked up to the boy and asked, 'Shurik, just how did you know it was us?'

'It was obvious! You see, the Fritzes don't walk around so boldly; they're more often driving around in vehicles, or else slink around on foot, just like dogs. But you? You're walking just like you're at home, that's how I knew.'

Zina, spotting Shurik's reddened hands, took off her mittens and handed them to the lad: 'Put them on, hero, or else your little hands are going to freeze.'

The boy, clutching his chest, took a step back from Stroyeva and slowly shook his head: 'I won't take them, Auntie! How will you hold a rifle with your bare hands? As for me, I can get by.' With that, he stuck his hands into the opposite sleeves of his old coat, while looking at the Russian female soldier with bright eyes.

Zina asked, 'But where do you live?'

'In the woods.'

'How?'

'Very simply. As the Gestapo began to herd our villagers to Germany, my Granny and I fled into the woods one night. Back in the summer I built a dugout, chopped lots of firewood, and saved spuds and salt.'

'Where are your Papa and Mama?'

'Papa's at war and the Germans took Mama away.'

Soldiers had gathered in a tight ring around Shurik and his grandmother. Each wanted to say a good word to the first Soviet citizens we had encountered on land liberated from the Germans. But we were in a real hurry: on the outskirts of Mestanovo, our advance guard was already trading shots with the enemy. The small, thin figure of the Russian lad and his clever, expressive eyes remained in my memory for the rest of my life. Even now, I can hear his parting words: 'Comrades! Be careful, the fascists are very evil!'

As soon as the scattering of shots was heard up ahead from Mestanovo, Kruglov ordered the 1st Rifle Company to outflank the Germans on the west, and the 3rd Rifle Company to outflank them on the east, in order to encircle them in the village. We snipers were ordered to pick off enemy machine-gunners and snipers.

The companies disappeared into the woods one after the other. The snipers paired off and headed off in different routes towards Mestanovo. Zina and I, reaching the birch tree that Shurik had pointed out, dropped to the ground. In front of us there stretched a snow-covered plain, which separated us from the village. It was impossible to spot a soldier dressed in a camouflage suit from here. We had to get to within at least 600 metres of the village, in order to see any Germans.

'Yosif, I'll start crawling towards that tall clump of weeds over there, while you keep a sharp watch for any nearby German snipers. I'll let you know when I reach that clump . . .'

Without waiting for my reply, Zina quickly crawled away. Soon her camouflage suit merged with the shroud of snow and I lost sight of her. I scrutinized every peg and fence post on the outskirts of Mestanovo, but I couldn't see even the flash of a gunshot or a German shifting position at a run.

'But what if Zina fails to notice a snow-covered mine?' My brain kept ticking over this frightful thought. 'Why hadn't I stopped her?' The blood was pounding in my temple so strongly that I didn't hear any shots. My eyes were watering from the strain, but I didn't have time to look to the side or even to wipe away a tear with my hand – I was afraid to miss the enemy sharpshooter, who might notice Zina and kill her. I wanted to crawl out after her as quickly as possible, to catch up with her, so as to never part from her again for even a second.

I continued to gaze intently first at the overgrown weeds, then at the buildings on the outskirts of Mestanovo. It seemed to me that an eternity had passed, but there was still no sign of Zina at the designated spot. I lost all patience. An insurmountable desire to be with her pushed me forward. Just then, the long stalks of the weeds stirred . . .

'Zina!' involuntarily exploded from my lips.

She lifted the gauze face covering of her hood, and her flushed face sharply stood out against the snow. I set off at a quick crawl, without looking around, in order to join her. After crawling some distance, I stopped to get my bearings: in front of me there was a small mound of snow, which blocked my view of the village. In the snow to the side of the mound were human tracks. Forgetting my caution, I set off at a run in a low crouch along these tracks.

'Get down! Crawl! Crazy, they'll see you!'

I fell into the snow and took a look around. Lying not far from me was Zina, or more accurately, I caught sight of the soles of her felt boots.

'Yosif, what happened?'

'I got worried . . . it will pass.'

'Me too. We won't ever part again in battle.'

It was now no further than 500 or 600 metres to Mestanovo, but where the Germans were hiding, we couldn't see. It seemed that the deep snow covering the roofs of the buildings was pressing their timbered walls into the earth with its weight. The snowy mantle covering the ground was up to the level of the windows.

'The Fritzes are obviously firing from the garrets. We'll have to crawl off to one side, in order to spot them,' I proposed.

'There's no need to crawl across the field, we'll keep watch on the streets and front yards of the homes from here,' Zina replied, warming the tips of the fingers on her left hand with her breath.

Somewhere quite nearby to the right and left, heavy and light machine guns opened up, accompanied by the sound of shots.

'Our guys have reached Mestanovo,' I thought with relief.

'Yosif, do you see that haystack next to the wall of the barn?'

'I see it; what of it?'

'Take a better look at it. It seems to me that straw is moving.'

'Keep an eye on it, and I'll keep watching the streets.'

At the moment when the troops of Kruglov's battalion had closed the ring around the village, volleys of *Katiusha* rockets streaked over our heads one after the other. Geysers of smoke and fire erupted on the streets and in the gardens, and several buildings burst into flame at once. A pair of light brown horses, harnessed to a two-horse sled, escaped the yard of one of the burning buildings and darted into the streets; they tore through the village in a wild gallop in our direction. Terrified by the shell explosions, the horses increased their pace. Clouds of steam billowed from their large nostrils. They raced past us directly across the field, and just when they ran out onto the road, there was an explosion. With a piercing whinny, the horses rose on their hind legs and collapsed to the ground.

'Yosif, look quickly, the haystack has come to life!'

Literally like baby chicks from under the wing of a hen, the heads of fascists poked out of the haystack. Then as if frightened by the appearance of a hawk, they simultaneously dropped back into the straw. Suddenly the haystack rose above the ground and began to turn in place. I managed to spot the back of one of the fascists. At that very second, Zina fired on the exposed back. The Nazi fell to the snow. One German leaped out of the haystack, and ran around the corner of the barn. Pressing against the wall, he started to look in our direction.

Reloading her rifle, I thought that Zina was going to shoot this fascist. She hesitated, plainly waiting for me to fire, but at this moment the German decided his fate on his own: he tore off his white camouflage cloak, and waving it over his head, he came running to meet the Soviet soldiers.

Fighting for this last German strongpoint flared up, which blocked approaches to the intersection of the Leningrad-Volosovo-Kingisepp roads from the north. The Nazis, surrounded on all sides in Mestanovo, fought with the desperation of the condemned. They were firing machine guns and mortars from the windows and garrets of the buildings. Everywhere you could hear rifle shots and bursts of submachine-guns, but the fighting still hadn't reached the point of hand-to-hand combat.

We were also shooting at the windows, from which German heavy and light machine guns were firing. Suddenly Zina tapped my arm: 'Do you see the Germans?' she asked. 'Just where are you looking! Over there next to the house by the tall tree; they're setting up a mortar.'

I had barely managed to pick out the mortar men when Zina fired. One of the Germans collapsed on his side, and the other two disappeared around a corner in a flash.

'That's better . . . They thought they could deploy a mortar in front of our eyes,' Zina said as she reloaded her rifle.

Every minute of fighting brought us closer to the point of hand-to-hand struggle. Then as if to mock us, it began to snow heavily. It interfered with our vision, so we couldn't see what the enemy was intending to do in the streets of the village.

'Yosif, we need to change positions; I can't see anything.'

We had not yet managed to shift position, when a company from Kruglov's battalion burst into the German strongpoint. Close-range fighting developed. Submachine-gun bursts, the explosions of hand grenades, a scattered firing from windows and from around the corner of homes and barns, and the shouts and cries of soldiers . . .

I set off at a run towards the barn with the haystack. Zina started after me. A machine gun opened up from somewhere, and the bullets began to crack all around me, but didn't hit me. Running up to the corner of the barn, I glanced back. She wasn't there.

'Zina!' I shouted.

There was no answer. I rushed back through the snow along my own tracks. Not far from the spot where we had been firing, I saw Zina: she was lying in the snow, her legs folded under her.

'Zina! Where are you wounded? What's wrong?'

She was silent. Her eyelashes quivered, but her eyes didn't open. Her ruddy face had grown pale, and her lips were tightly compressed. She was dead . . . How long I lay there beside her, my face buried in the snow, I don't recall. I didn't hear it when the final shot rang out on the streets of Mestanovo. With the fall of darkness, I took the arms of my faithful combat-friend and tenderly crossed them on her chest. Then I lifted her body like it was something most precious, and carried the woman, whom my motherless son had called Mama, into the village. Naydenov met me on the street. He quietly removed his fur cap from his head, pressed his lips together, and followed me to where the bodies of our collected fallen comrades were lying beside a garden. I gently laid the body of Zina next to them.

Kruglov removed her Party card and soldier's booklet from her breast pocket. In it, he also found a bloodstained photograph of Zinaida Stroyeva in a military uniform and silently handed it to me . . .

Chapter Thirty-one

Familiar Places

Short are the soldier's minutes when saying goodbye to his comrade-friends who have fallen in battle. Head hastily uncovered, on bended knee by the fraternal grave, you furtively wipe away a burning tear, squint towards the west, and once again you're taking the road towards new battles.

Major Kruglov's battalion was delayed in the liberated Mestanovo, waiting for the remaining battalions of the 602nd Regiment to come up. We spent the night in the badly damaged homes and barns. At dawn on 27 January, we moved out and with a swift thrust cut the Leningrad-Kingisepp highway in the vicinity of Kirkovitsa. Having hurled the Nazis from the road, we pursued the retreating foe without pause across a field. By evening we reached the banks of the Suma River. But we didn't have a chance to rest.

The battalion received a new assignment: to drive the Germans out of Kaibolovo and link up with neighbouring units, who were operating along the highway and the Kotly-Udasolov railroad. But troops of the 2nd Shock Army forestalled this mission: before our approach, they had already kicked the Germans out of Kaibolovo, forced a crossing of the Suma River, and were already fighting for the intersection of the highway and railroad on the approaches to the settlement of Kikhtolka.

Passing through this little village, where battle had just been raging, we saw a familiar scene: wrecked and abandoned combat equipment, both ours and the enemy's, scattered everywhere, and soldiers' corpses at almost every step. A woman was standing alone in front of a demolished home, holding a small bundle. Gazing at the ruins, she was crying . . .

Our battalion moved out down the Suma River and stopped at the edge of a forest in one of the bends of the river. Here we could rest, have a cup of hot tea, and if circumstances permitted, even doze for an hour.

Naydenov and I – after Zina's death, he never left my side – scraped the snow away from the roots of a low birch tree, spread out a tent half, and sheltered from the wind by it, we lit our alcohol burner. Sergey opened a can of food, sliced some bread, and pulled out his flask: 'Osip, you need to drink a cup, or else your insides will get all twisted up.'

'I don't feel like it, Seryozha.'

'Buck up; after all, you know you can't bring her back.'

'Sergey, I beg you, don't feel sorry for me; I'll manage.'

'And you don't get sore! The entire battalion is grieving. The guys are talking only about Stroyeva.' Naydenov gave a dismissive wave of his hand, poured up a cup of vodka, and downed it.

Kruglov, Romanov and an artillery captain showed up on the edge of the woods. They were talking something over in low voices.

Naydenov hailed them with an invitation: 'Come have breakfast with us, Comrade Commanders!'

'If you treat us to something warm, guys, I'll accept with full satisfaction,' Kruglov answered, as he squatted down beside the burner.

Cautiously sipping the boiling tea from the cup, Kruglov kept casting sideways glances at me. I saw, or more accurately, sensed his gaze and waited for a question, but the Major kept silent. Romanov tossed down some vodka and ate a slice of bread and sausage with gusto. The artilleryman, insisting that he had already eaten breakfast, sat on the corner of the tent half and had a smoke.

Kruglov put away his cup and asked the artilleryman, 'Do you, Captain, know these places?'

'No, why?'

'Each step reminds me of the year 1941. We retreated along these roads and through these fields. It's hard to think of those that gave up, without waiting for the present day to arrive.'

'I served with the Southern Front; it wasn't easy for us either to fall back to the Volga.'

The commanders fell silent, each thinking about his own path that he had taken through these years.

Breaking branches in his way, the regiment commander's runner Sergeant Bazanov came crashing through the woods towards us. Panting, he handed a note to Kruglov and said, 'The Germans have brought up fresh tank and infantry units. A counter-attack is expected.'

Kruglov ran his eyes over the lines of the note, then curtly told Bazanov, 'Tell the regiment commander that his order will be carried out. Go.'

Viktor Vladimirovich pulled a map out of his map case, carefully unfolded it on his lap, and then turned to the artillery captain: 'Aleksandr Vasil'evich, let's shove off to the other side of the river, ah?'

'It's possible.'

'Can you cross with your guns or support us? We'll be waiting for you right here on these knolls,' Kruglov said, pointing to a spot on the map.

The artilleryman also pulled out a map and noted the knolls on the approaches to the settlement of Kikhtolka: 'Comrade Major, we'll need your help getting across the river: the banks are quite steep and the ice is still thin. Once there, we'll manage.'

'You won't be late?'

'What are you saying? My guys are strong, we'll be on time!'

Kruglov handed the note to the regiment's artillery commander: 'Read it, but don't forget – I'll be waiting for you.' The captain departed.

Kruglov turned to Romanov: 'Petr Vladimirovich, take your eagles and go help the artillerymen, while I lead the remaining companies to those knolls. You catch up with us.'

I didn't know what combat assignment the battalion was to execute, but I knew firmly that each of us was ready to do anything to destroy the German-fascist forces in front of Leningrad. Kruglov stood up. Thanking us for the tea, the commanders left.

Just an hour later, a battalion of anti-tank guns had already been transferred to the western bank of the Suma River. Kruglov's battalion, crossing the river, deployed into a combat formation and advanced. We could hear shell explosions to the right of us beyond some woods, and frequent rifle and machine-gun firing. To the left of us there was not a sound, and in front of us – a complete mystery. We moved with great caution, expecting an enemy attack. Skirting a bend in the river, we stopped at the foot of an elevation, waiting for the return of our scouts. The soldiers quickly dug into the snow, taking shelter from the wind and enemy eyes. Kruglov was sitting in the snow a couple of metres away from Naydenov and me, leaning with his shoulder against a boulder. He was looking through binoculars in the direction of a bridge across the Suma.

The low ridge in front was unoccupied by the enemy. We quickly clambered up it and found ourselves next to a dirt road, which ran along the Kotly-Veymarn railroad tracks.

Naydenov and I settled into a little place on the slope of a small gully, at the foot of a tall poplar. From this position we could keep not only the dirt road under observation, but also a section of the main road as it approached the bridge across the Suma River.

'Osip, do you know this area?'

'Of course I know! I'll never forget these places. The graves of many of my combat-friends, who fell back in 1941, are here.'

'I see . . . and where do that high road and railroad lead?'

'To Kingisepp.'

'How much farther to the city?'

'About 12 to 15 kilometres.'

'We'll get there soon.'

'So you say,' rose the voice of Gavrila, whose machine gun was in an emplacement dug out of the snow about 5 metres away from us.

'Forget those words "so you say", Gavrila,' Sergey hissed angrily. 'Now that we've started, we'll not only get to Kingisepp, but to Berlin itself!'

The machine-gunner was silent. Naydenov, not taking his eye from his telescopic sight, nudged me with his shoulder:'Do you see it?'

'Where? What?'

'Over there on the second knob – men in cloaks.'

'Don't shoot. We have to clarify. They may be our guys.'

The soldiers in camouflage suits, armed with submachine-guns, sometimes disappeared from view in the bushes, and then would reappear again. Crouching low, they were running from piece of cover to piece of cover, making their way in our direction.

'Seryozha, you keep an eye on them, and I'll report to the battalion commander.'

Major Kruglov didn't know whose scouts these were. I returned to Naydenov.

'Did you find out?' Sergey asked.

'The battalion commander didn't know if they are our scouts or the enemy's. He ordered us to keep them under observation. Where are they?'

'They've gathered over there by the trunk of that birch tree. They're looking all around like barn owls.'

The unknown soldiers slid on their backsides down the knoll one after the other and stopped behind a bush, conversing with each other and pointing in different directions. There were five of them.

Keeping my sight zeroed in on the one who was plainly in command, I waited. Where were they going? What were their intentions? Naydenov, like I was doing, followed the scouts' every movement.

After a short conference, two of the scouts ran at full speed through a gully in our direction and took cover at the foot of a rise. The remaining three men stayed put and looked in our direction, and then one of them began to climb to the top of the knoll. It became clear to me that the unidentified soldiers were creating a human chain for visual signalling, in order to report back quickly on observed enemy movements.

'We need to break this living chain,' Naydenov muttered.

'Let's wait another minute. We have time.'

I turned my attention back to the two men who had remained in place. One of them dug into his breast pocket for something and threw back the hood of the camouflage jacket. I made out a star on the man's fur cap. I involuntarily took in a sharp breath.

'Ours!' Naydenov exclaimed, wiping his forehead with his sleeve. 'I was just about to fire . . .'

My throat clutched with the thought that I might have killed one of my own in haste. I removed my numb hand from my rifle stock and shifted the position of my frozen body. Five minutes hadn't passed, when Kruglov came by our observation post with the artillery captain and two artillery scouts.

'Beyond this little hill about 500 metres away, camouflaged tanks are parked in the undergrowth along both sides of the dirt road,' a scout reported. 'How many of them?' the Captain asked.

'We saw eight tanks and four self-propelled guns.'

'Any infantry?'

'No.'

'Did you go beyond the railroad embankment?'

'No.'

'Who remained to keep watch?'

'Sergeant Volodin.'

'What have those Germans thought up? It would be good to blanket them where they're standing,' the Captain said to Kruglov.

'Not bad at all. But we have an order from the regiment commander. We don't have the authority to act on our own.'

'We'll inform the command, let it call in the air force. I'll be right back.' With that, the artilleryman slithered away on his belly towards a radio.

'The enemy's plan is clear,' Kruglov spoke up in reflection, addressing no one in particular. 'The Nazis want to throw us back to Volosovo, in order to clear a path for the withdrawal of their baggage train, trapped by us in a bottleneck on the Volosovo-Begunitsy highway. But those times have passed: we won't give back what we've taken.'

Listening to Kruglov, I looked through my telescopic sight at the prone Sergeant Volodin, who was lying next to a birch tree; I was thinking with horror that I might have killed this man. I didn't notice when Kruglov and the artillery scouts left us. Suddenly, a powerful explosion ripped through the air: little saplings, like blades of grass, were blown to the ground, striking each other with their bare branches. Above our heads, the trunk of the poplar shook, sending heavy clumps of snow showering down.

'They blew up the bridge on the Suma! Ehh, our guys didn't manage to repulse them,' Naydenov said, unfastening his grenade bag. 'Plainly, that's the Germans' signal to attack.'

Aircraft were already duelling overhead. The artillery was still silent.

'Where the hell were you devils? I've been searching for you for half an hour!'

I glanced back. It was the sniper Bodrov. 'What's happened?' Naydenov asked.

'There's a letter for you from home.'

A joyous smile creased Sergey's weathered face, and his eyes lit up. I wasn't expecting any letters, but whenever comrades received a letter, I was seized by a different joy, as if a tender, warm word from someone else's life had arrived in the front line for me as well.

However, Naydenov hadn't even had time to open the envelope when the Nazis launched their counter-attack. The first shells, passing overhead, exploded on the edge of the forest, right where we had enjoyed breakfast that morning.

Suddenly swarms of Germans rose from behind the railroad embankment directly in front of us, as if they had emerged from the ground. As if racing each other, they ran up to the dirt road and dropped into the snow. But for some reason they weren't looking in our direction, but in the direction of where our scouts had discovered the tanks. I thought, 'They're waiting for the tanks to come up, so they can resume the attack under their cover.' I looked over at the machine-gunner Gavrila. He was lying behind his machine gun, ready to fire, never taking his eyes off the Germans.

'Why is our artillery being silent?' Naydenov asked. He knew perfectly well that I was just as informed as he was about the situation, but in those minutes when you see the foe in front of you and you are sitting in ambush and anxious for the time to kill him – at such a moment a man wants to say at least one word to someone.

'I don't know, Seryozha.'

'Now's the time to smash them, while they're lying in the snow like seals,' Naydenov added, tucking the envelope under his cap.

I threw a momentary glance at Sergey. The roving smile had faded from his unshaven face, his thick eyebrows were frowning, and his eyes glittered through the narrow slits of his lids. This gleam promised nothing good.

The artillery scout, whom I had continued to check on from time to time, suddenly hastily crawled away from the trunk of the birch tree next to which he had been lying and rolled head over heels down the slope. Reaching his comrades in this fashion, who had been lying in the snow in some low bushes, he said something to them, and they all started off at a run in our direction.

'The guys have noticed something. Just wait, now the attack will begin,' Naydenov whispered, tugging his cap down over his ears.

At this moment, six 'Shturmoviki' ground-attack planes emblazoned with red stars emerged from behind the woods. Flying at treetop level, the pilots strafed the German infantry that was lying in the snow with their cannons and machine guns, as if stitching them to the place. Then as if dissatisfied with the work they had done, they turned and fired their cannons at the tanks and self-propelled guns before disappearing.

The Nazis, like crabs dumped out onto the sand, started crawling in different directions. Some of them headed for the railroad embankment, others strove to obtain cover from their tanks, while many remained lying where they were, their faces pressed into the snow.

'Our pilots really gave it to them,' Sergey said, warming the tips of his fingers with his breath.

'Our air force isn't dozing, but when will the artillery begin? We've been lying in the snow for two hours now, and my skin is starting to crack,' Gavrila responded.

'Keep your trap shut, while there's nothing to do.'

'Damn it, I'm speaking seriously.'

'Well, then chatter your teeth, that will help.'

Suddenly on the banks of the river, close to the ruins of the blown-up bridge, a fierce clash erupted. Artillery fire swelled on both sides. Quite nearby, beyond the little knoll in the direction of the high road, tank engines began to rumble and somewhere in that vicinity, an enemy Nebelwerfer began to shriek.

'Our *Katiushas* are still being silent; they're being cunning, the beauties . . .' Naydenov said, slipping his fingers beneath his cap and feeling the letter from his Svetlana. But as if he had touched an exposed electrical current, he jerked away his hand and grabbed his rifle: 'Osip, look, Fritzes have appeared on that knoll where our scout was lying.'

'Don't shoot,' a stern voice warned us. It was Romanov. We hadn't noticed it when he had crawled up to our position. 'One premature shot might cost us too dearly. We're going to wait for them to attack, and then we'll strike them in the flank. Yes, what an attack!' the commander continued, never taking his eyes from his binoculars. 'It's just a shadow of their former attacks! In '41, you remember, they didn't bother to take cover and crawl from bush to bush; they came right at us in columns to the beat of drums. Now in front of us are only fragments of the former fascist army.'

Only now did I notice that anti-tank riflemen had taken positions to the right and left of us. The long barrels of their weapons were lying on the snow like quills. Listening to Romanov, I kept my eyes on the foe, lying just 500 metres away from us.

'The fascist strength, Lieutenant, is still great.' I glanced around, having heard the familiar voice of Kruglov. He was lying 2 metres behind me together with the artillery captain. 'If you say instead,' the Major continued, 'that the combat spirit of the Nazi soldier has become a bit tattered, with this I would agree. They still have certain strength, though we have become a different army. You see with what caution they're preparing to attack us. We will have a tough fight with these remnants, in order to prevent them from freeing their baggage train.'

'Comrade Commander, tanks!'

'Aha! They've started to move,' Kruglov said loudly. Then in a whisper he said something to the commander of the anti-tank rifle platoon and crawled off together with the artillery captain.

The enemy's lead tank, emerging from cover onto the dirt road, spun in place and dashed in the direction of the highway.

'They're aiming at our flank,' Naydenov said.

The enemy's remaining seven tanks, which were carrying submachine-gunners, repeated the lead tank's manoeuvre.

'Why are our artillerymen and anti-tank riflemen just admiring them?' Gavrila said, pulling the case with the ammunition belts a little closer to the machine gun. 'Now is the very time to fire on the devils.'

'Shut up, you bore; this is stomach-churning enough even without you!' Sergey interrupted the machine-gunner.

Suddenly the Germans who had been lying on the elevation in front of us rose to their feet with a cry: 'Lia–lia–lia' – and rushed down the slope at a run towards the bend in the river, targeting the flank of our units that were attacking towards Pruzhnitsy. Overtaking their infantry, the tanks with the assault infantry on board rolled at full speed towards the Suma River.

Following the tanks, more and more throngs of Germans emerged at a run from behind the railroad embankment. Encouraging themselves with shouts and firing into the air, they were running to keep up with the tanks. For the first time in the war, I was witnessing a German attack under way as if from the sidelines.

'Really do we also attack the enemy with such fury?' I thought to myself, watching a Nazi officer moving with a pistol in his hand. He was striding through the powdery snow with a bold step, his head tilted forward.

'Fire!' Romanov's order rang out.

The command was immediately drowned out by the roar of dozens of heavy and light machine guns. Shells streaked towards the tanks, and anti-tank rifles began to bark.

The Lieutenant grabbed his pistol from its holster, and waving it over his head, shouted: 'Comrades, after me! Uraaah!' The troops of Romanov's company rushed towards the dirt road, cutting off the Germans' path to shelter behind the railroad embankment.

'Look! Look! One has started smoking!' the anti-tank riflemen began to cry in chorus.

The commander's voice interrupted the general delight: 'Why are you howling for no reason? What if it's laying down a smokescreen to conceal the infantry?'

Everyone went silent. One could hear only rare rifle shots.

The flank attack of the remaining companies of Kruglov's battalion stopped the enemy's advance. The Nazi officer was already lying on the ground, his arms outspread. The Germans, falling back while returning fire, tried to take cover behind the railroad embankment from which they had set out, but winding up under the fire of Romanov's company, they took to their heels in the direction of the settlement of Pruzhnitsy.

Two tanks were burning. One with a broken track was spinning in circles like a chained dog.

Pursuing on the heels of the Germans, we advanced to a point close to the settlement. Here a brief mêlée flared up. It was the most savage of all the ones in which I was involved during the war. The Nazis, squeezed by our forces from three directions, fought with the wild ferocity of the condemned. They were shooting their own wounded, and finished with suicides. The few we managed to capture were all dying from mortal wounds, groaning and requesting help in Russian.

'Who are they? What kind of terrible people are they?' Naydenov asked, looking down on the dying faces of the soldiers dressed in Nazi coats.

They were Vlasovites!

* * *

The regiments of the 109th Rifle Division pursued the retreating enemy until complete nightfall. Major Kruglov's battalion halted on the approach to the Salka River, but only to hear the reading of an order of the Supreme High Command, addressed to the troops of the Leningrad and Volkhov Fronts. Listening to the order, I mentally pictured the wild celebrations of the Leningraders. The soldiers and commanders held their breath as they caught every word, fearing even to shift their weight from one foot to the other, in order not to disrupt this triumphant moment.

How can one hide the joy, when it fills the heart and lights up the faces of people like the early morning sun? It wipes away the soldier's fatigue, and inspires him to new combat feats.

That night, we received replacements. The machine-gunner Maksim Maksimovich Maksimov also returned from the hospital. We vied with each other to ask him to tell us about Leningrad: how was the city living now? Had he witnessed the first salute to our achievements?

Here's what he told us:

It is impossible, my brothers, to describe in words what I saw on the streets of the city on that day. Complete strangers were embracing each other, crying and laughing, and almost smothered us soldiers with embraces. One elderly woman hugged me and told me through her tears, 'Sonny, I'm embracing not only you in joy, but our entire army; my thanks to it!' And of course it had to happen to me – I've never cried in my life, but there and then, just like I'm in front of you now, I practically broke down in front of other people. I swallowed my tears, but the woman caressed me on the shoulder with her gaunt hand, just like I was a little lad, and said, 'You, my dear, don't swallow your tears; we've swallowed enough of them, but now we can celebrate from the bottom of our souls.' I don't know whose hands filled the pockets of my greatcoat with cigarettes, matches, pieces of chocolate and candy. Just kill me because I can't remember how, but a bottle of Russian bitters and these here woollen mittens were tucked down the front of my coat. Even more, look, I found a new pipe in my pocket. Likely, an uncle somehow guessed to stick one in there . . . That's fortunate.

Maksimov lit his pipe, took a look around us and continued: 'And just as soon as the first volley of the artillery salute thundered, well, my brothers, the people went totally crazy: they shouted, danced, and threw their arms into the air, where colourful fireworks were bursting. It was the first time in my life that I managed to witness such great human joy . . .'

Maksimov stopped talking. He carefully looked around his audience, searching for someone with his eyes, and then nudged me with his elbow: 'Osip, where's Zina? I have a little gift for her.'

I stood quietly, my head lowered. Maksimych wanted to say something, but just dallied for a moment in his spot, as if trying to recall where he needed to go, gave a wave of his hand, and then without looking at any of the comrades gathered around him, hastily stalked off to his machine gun.

At dawn on 29 January, Major Kruglov's battalion marched directly off-road through the snow to the banks of the Salka River, which was familiar to us from 1941. On our way, we saw guns, tanks and transports parked in bushes, in gullies, behind the railroad embankment – wherever it was possible to hide from enemy eyes. Two *Katiusha* rocket-launching trucks were parked under a bridge. Maksimych, having set up his machine gun, walked over to them: 'Look at these beauties, fellows. Thank you from a Russian soldier, my sweeties, for your help and your sharp tempers.'

The sun rose. A panorama lay in front of our eyes, familiar to us from our battles in these places in 1941. Only then it was summer, and now it was winter. Then we were retreating, but now we were punishing the enemy severely. To our right, tall, majestic fir trees were standing as if enchanted, supporting large layers of snow on the green needles of their branches. In the silence, there were the distinct sounds of woodpeckers. In a clump of willows on the opposite riverbank, some sort of bright red little bird was fluttering around.

From behind the treetops, glittering in the sunlight, flew squadrons of red-starred bombers, one after the other, and high above them and to the sides in the clear sky, fighters were prowling like bees; the air was filled with the powerful roar of their engines. It sounded like the threatening voice of retribution – a just punishment for all the enemy's atrocities. The bird in the willows was flushed into the air, and as if diving into the air waves, flew off into the forest. Behind us, on the ground, tank engines were rumbling. The self-propelled guns had elevated their gun barrels, as if sniffing the air. The *Katiusha* rocket-launchers raised their rails and aimed them in the direction of Opol'e. With the sight of such menacing combat equipment and the excited faces of the comrades lying nearby, a combat fervour began to burn in the veins like an unseen flame.

Major Kruglov's battalion under the cover of the tanks and self-propelled guns crushed a light screening force on the Germans' left flank, bypassed the enemy strongpoint in Opol'e, and seized a key intersection of the highway and a dirt road in the enemy rear, thereby blocking the enemy's path of retreat to the Luga River and to the city of Kingisepp.

Some 3 kilometres to the east of us, Opol'e was burning. There, tanks, aircraft and the regiments of the 109th Rifle Division were finishing off the Nazis, who were being squeezed from three sides.

Maksimych went up to Romanov: 'Comrade Company Commander, why are we just admiring from the sidelines, while our comrades are fighting, ah?'

'Don't worry, Maksimych, they won't get around us.'

The machine-gunner scratched the back of his head, glancing askance at his laughing comrades.

'War, Mak-symich, is w-war. As they say, ever'one will 'ave a turn,' Gavrila said, slurring his words.

'Anyone can talk about this but you, Gavrila,' Naydenov sharply replied. 'Look at yourself: over the past several days you've turned into a sour melon from that stinking rum you've been chugging. Even your nose has swelled and your eyes are red. Eh! Watch out, it won't lead to anything good.'

Gavrila disdainfully waved Naydenov off and snapped back: 'Watch out yourself, sniper, or we'll do something with those whiskers . . .'

Romanov looked vigilantly at the machine-gunner and bit off his words: 'You, Gavrila, get rid of that rum! I'm not saying this for the first time. Now step away from the machine gun.'

'Calm and endurance are the soldier's attire. But a mug of rum makes a fortress, d'you know it?' Gavrila said gruffly, moving away from the machine gun.

No one supported him.

Far from Kingisepp, two black specks appeared on the highway and began to approach us – German motorcyclists. Lieutenant Romanov ordered Bodrov and me to exchange our sniper rifles for captured sub-machine-guns and to lower the rail crossing gate across the highway, and for everyone else to take cover. The commander thoroughly checked our equipment, and then said: 'Not a word; let me handle them.'

'What's the Lieutenant brewing up?' Bodrov whispered to me, watching Romanov saunter along the road.

'I don't know, we'll wait and see.'

Two hefty Nazi motorcyclists, their faces reddened by the cold and high-speed run, slowed to a stop when they saw us and the lowered crossing gate.

'Password?' Romanov asked them in German.

The Germans gave it.

'Where are you going?'

'To Opol'e.'

'What the hell do you need there? You can see it's a hot place there.'

'A dispatch from General Kester.'[5]

'That's a different matter. Come with me.'

Without looking back, Romanov walked away in the direction of the railroad hut, next to which a rather substantial dugout had been constructed; plainly, the Germans manning the control post at the rail crossing had lived in it. The motorcyclists hopped off their machines, ducked under the striped arm of the crossing gate and jogged after Romanov. I didn't see them again.

One after the other, tank and self-propelled gun commanders came running out of their concealment; men started bustling about, and engines started up. The battalion prepared for battle. Romanov reappeared, and catching sight of us still standing on the road, shouted: 'Guys! The masquerade is over. Get your rifles, but don't toss away your submachine-guns; a nice bit of work awaits us. Two battalions of Germans are hurrying to the help of their own in Opol'e. Do you understand?'

I found Naydenov next to Maksimov's machine gun. They had been setting up the machine gun at the former position of an enemy anti-aircraft battery between the dirt road and railroad.

Someone shouted: 'Germans behind us!'

Confusion rippled through our combat formations. The soldiers and commanders were turning around to face from the west to the east, while some were running from place to place, searching for any new cover. Naydenov grabbed the heavy machine gun into his arms like it was a bundle of straw, and carried it away towards the railroad track. We, not having had time to disperse effectively, saw Germans running from the direction of Opol'e on both sides of the highway. They dropped to one knee for a moment and fired at their pursuers, then began running again.

'Our guys in Opol'e really gave it to them. Look how they're running – like their feet are on fire.'

The Germans, snapping back at their pursuers with ferocity, fell back

5. I have been unable to identify this German general. It is possible that he was commanding the 10th Luftwaffe Field Division at the time, which was largely destroyed around Opol'e at this point.

in the direction of the railroad in order to find cover behind its embankment and blunt the Russian attack. Major Kruglov, having waited for the Nazis to emerge from a depression and into the open, gave the order: 'Fire!'

The Germans, hearing the machine-gun fire and accompanying volleys of rifle shots behind their backs, were seized with panic and began running to and fro in the kill zone. But where and how could the foe find cover, when a torrent of bullets was lashing him from all sides?

The forward elements of our division's 456th Rifle Regiment reached us. The final enemy strongpoint on the approaches to Kingisepp and the Luga River was taken.

Kruglov met with a short captain with an eagle's nose and quick, falcon-like eyes, and asked: 'Grisha, was it you and your heroes putting the spurs to the Germans from Opol'e?'

'It was me. Thanks, Viktor, for your help. I never thought or even guessed that I would meet you here, especially in these circumstances!'

'What doesn't happen in war?'

These were the fleeting meetings of brothers-in-arms on the path of war. Having hardly had time to exchange greetings, they were again moving along different roads, but towards one goal. Later I found out that Kruglov had served together with this captain on the Finnish sector of the front.

Towards evening we reached the junction of two rivers, the Salka and Kikhtolka. We stopped to rest in the immediate proximity of the Kingisepp-Krikkovo road.

These were familiar places! They reminded me of so much: here during the August battles of 1941, Vasiliy Yershov had shot down the first enemy bomber with a burst from his machine gun. Here was the very same birch tree by the side of the road, near which the nurse Shura had danced the Kamarinskaya [a traditional Russian dance] to the clamorous voices of the spectators standing two deep and the whoops of her combat-friends, fellow people's militia members. From here we had gone on our first combat patrol. Here we had really learned how to fight . . . A fine thing – memory!

Chapter Thirty-two

Caring Hands

The morning of 30 January . . . the sunlight had still not touched the earth, but had only gilded the sparse clouds, when an airplane appeared in the frosty sky. It was flying, lit by the bright rays of the sun, alone and beautiful, like the fairytale firebird. It was a Soviet artillery spotter plane. On the ground there was not a sound or a rustle. The calm was silent and disquieting. Everyone was waiting for the start of the attack. Seeing our airplane in the sky, the soldiers and commanders tightened their belts a notch and grabbed their weapons.

Maksimov set up his machine gun on a sled, covered it with a camouflage smock, and crawled over to our position in a shell hole. Taking a seat next to Naydenov, he started to roll a cigarette.

The moment of the resumption of combat was approaching. We were sitting around a dying campfire. The golden embers, like the eyes of a person nodding off, were covered with a soft shroud of ashes. A sudden breeze whisked away this silvery shroud and hurled it onto the flap of a soldier's greatcoat.

From the depths of our position, several hundred guns struck at once. An arc of fire, as if resting on the earth, spanned the banks of the Luga.

In front of us, and above and below our position on the river, flashes of artillery fire and explosions twinkled and danced. Our artillery and bombers were concentrating their blows on two of the Germans' strongpoints: Aleksandrovskaya Gorka and Sala.

Kruglov's battalion was pinned down on the bank in the gap between these two strongpoints. A smooth, icy surface stretched in front of us.

'Fedor, come here!' Maksimych shouted to an ammo-bearer. 'Gavrila has been hit!'

This time the German rum had played a bad joke on Gavrila: he had been trying to carry cases of ammunition belts to a different spot, but had stumbled and fallen on a piece of level ground, where an enemy shell fragment had found him.

Naydenov continued to fire. The river ice was cracking and breaking, as if its banks had become too narrow; chunks of ice and geysers of water flew into the air under the impacts of bombs and shells.

We could hear an irregular machine-gun and rifle fire and the sharp cries of men. These were soldiers of the neighbouring company who had first stepped out onto the river ice.

Now our turn arrived. Naydenov was running next to me. Leaping over the jagged pieces of ice, we approached the western bank of the river, which was shrouded with smoke. Somewhere quite nearby, bullets were pattering and shells were bursting, flinging icy water and ice chips into the faces of the men running across the ice.

Shots sounded to the right, left and behind us, and we could hear the encouraging shouts of officers. The heart and mind were both filled with a single, all-encompassing desire: to get off the ice as quickly as possible onto firm land and enter into battle!

Naydenov, Maksimov with the machine-gun detachment and a group of soldiers from Romanov's company all reached the opposite bank of the river at the same time. A hand-to-hand mêlée was already under way there; you could hear the dull thuds of striking rifle butts, yells and curses, brief submachine-gun bursts and solitary rifle and pistol shots, and the groans of the wounded. There were no entrenchments here. There was not even any snow.

The savage, bloody struggle of men was going on in a blackened field, which had been ploughed up by shells and bombs. In the course of one hour, the regiments of the 109th Rifle Division forced a crossing of the Luga River, drove the Germans from their strongpoint of Sala, and firmly fortified the line they had gained.

The Germans did everything to try to hurl us back into the river. They kept introducing fresh rifle and tank units into the battle. The howl of engines in the sky never subsided. In the first hour of the battle, we were fighting against Nazis of their 61st Infantry Division. By evening, troops of the German 11th Infantry Division had launched three counter-attacks against us. That night, we were engaged against fascists of the 207th Security Division.

The Soviet forces, having broken the enemy's line of defences at the strongpoints on the left bank of the river, threatened to trap the Nazis against the coastline of the Gulf of Narva. All night long, the Germans rained a destructive fire from artillery and Nebelwerfers on our flanks from the villages of Izvoz and Aleksandrovskaya Gorka. With the break of dawn they again counter-attacked. This time it was the 11th SS Panzergrenadier Division *Nordland*.

I had previously heard about this particular division more than once, and now it was our turn to meet these Nazi volunteers on the banks of the Luga River. They attacked aggressively, to say the least. They kept coming in the face of the machine-gun fire, with no regard for their losses. However, we also didn't give them any errors to exploit, and we fought with the stubbornness of avengers.

'They keep coming and coming, the vultures!' Maksimych said, replacing the boiling water in the jacket of his machine gun. I was filling ammo belts for him.

Some 5 metres away from us, Naydenov was firing from a captured German heavy machine gun. On the left side of the machine gun, there was a pile of emptied metal ammunition belts, but Sergey kept loading and loading fresh ones, never ceasing fire. Captain Morozov's companies began to buckle under the enemy pressure and fall back.

'Brothers! Where are you going? Hold on, or else the vermin will toss us back onto the ice!'

'We don't have the strength, old man. They're mowing us down,' someone's voice called back.

A terrible threat was now hanging over our positions. The *Katiushas* never ceased firing on the attacking foe for a moment.

'That's the third attack we're driving back! All the same you won't take us!' Sergey shouted in the direction of the Germans. [Actually, the 11th SS Panzergrenadier Division *Nordland* consisted largely of foreign volunteers, mainly Scandinavians, but also *volksdeutsch* from Romania, Danish, Dutch, Estonian and other volunteers from around Europe.]

'Hang in there, buddy! Otherwise, it's thumbs down for us,' Maksimych calmly said.

The strongpoints of Aleksandrovskaya Gorka and Izvoz were burning. Suddenly, the SS troops in the field broke off the attack and took to their heels in disarray towards Narva. This turning-point in the battle occurred so unexpectedly, that for some time we were stunned – we didn't even fire at the backs of the fleeing enemy. Everything became clear, when we saw Soviet T-34 tanks tearing across the field.

The exhausted soldiers began to step across the snowy, idle field to follow the tanks. We paused only to receive some bread, and we ate while on the move.

Towards evening we attacked the enemy in Dubrovka from the march. We cut the railroad and main road between Kingisepp and Ivangorod.

We spent the night in some woods. Sergeant Bazanov in a fire-break lit a bundle of dry brushwood: 'Aaaah, guys! Come warm your paws. That's enough playing leapfrog with the Fritzes. Build some bonfires in the shell craters.'

Comrades were walking up to the fire, removing their boots, and taking a seat on some fir logs by the fire, drying their foot wrappings and mittens. Some, having warmed their hands, immediately began to fall asleep in the snow, without even finishing a cigarette.

Looking at the blazing fire, I thought back to 1941 and the endless days of our retreat. At that time, we were even afraid at night to strike a match in an exposed place.

Our artillery and air force pounded Ivangorod and Narva all night long. Kingisepp was burning. There were still the sounds of street fighting coming from there.

Maksimych spread out a tent-half on the snow, disassembled his machine gun, and began quietly cleaning the powder-blackened parts one after the other. Naydenov was helping him. I involuntarily recalled Uncle Vasya, who loved to make sure his weapon was clean and in working order. None of the comrades broke the silence, even though there was something for us to talk about: after all, over the fifteen days of our offensive thus far, the adversary had been thrown back from the walls of Leningrad by 100–150 kilometres, whereas during their offensive back in 1941, it had taken the Germans three months to cover the same distance! However, the death of comrades dimmed our joy.

On the morning of 5 February 1944, Major Kruglov's battalion, pursuing the retreating enemy, moved right up to the Narva River south of Ivangorod. These were the very places, where I had first seen a fascist soldier in July 1941, and had killed my first Nazi.

We spent the entire day in some woods, waiting for the artillery to move up. It had trouble keeping up with the rapid advance that the rifle units were making.

Naydenov and I were sitting on the edge of a broad forest ravine close to the battalion command post. Tanks were moving in column along the bottom of the ravine. The lead tank stopped, and a youngish lieutenant's head popped out of the turret hatch and shouted: 'Comrades, can you tell me where the nearest ford across the Narva is around here?'

I slid down to the bottom of the ravine to give the tanker directions. Suddenly the tank shook and everything around me began to swim . . . I began to lose consciousness. There was a loud ringing in my ears. I wasn't feeling any pain and tried to regain my senses, but the entire ground in front of me was starting to whirl crazily like some sort of fantastic dance, and I blacked out.

I came to only from the touch of someone's tender hands on my face. I tried to open my eyes wide, so I could see the person to whom these caring hands belonged, but I couldn't. As before, I was surrounded by complete darkness. I was laying face-up on some hard surface. A terrible buzzing filled my ears, which drowned out all other sounds. All of this was repeated many times, before a moment of some sort of consciousness arrived. Just at that moment, I again felt the touch of someone's tender hands. Who was this person, whose hands were these?

I began to hear certain sounds more and more often, still indistinct and remote, like the echo of human voices and wavering musical chords. They would totally disappear, and then reappear again. Then suddenly in these not fully distinct sounds I caught the words: 'He'll live.' Then everything wavering, intermittent and barely recognizable faded out again . . . I was again standing by the solitary birch tree on the side of the road close to the Salka River. My combat comrades and friends, however, were walking away from me further and further, while I was standing as if chained to the spot, with no strength to tear my feet from the earth, to take even a single step to go after my friends . . . I had to catch up with them!

. . . Then suddenly I was home, surrounded by my family: my wife was handing me a white shirt and tie: 'Yosif, you still haven't changed? How have you forgotten, today is Vitya's birthday! Pull yourself together, guests will be arriving soon.'

I leaned towards my wife, in order to take the tie from her, but I couldn't reach it . . . Someone's powerful hands were holding me by the shoulders . . . From under a white hood that fell just above her eyes, Zina was looking at me. Her face was ruddy from the cold. Reaching for me, she was saying something important about Volodya . . .

Once again I woke up to a touch on my face from the same tender hands. Such hands they were! Like a warm breath, they touched my cheek, my forehead, ran across my lips and tickled my chin . . . They removed an impenetrable mask from my head, and roused me back to life.

My first wish was to see this person, who was so attentively caring for me. I also wanted to regain control of my tongue again as quickly as possible – it seemed wooden and so swollen, that it not only interfered with my speech, but also made it difficult to swallow my saliva. I tried to move an arm, but I couldn't. My arms wouldn't obey; they were lying along my body like two sticks. I tried to turn, but something prevented me: I was tightly bound to a wooden board. The only thing that was confirming my faith in life was the thought that my senses were no longer wandering aimlessly, and things were becoming clear again.

One day I saw the door to the room cautiously swing open, and a girl with brown pigtails, about 14 years of age, entered the room sideways, holding a basin. She was dressed in school clothing. On tiptoes, almost without a sound, she slipped between the beds and came towards me. When she reached me, she carefully laid the basin on a stool. With serious concern, the girl examined my bound body on the board from my feet to my head. Giving a sigh, she pulled a piece of gauze from the front pocket of her apron, dipped it into the water, squeezed it in her little fist, and then carefully, as if I was fragile glass, began to wipe my face. Only then did I understand to whom these caring hands belonged.

I so wanted to ask her for her name, and to find out where she was from . . . But how could I do this? My tongue still felt like it was wooden. When the unfamiliar little lady took my right hand into hers, I gave her little fingers a light squeeze. The girl instantly looked up at my face, and seeing something like a smile on it, she flew like a swallow headlong out of the ward. From the corridor, I could hear a child's joyfully excited voice: 'Aleksandra Kuz'minichna, he squeezed my hand and smiled. I'm so happy!'

'You know I told you, Valyusha, that he would live.'

'I remember, I remember everything, Aleksandra Kuz'minichna, but he's so weak, he can't eat, and he's been lying on that board for so long – I felt sorry for him . . .'

'Valyusha, he'll have to lie on that board for two more days, that doesn't frighten us, but how are we going to return his ability to speak?'

'If he only survives . . . a mother will understand her son even without words,' I heard a third woman's voice say.

. . . Three months later I dropped by the ward, dressed in a brand new military uniform, in order to say goodbye to my comrades still there and to shake the little courageous hand of the Leningrad schoolgirl Valentina Avdeyeva, the worn, wrinkled hand of Major of Medical Services Dr. Aleksandra Kuz'minichna Yas'kevich, and to tightly hug the nanny Agrafena Konstantinovna Prudnikova, who had been loved by all the patients.

The comrades, saying their farewells to me, seemingly paid no attention to my trembling hand. Stammering, I pronounced my parting words with difficulty . . . Friends with Red Cross armbands escorted me like I was their own brother, and the dear nanny Agrafena cried . . .

I stepped out into the street. The April sun and fresh air were dizzying. It was hard to walk. I leaned against the wall of a building and looked around. On the Moika embankment, blackbirds were raising a cheerful racket as they repaired their nests from the previous year. The sounds of music carried from the street loudspeakers.

*   *   *

In the Oktiabr'sky District Committee, I was shown into a commissar's office. A stoop-shouldered man with grey hair and tired eyes was seated behind a writing desk. He was looking over some sort of papers. The attendant laid my papers in front of him and left. The commissar gazed at me, and then read the documents attentively. For a long time, he asked me about my combat path – from the first battle on the Narva River to my last wounding. He showed a lot of interest in the successes of my sniper trainees, and then seemingly casually asked: 'Do you have any family in the city?'

'No.'

Tightly shaking my hand, with a restrained, soft smile he told me: 'You'll reside in our district. Have a rest. If you're needed – we'll call you.'

Index